"*Washington Rules* is the author's shorthand for the American conviction that we always represent the good and the pure in international affairs. His powerful book clearly demonstrates how threadbare this idea has become."

—CHALMERS JOHNSON, author of the
Blowback Trilogy and *Dismantling the Empire*

"*Washington Rules* dissects the convictions that have turned the United States into a warrior nation—a country devoted to military solutions that do little, if anything, to enhance its security or advance the well-being of its citizens or the foreign peoples on whom we inflict our illusory benevolence. A brilliant historian's analysis of what ails America, this book should be read not only by every national officeholder but by all who care about America's future safety and prosperity."

—ROBERT DALLEK, author of *The Lost Peace: Leadership in a
Time of Horror and Hope, 1945–1953*

"Engaging and insightful . . . A timely analysis and critique of contemporary and historical defense policies . . . Thought provoking."

—*The Washington Times*

"Against a national strategy gone astray, Bacevich offers a unique combination of rigorous analysis and emotion-powered protest. May it be widely read, may it disenthrall us from the academic generals, militant academics, and cynical politicians who insist that we must invest blood and treasure in mud-brick Afghan villages, while China invests in advanced technology."

—EDWARD N. LUTTWAK, author of
The Grand Strategy of the Byzantine Empire

WASHINGTON
RULES

Also by Andrew J. Bacevich

The Limits of Power:
The End of American Exceptionalism

The Long War:
A New History of U.S. National Security Policy
Since World War II

The New American Militarism:
How Americans Are Seduced by War

American Empire:
The Realities and Consequences
of U.S. Diplomacy

The Imperial Tense:
Prospects and Problems
of American Empire

WASHINGTON RULES

AMERICA'S PATH
TO PERMANENT WAR

ANDREW J. BACEVICH

METROPOLITAN BOOKS

HENRY HOLT AND COMPANY

NEW YORK

Metropolitan Books
Henry Holt and Company, LLC
Publishers since 1866
175 Fifth Avenue
New York, New York 10010
www.henryholt.com

Metropolitan Books® and ⊞® are registered trademarks of Henry Holt and
Company, LLC.

Distributed in Canada by H. B. Fenn and Company Ltd.

Library of Congress Cataloging-in-Publication Data

Bacevich, Andrew J.
    Washington rules : America's path to permanent war / Andrew J.
Bacevich.—1st ed.
        p. cm.
    Includes bibliographical references and index.
    ISBN 978-0-8050-9422-0
    1. United States—Foreign relations—Decision making.   2. United
States—Military policy—Decision making.   3. Consensus (Social
sciences)—United States.   I. Title.
    JZ1480.B335 2010
    355'.033573—dc22   2010006302

Henry Holt books are available for special promotions and premiums.
For details contact: Director, Special Markets.

Originally published in hardcover in 2010 by Metropolitan Books

First paperback edition 2011

Designed by Meryl Sussman Levavi

Printed in the United States of America

1 3 5 7 9 10 8 6 4 2

TO MY DARLING DAUGHTERS

Jennifer Maureen

Amy Elizabeth

Kathleen Therese

Suffer us not to mock ourselves with falsehood.

T. S. Eliot, "Ash Wednesday" (1930)

CONTENTS

WASHINGTON RULES

INTRODUCTION: SLOW LEARNER

WORLDLY AMBITION INHIBITS TRUE LEARNING. ASK ME. I know. A young man in a hurry is nearly uneducable: He knows what he wants and where he's headed; when it comes to looking back or entertaining heretical thoughts, he has neither the time nor the inclination. All that counts is that he is going somewhere. Only as ambition wanes does education become a possibility.

My own education did not commence until I had reached middle age. I can fix its start date with precision: For me, education began in Berlin, on a winter's evening, at the Brandenburg Gate, not long after the Berlin Wall had fallen.

As an officer in the U.S. Army I had spent considerable time in Germany. Until that moment, however, my family and I had never had occasion to visit this most famous of German cities, still littered with artifacts of a deeply repellent history. At the end of a long day of exploration, we found ourselves in what had, until just months before, been the communist East. It was late and we were hungry, but I insisted on walking the length of the Unter den Linden, from the River Spree to the gate itself. A cold rain was falling and the pavement glistened. The buildings lining the avenue, dating from the era of Prussian kings, were dark, dirty, and pitted. Few people were about. It was hardly a night for sightseeing.

For as long as I could remember, the Brandenburg Gate had been the preeminent symbol of the age and Berlin the epicenter of contemporary history. Yet by the time I made it to the once and future German capital, history was already moving on. The Cold War had abruptly ended. A divided city and a divided nation had reunited.

For Americans who had known Berlin only from a distance, the city existed primarily as a metaphor. Pick a date—1933, 1942, 1945, 1948, 1961, 1989—and Berlin becomes an instructive symbol of power, depravity, tragedy, defiance, endurance, or vindication. For those inclined to view the past as a chronicle of parables, the modern history of Berlin offered an abundance of material. The greatest of those parables emerged from the events of 1933 to 1945, an epic tale of evil ascendant, belatedly confronted, then heroically overthrown. A second narrative, woven from events during the intense period immediately following World War II, saw hopes for peace dashed, yielding bitter antagonism but also great resolve. The ensuing stand-off—the "long twilight struggle," in John Kennedy's memorable phrase—formed the centerpiece of the third parable, its central theme stubborn courage in the face of looming peril. Finally came the exhilarating events of 1989, with freedom ultimately prevailing, not only in Berlin, but throughout Eastern Europe.

What exactly was I looking for at the Brandenburg Gate? Perhaps confirmation that those parables, which I had absorbed and accepted as true, were just that. Whatever I expected, what I actually found was a cluster of shabby-looking young men, not German, hawking badges, medallions, hats, bits of uniforms, and other artifacts of the mighty Red Army. It was all junk, cheaply made and shoddy. For a handful of deutsche marks, I bought a wristwatch emblazoned with the symbol of the Soviet armored corps. Within days, it ceased to work.

Huddling among the scarred columns, those peddlers—almost certainly off-duty Russian soldiers awaiting redeployment home—constituted a subversive presence. They were loose ends of a story that was supposed to have ended neatly when the Berlin Wall came down. As we hurried off to find warmth and a meal, this disconcerting encounter stuck with me, and I began to entertain this possibility: that the truths I had accumulated over the previous twenty years as a professional soldier—especially truths about the Cold War and U.S. foreign policy—might not be entirely true.

By temperament and upbringing, I had always taken comfort in orthodoxy. In a life spent subject to authority, deference had become a deeply ingrained habit. I found assurance in conventional wisdom. Now, I started, however hesitantly, to suspect that orthodoxy might be a sham. I began to appreciate that authentic truth is never simple and that any version of truth handed down from on high—whether by presidents, prime ministers, or archbishops—is inherently suspect. The powerful, I came to see, reveal truth only to the extent that it suits them. Even then, the truths to which they testify come wrapped in a nearly invisible filament of dissembling, deception, and duplicity. The exercise of power necessarily involves manipulation and is antithetical to candor.

I came to these obvious points embarrassingly late in life. "Nothing is so astonishing in education," the historian

Henry Adams once wrote, "as the amount of ignorance it accumulates in the form of inert facts."[1] Until that moment I had too often confused education with accumulating and cataloging facts. In Berlin, at the foot of the Brandenburg Gate, I began to realize that I had been a naïf. And so, at age forty-one, I set out, in a halting and haphazard fashion, to acquire a genuine education.

Twenty years later I've made only modest progress. This book provides an accounting of what I have learned thus far.

★

In October 1990, I'd gotten a preliminary hint that something might be amiss in my prior education. On October 3, communist East Germany—formally the German Democratic Republic (GDR)—ceased to exist and German reunification was officially secured. That very week I accompanied a group of American military officers to the city of Jena in what had been the GDR. Our purpose was self-consciously educational—to study the famous battle of Jena-Auerstädt in which Napoleon Bonaparte and his marshals had inflicted an epic defeat on Prussian forces commanded by the Duke of Brunswick. (The outcome of that 1806 battle inspired the philosopher Hegel, then residing in Jena, to declare that the "end of history" was at hand. The conclusion of the Cold War had only recently elicited a similarly exuberant judgment from the American scholar Francis Fukuyama.)

On this trip we did learn a lot about the conduct of that battle, although mainly inert facts possessing little real educational value. Inadvertently, we also gained insight into the reality of life on the far side of what Americans had habitually called the Iron Curtain, known in U.S. military vernacular as "the trace." In this regard, the trip proved nothing less than revelatory. The educational content of this excursion would—for me—be difficult to exaggerate.

As soon as our bus crossed the old Inner German Border, we entered a time warp. For U.S. troops garrisoned throughout Bavaria and Hesse, West Germany had for decades served as a sort of theme park—a giant Epcot filled with quaint villages, stunning scenery, and superb highways, along with ample supplies of quite decent food, excellent beer, and accommodating women. Now, we found ourselves face-to-face with an altogether different Germany. Although commonly depicted as the most advanced and successful component of the Soviet Empire, East Germany more closely resembled part of the undeveloped world.

The roads—even the main highways—were narrow and visibly crumbling. Traffic posed little problem. Apart from a few sluggish Trabants and Wartburgs—East German automobiles that tended to a retro primitivism—and an occasional exhaust-spewing truck, the way was clear. The villages through which we passed were forlorn and the small farms down at the heels. For lunch we stopped at a roadside stand. The proprietor happily accepted our D-marks, offering us inedible sausages in exchange. Although the signs assured us that we remained in a land of German speakers, it was a country that had not yet recovered from World War II.

Upon arrival in Jena, we checked into the Hotel Schwarzer Bär, identified by our advance party as the best hostelry in town. It turned out to be a rundown fleabag. As the senior officer present, I was privileged to have a room in which the plumbing functioned. Others were not so lucky.

Jena itself was a midsized university city, with its main academic complex immediately opposite our hotel. A very large bust of Karl Marx, mounted on a granite pedestal and badly in need of cleaning, stood on the edge of the campus.

Briquettes of soft coal used for home heating made the air all but unbreathable and coated everything with soot. In the German cities we knew, pastels predominated—houses and apartment blocks painted pale green, muted salmon, and soft yellow. Here everything was brown and gray.

That evening we set out in search of dinner. The restaurants within walking distance were few and unattractive. We chose badly, a drab establishment in which fresh vegetables were unavailable and the wurst inferior. The adequacy of the local beer provided the sole consolation.

The following morning, on the way to the battlefield, we noted a significant Soviet military presence, mostly in the form of trucks passing by—to judge by their appearance, designs that dated from the 1950s. To our surprise, we discovered that the Soviets had established a small training area adjacent to where Napoleon had vanquished the Prussians. Although we had orders to avoid contact with any Russians, the presence of their armored troops going through their paces riveted us. Here was something of far greater immediacy than Bonaparte and the Duke of Brunswick: "the other," about which we had for so long heard so much but knew so little. Through binoculars, we watched a column of Russian armored vehicles—BMPs, in NATO parlance—traversing what appeared to be a drivers' training course. Suddenly, one of them began spewing smoke. Soon thereafter, it burst into flames.

Here was education, although at the time I had only the vaguest sense of its significance.

★

These visits to Jena and Berlin offered glimpses of a reality radically at odds with my most fundamental assumptions. Uninvited and unexpected, subversive forces had begun to infiltrate my consciousness. Bit by bit, my worldview started to crumble.

That worldview had derived from this conviction: that American power manifested a commitment to global leadership, and that both together expressed and affirmed the nation's enduring devotion to its founding ideals. That American power, policies, and purpose were bound together in a neat, internally consistent package, each element drawing strength from and reinforcing the others, was something I took as a given. That, during my adult life, a penchant for interventionism had become a signature of U.S. policy did not—to me, at least—in any way contradict America's aspirations for peace. Instead, a willingness to expend lives and treasure in distant places testified to the seriousness of those aspirations. That, during this same period, the United States had amassed an arsenal of over thirty-one thousand nuclear weapons, some small number of them assigned to units in which I had served, was not at odds with our belief in the inalienable right to life and liberty; rather, threats to life and liberty had compelled the United States to acquire such an arsenal and maintain it in readiness for instant use.[2]

I was not so naïve as to believe that the American record had been without flaws. Yet I assured myself that any errors or misjudgments had been committed in good faith. Furthermore, circumstances permitted little real choice. In Southeast Asia as in Western Europe, in the Persian Gulf as in the Western Hemisphere, the United States had simply done what needed doing. Viable alternatives did not exist. To consent to any dilution of American power would be to forfeit global leadership, thereby putting at risk safety, prosperity, and freedom, not only our own but also that of our friends and allies.

The choices seemed clear enough. On one side was the

status quo: the commitments, customs, and habits that defined American globalism, implemented by the national security apparatus within which I functioned as a small cog. On the other side was the prospect of appeasement, isolationism, and catastrophe. The only responsible course was the one to which every president since Harry Truman had adhered.

For me, the Cold War had played a crucial role in sustaining that worldview. Given my age, upbringing, and professional background, it could hardly have been otherwise. Although the great rivalry between the United States and the Soviet Union had contained moments of considerable anxiety—I remember my father, during the Cuban Missile Crisis, stocking our basement with water and canned goods—it served primarily to clarify, not to frighten. The Cold War provided a framework that organized and made sense of contemporary history. It offered a lineup and a scorecard. That there existed bad Germans and good Germans, their Germans and our Germans, totalitarian Germans and Germans who, like Americans, passionately loved freedom was, for example, a proposition I accepted as dogma. Seeing the Cold War as a struggle between good and evil answered many questions, consigned others to the periphery, and rendered still others irrelevant.

Back in the 1960s, during the Vietnam War, more than a few members of my generation had rejected the conception of the Cold War as a Manichean struggle. Here too, I was admittedly a slow learner. Yet having kept the faith long after others had lost theirs, the doubts that eventually assailed me were all the more disorienting.

Granted, occasional suspicions had appeared long before Jena and Berlin. My own Vietnam experience had generated its share, which I had done my best to suppress. I was, after all, a serving soldier. Except in the narrowest of terms, the military profession, in those days at least, did not look kindly on nonconformity. Climbing the ladder of career success required curbing maverick tendencies. To get ahead, you needed to be a team player. Later, when studying the history of U.S. foreign relations in graduate school, I was pelted with challenges to orthodoxy, which I vigorously deflected. When it came to education, graduate school proved a complete waste of time—a period of intense study devoted to the further accumulation of facts, while I exerted myself to ensuring that they remained inert.

Now, however, my personal circumstances were changing. Shortly after the passing of the Cold War, my military career ended. Education thereby became not only a possibility, but also a necessity.

In measured doses, mortification cleanses the soul. It's the perfect antidote for excessive self-regard. After twenty-three years spent inside the U.S. Army seemingly going somewhere, I now found myself on the outside going nowhere in particular. In the self-contained and cloistered universe of regimental life, I had briefly risen to the status of minor spear carrier. The instant I took off my uniform, that status vanished. I soon came to a proper appreciation of my own insignificance, a salutary lesson that I ought to have absorbed many years earlier.

As I set out on what eventually became a crablike journey toward a new calling as a teacher and writer—a pilgrimage of sorts—ambition in the commonly accepted meaning of the term ebbed. This did not happen all at once. Yet gradually, trying to grab one of life's shiny brass rings ceased being a major preoccupation. Wealth, power, and celebrity became not aspirations but subjects for critical analysis. History—especially the familiar narrative of the Cold War—no longer offered answers; instead, it posed perplexing riddles. Easily the most nagging was this one: How could I have so profoundly misjudged the reality of what lay on the far side of the Iron Curtain?

Had I been insufficiently attentive? Or was it possible that I had been snookered all along? Contemplating such questions, while simultaneously witnessing the unfolding of the "long 1990s"—the period bookended by two wars with Iraq when American vainglory reached impressive new heights—prompted the realization that I had grossly misinterpreted the threat posed by America's adversaries. Yet that was the lesser half of the problem. Far worse than misperceiving "them" was the fact that I had misperceived "us." What I thought I knew best I actually understood least. Here, the need for education appeared especially acute.

George W. Bush's decision to launch Operation Iraqi Freedom in 2003 pushed me fully into opposition. Claims that once seemed elementary—above all, claims relating to the essentially benign purposes of American power—now appeared preposterous. The contradictions that found an ostensibly peace-loving nation committing itself to a doctrine of preventive war became too great to ignore. The folly and hubris of the policy makers who heedlessly thrust the nation into an ill-defined and open-ended "global war on terror" without the foggiest notion of what victory would look like, how it would be won, and what it might cost approached standards hitherto achieved only by slightly mad German warlords. During the era of containment, the United States had at least maintained the pretense of a principled strategy; now, the last vestiges of principle gave way to fantasy and opportunism. With that, the worldview to

which I had adhered as a young adult and carried into
middle age dissolved completely.

★

What should stand in the place of such discarded convictions? Simply inverting the conventional wisdom, substituting a new Manichean paradigm for the old discredited
version—the United States taking the place of the Soviet
Union as the source of the world's evil—would not suffice.
Yet arriving at even an approximation of truth would entail
subjecting conventional wisdom, both present and past, to
sustained and searching scrutiny. Cautiously at first but with
growing confidence, this I vowed to do.

Doing so meant shedding habits of conformity acquired
over decades. All of my adult life I had been a company
man, only dimly aware of the extent to which institutional
loyalties induce myopia. Asserting independence required
first recognizing the extent to which I had been socialized
to accept certain things as unimpeachable. Here then were
the preliminary steps essential to making education acces-
sible. Over a period of years, a considerable store of debris
had piled up. Now, it all had to go. Belatedly, I learned that
more often than not what passes for conventional wisdom
is simply wrong. Adopting fashionable attitudes to demonstrate one's trustworthiness—the world of politics is flush
with such people hoping thereby to qualify for inclusion in
some inner circle—is akin to engaging in prostitution in
exchange for promissory notes. It's not only demeaning
but downright foolhardy.

This book aims to take stock of conventional wisdom in
its most influential and enduring form, namely the package
of assumptions, habits, and precepts that have defined the
tradition of statecraft to which the United States has adhered

since the end of World War II—the era of global dominance now drawing to a close. This postwar tradition combines two components, each one so deeply embedded in the American collective consciousness as to have all but disappeared from view.

The first component specifies norms according to which the international order ought to work and charges the United States with responsibility for enforcing those norms. Call this the American credo. In the simplest terms, the credo summons the United States—and the United States alone—to lead, save, liberate, and ultimately transform the world. In a celebrated manifesto issued at the dawn of what he termed "The American Century," Henry R. Luce made the case for this spacious conception of global leadership. Writing in *Life* magazine in early 1941, the influential publisher exhorted his fellow citizens to "accept wholeheartedly our duty to exert upon the world the full impact of our influence for such purposes as we see fit and by such means as we see fit." Luce thereby captured what remains even today the credo's essence.[3]

Luce's concept of an American Century, an age of unquestioned American global primacy, resonated, especially in Washington. His evocative phrase found a permanent place in the lexicon of national politics. (Recall that the neoconservatives who, in the 1990s, lobbied for more militant U.S. policies named their enterprise the Project for a New American Century.) So, too, did Luce's expansive claim of prerogatives to be exercised by the United States. Even today, whenever public figures allude to America's responsibility to lead, they signal their fidelity to this creed. Along with respectful allusions to God and "the troops," adherence to Luce's credo has become a de facto prerequisite for high office. Question its claims and your prospects of being heard in the hubbub of national politics become nil.

Note, however, that the duty Luce ascribed to Americans has two components. It is not only up to Americans, he wrote, to choose the purposes for which they would bring their influence to bear, but to choose the means as well. Here we confront the second component of the postwar tradition of American statecraft.

With regard to means, that tradition has emphasized activism over example, hard power over soft, and coercion (often styled "negotiating from a position of strength") over suasion. Above all, the exercise of global leadership as prescribed by the credo obliges the United States to maintain military capabilities staggeringly in excess of those required for self-defense. Prior to World War II, Americans by and large viewed military power and institutions with skepticism, if not outright hostility. In the wake of World War II, that changed. An affinity for military might emerged as central to the American identity.

By the midpoint of the twentieth century, "the Pentagon" had ceased to be merely a gigantic five-sided building. Like "Wall Street" at the end of the nineteenth century, it had become Leviathan, its actions veiled in secrecy, its reach extending around the world. Yet while the concentration of power in Wall Street had once evoked deep fear and suspicion, Americans by and large saw the concentration of power in the Pentagon as benign. Most found it reassuring.

A people who had long seen standing armies as a threat to liberty now came to believe that the preservation of liberty required them to lavish resources on the armed forces. During the Cold War, Americans worried ceaselessly about falling behind the Russians, even though the Pentagon

consistently maintained a position of overall primacy. Once
the Soviet threat disappeared, mere primacy no longer suf-
ficed. With barely a whisper of national debate, unambigu-
ous and perpetual global military supremacy emerged as
an essential predicate to global leadership.

Every great military power has its distinctive signature.
For Napoleonic France, it was the *levée en masse*—the people
in arms animated by the ideals of the Revolution. For Great
Britain in the heyday of empire, it was command of the seas,
sustained by a dominant fleet and a network of far-flung
outposts from Gibraltar and the Cape of Good Hope to
Singapore and Hong Kong. Germany from the 1860s to the
1940s (and Israel from 1948 to 1973) took another approach,
relying on a potent blend of tactical flexibility and operational audacity to achieve battlefield superiority.

The abiding signature of American military power since
World War II has been of a different order altogether. The
United States has not specialized in any particular type of
war. It has not adhered to a fixed tactical style. No single
service or weapon has enjoyed consistent favor. At times,
the armed forces have relied on citizen-soldiers to fill their
ranks; at other times, long-service professionals. Yet an examination of the past sixty years of U.S. military policy and
practice does reveal important elements of continuity. Call
them the sacred trinity: an abiding conviction that the minimum essentials of international peace and order require the
United States to maintain a *global military presence*, to configure its forces for *global power projection*, and to counter existing or anticipated threats by relying on a policy of *global
interventionism*.

Together, credo and trinity—the one defining purpose,
the other practice—constitute the essence of the way that
Washington has attempted to govern and police the Ameri-

can Century. The relationship between the two is symbiotic. The trinity lends plausibility to the credo's vast claims. For its part, the credo justifies the trinity's vast requirements and exertions. Together they provide the basis for an enduring consensus that imparts a consistency to U.S. policy regardless of which political party may hold the upper hand or who may be occupying the White House. From the era of Harry Truman to the age of Barack Obama, that consensus has remained intact. It defines the rules to which Washington adheres; it determines the precepts by which Washington rules.

As used here, Washington is less a geographic expression than a set of interlocking institutions headed by people who, whether acting officially or unofficially, are able to put a thumb on the helm of state. Washington, in this sense, includes the upper echelons of the executive, legislative, and judicial branches of the federal government. It encompasses the principal components of the national security state— the departments of Defense, State, and, more recently, Homeland Security, along with various agencies comprising the intelligence and federal law enforcement communities. Its ranks extend to select think tanks and interest groups. Lawyers, lobbyists, fixers, former officials, and retired military officers who still enjoy access are members in good standing. Yet Washington also reaches beyond the Beltway to include big banks and other financial institutions, defense contractors and major corporations, television networks and elite publications like the *New York Times*, even quasi-academic entities like the Council on Foreign Relations and Harvard's Kennedy School of Government. With rare exceptions, acceptance of the Washington rules forms a prerequisite for entry into this world.

My purpose in writing this book is fivefold: first, to trace the origins and evolution of the Washington rules—both the credo that inspires consensus and the trinity in which it finds expression; second, to subject the resulting consensus to critical inspection, showing who wins and who loses and also who foots the bill; third, to explain how the Washington rules are perpetuated, with certain views privileged while others are declared disreputable; fourth, to demonstrate that the rules themselves have lost whatever utility they may once have possessed, with their implications increasingly pernicious and their costs increasingly unaffordable; and finally, to argue for readmitting disreputable (or "radical") views to our national security debate, in effect legitimating alternatives to the status quo. In effect, my aim is to invite readers to share in the process of education on which I embarked two decades ago in Berlin.

The Washington rules were forged at a moment when American influence and power were approaching their acme. That moment has now passed. The United States has drawn down the stores of authority and goodwill it had acquired by 1945. Words uttered in Washington command less respect than once was the case. Americans can ill afford to indulge any longer in dreams of saving the world, much less remaking it in our own image. The curtain is now falling on the American Century.

Similarly, the United States no longer possesses sufficient wherewithal to sustain a national security strategy that relies on global military presence and global power projection to underwrite a policy of global interventionism. Touted as essential to peace, adherence to that strategy has propelled the United States into a condition approximating perpetual war, as the military misadventures of the past decade have demonstrated.

To anyone with eyes to see, the shortcomings inherent in

the Washington rules have become plainly evident. Although those most deeply invested in perpetuating its conventions will insist otherwise, the tradition to which Washington remains devoted has begun to unravel. Attempting to prolong its existence might serve Washington's interests, but it will not serve the interests of the American people.

Devising an alternative to the reigning national security paradigm will pose a daunting challenge—especially if Americans look to "Washington" for fresh thinking. Yet doing so has become essential.

In one sense, the national security policies to which Washington so insistently adheres express what has long been the preferred American approach to engaging the world beyond our borders. That approach plays to America's presumed strong suit—since World War II, and especially since the end of the Cold War, thought to be military power. In another sense, this reliance on military might creates excuses for the United States to avoid serious engagement: Confidence in American arms has made it unnecessary to attend to what others might think or to consider how their aspirations might differ from our own. In this way, the Washington rules reinforce American provincialism—a national trait for which the United States continues to pay dearly.

The persistence of these rules has also provided an excuse to avoid serious self-engagement. From this perspective, confidence that the credo and the trinity will oblige others to accommodate themselves to America's needs or desires—whether for cheap oil, cheap credit, or cheap consumer goods—has allowed Washington to postpone or ignore problems demanding attention here at home. Fixing Iraq or Afghanistan ends up taking precedence over fixing Cleveland and Detroit. Purporting to support the troops in their crusade to free the world obviates any obligation to assess the implications of how Americans themselves choose to exercise freedom.

When Americans demonstrate a willingness to engage seriously with others, combined with the courage to engage seriously with themselves, then real education just might begin.

1

The Advent of Semiwar

Speaking to the throngs gathered in Chicago's Grant Park on the night of his election to the presidency, Barack Obama summoned his fellow citizens "to put their hands on the arc of history and bend it once more toward the hope of a better day."[1] That history has a readily apparent direction and that Americans are called upon to determine its trajectory are propositions his listeners likely took for granted. Americans have long since become accustomed to their leaders making such claims.

Bending the arc of history necessarily entails vast exertions on a sustained basis. It likewise implies a capacity to discern the arc's proper shape. It assumes not only the possession of great power, but also a willingness to expend that power so as to ensure the accomplishment of history's purposes.

In what was billed as her first major foreign policy address, Hillary Clinton, Obama's secretary of state, made the point explicitly. Citing with approval the famous words of Revolutionary-era radical Tom Paine—"We have it within our power to begin the world over again"—Clinton went on to declare, "Today . . . we are called upon to use that power."[2]

This self-adulatory vision captures the essence of what Americans commonly understand by the phrase *global leadership*. In his speech, Obama was implicitly affirming his commitment to everything signified by that phrase. Change was coming to America but that did not mean the United States was about to shirk its responsibilities. On the contrary.

Since taking office, President Obama has acted on many fronts to adjust the way the United States exercises that leadership. Yet these adjustments have seldom risen above the cosmetic. When it comes to fundamentals, he has stood firm. The national security consensus to which every president since 1945 has subscribed persists. On this score, change has not come to America.

Once installed in office, President Obama and his chief lieutenants wasted little time in signaling their allegiance to this consensus and to the four assertions on which it rests. Every president since Harry Truman has faithfully subscribed to these four assertions and Obama is no exception.

First, the world must be organized (or shaped). In the absence of organization, chaos will surely reign.

Second, only the United States possesses the capacity to prescribe and enforce such a global order. No other nation has the vision, will, and wisdom required to lead. Apart from the United States, no other nation or group of nations (and certainly no supra-national institution) can be entrusted with that role. Leadership in this sense implies that Washington demonstrate a voracious appetite for taking on new obligations, never acknowledging that limits exist on how much Americans can afford. Once shouldered, obligations become permanent—the consequences of pulling out of Afghanistan after 1989 demonstrating the penalty that results from violating this dictum.

Third, America's writ includes the charge of articulating the principles that should define the international order. Those principles are necessarily American principles, which possess universal validity. That specific American principles may themselves evolve in no way compromises their universality. However much American attitudes regarding nuclear weapons or noncombatant casualties or women's rights may change, the most recent articulation of principle is the one that counts and to which others must conform.

Finally, a few rogues and recalcitrants aside, everyone understands and accepts this reality. Despite pro forma grumbling, the world wants the United States to lead. Indeed, what keeps world leaders up at night is the possibility that Americans may someday tire of the responsibilities that history plainly intends them to bear and which they are so admirably equipped to fulfill.

Mainstream Republicans and mainstream Democrats are equally devoted to this catechism of American statecraft. Little empirical evidence exists to demonstrate its validity, but no matter: When it comes to matters of faith, proof is unnecessary. In American politics, adherence to this creed qualifies as a matter of faith. In speeches, state papers, and official ceremonies, public figures continually affirm and reinforce its validity. Like the sales pitches woven into commercial TV programming, it is both omnipresent and hidden in plain sight.

Mainstream Republicans and Democrats are also committed to the proposition that implementing this creed entails the exercise of power. In this regard, singular responsibilities require singular prerogatives. Not content simply to deflect threats, Washington seeks to remove them. Rather than waiting on events, national security elites favor an activist posture. The misleadingly named Department of Defense serves in fact as a Ministry of Global Policing.

When it comes to projecting power, the United States exempts itself from norms with which it expects others to comply. The notorious Bush Doctrine of preventive war provides the ultimate expression of the prerogatives to which Washington lays claims. Yet in promulgating the doctrine that bears his name, George W. Bush was adhering to a well-established practice. Ever since 1904 when Theodore Roosevelt enunciated his famous "corollary" to the Monroe Doctrine—asserting authority to "exercise international police power" throughout the Caribbean whenever the United States found evidence of "chronic wrongdoing"— his successors have played variations of TR's theme. The eponymous doctrines of Presidents Truman, Eisenhower, Carter, and Reagan number among the results.[3]

That the United States should also maintain a far-flung network of bases and other arrangements to facilitate intervention abroad emerges as an essential predicate. Whereas the United States once erected bases in places like Hawaii, Panama, or the Philippines to defend outposts of empire, for decades now a central purpose of "forward presence" has been to project power anywhere on earth. As a result, Americans have long since become accustomed to the stationing of U.S. troops in far-off lands. This global military presence is ostensibly essential to the defense of American freedom even in places where the actual threat to American freedom is oblique or imaginary.

Precisely because American purposes express the collective interests of humankind, Washington expects others to view U.S. military power, the Pentagon's global footprint, and an American penchant for intervention not as a matter of concern but as a source of comfort and reassurance. The good intentions inherent in the credo of American global leadership render the triad of principles defining U.S. military practice benign.

Americans take all this for granted and so are blind to its significance. Like corruption or hypocrisy, this national security consensus has long since become part of the wallpaper of national life, attracting attention only when some especially maladroit escapade comes to light.

What makes headlines is not a congressman accepting bribes, but that he stashes the cash in his kitchen freezer. That a married senator keeps a mistress on the side qualifies as a bit ho-hum; that he's trumpeted his devotion to family values as a member of Promise Keepers and was in the forefront of those demanding Bill Clinton's impeachment over the Lewinsky affair gives the story its special juice. So, too, with the Washington rules: It's only when something especially egregious occurs—most commonly a botched war—that members of the public take notice, and even then only briefly. That the Washington rules *are* the problem rather than offering the solution to problems seldom commands any attention.

For some comparative perspective, consider this possibility: In light of his country's status as a rising power, China's minister of defense announces plans to

- increase Chinese military spending so that annual expenditures by the People's Liberation Army (PLA) will henceforth exceed the combined defense budgets of Japan, South Korea, Russia, India, Germany, France, and Great Britain.
- create a constellation of forward-deployed PLA garrisons in strategically sensitive areas around the world,

including, say, Latin America, expressing the global range of Chinese interests.

- negotiate access agreements and overflight rights with dozens of nations to facilitate humanitarian intervention and augment the PLA's ability to assist in maintaining global stability.
- partition Planet Earth into sprawling territorial commands, with one four-star Chinese general assigned responsibility for the Asia Pacific, another for Africa, a third for the Middle East, and so on—to include a Chinese North America Command, charged with monitoring conditions on that continent, and a Chinese Space Command responsible for the cosmos.
- institute a vigorous program of war games and exercises in countries around the world, to include the Western Hemisphere, while maintaining in instant readiness the land, air, and naval forces needed to convert such games and exercises into combat operations.
- form a PLA Long-Range Strike Force, capable on very short notice of conducting intercontinental attacks, employing conventional or nuclear weapons or operating in cyberspace.

No doubt the defense minister would caution other nations not to view this program as posing any threat, the People's Republic being sincerely committed to living in harmony with others. The minister might even argue that China, both a venerable civilization and a vigorous, rising nation-state, has an inherent responsibility to contribute to global stability. Few observers in the United States (or elsewhere for that matter) would take comfort in such assurances. In Washington, Tokyo, Moscow, and other capitals, China's true intentions might be subject to debate, but no responsible official would accept the assertion that such a huge investment in military power reflected China's desire to advance the cause of peace. The rhetorical camouflage would fool no one.

The imaginary Chinese program described above pales in comparison to the existing military posture of the United States. Some highlights of that posture include the following:

- With current Pentagon outlays running at something like $700 billion annually, the United States spends as much or more money on its military than the entire rest of the world combined.[4]

- The United States currently has approximately 300,000 troops stationed abroad, again more than the rest of the world combined (a total that does not even include another 90,000 sailors and marines who are at sea);[5] as of 2008, according to the Department of Defense, these troops occupied or used some 761 "sites" in 39 foreign countries, although this tally neglected to include many dozens of U.S. bases in Iraq or Afghanistan;[6] no other country comes even remotely close to replicating this "empire of bases"—or to matching the access that the Pentagon has negotiated to airfields and seaports around the world.[7]

- The Pentagon has divvied up the planet (and universe) into "unified commands," each headed by a four-star general or admiral. *Pacific Command*, "committed to preserving the security, stability, and freedom" of the Asia-Pacific region, polices a region comprising 50 percent of the earth's surface, and more than half of its population;[8] *Central Command*, spanning the Greater Middle East, currently presides over wars in Iraq, Afghanistan, and Pakistan as it seeks "to promote security, stability, and prosperity";[9] *European*

Command, established in Germany at the end of World War II, remains committed to the proposition that a need exists "for continuing and expanded U.S. engagement throughout the command's area of focus";[10] *Africa Command*, created in 2007, conducts "military-to-military programs, military-sponsored activities, and other military operations" in fifty-three nations in order "to promote a stable and secure African environment";[11] *Southern Command*, encompassing Central and South America and the Caribbean, strives to "ensure stability," "enhance security," and "enable partnerships";[12] *Northern Command*, established in the wake of 9/11, tends to North America; and, by no means least of all, *Space Command*, responsible for the biggest region of all, conducts "joint space operations," including "Space Force Support, Space Force Enhancement, Space Force Application, and Space Force Control."[13]

- Each of the six regional commands manages its own frenetic schedule of war games, command post exercises, workshops, conferences, seminars, training missions, and disaster relief operations, all conducted under the rubric of "engagement"; Pacific Command's program of recurring exercises, for example, includes Talisman Saber, Tandem Thrust, Kingfisher, Crocodile, Cobra Gold, Balikatan, Keen Sword, Keen Edge, and Rim of the Pacific, a list that does not include the seven hundred ship visits made each year throughout the region by units of the Navy's Pacific Fleet.[14]

- Finally, not to be forgotten, is *Strategic Command*—formerly known as Strategic Air Command—with its sea- and land-based ballistic missiles and its fleet of long-range bombers standing ready "to deliver integrated kinetic and non-kinetic effects to include nuclear and information operations" anywhere in the world at any time;[15] information operations is a euphemism for cyberwarfare, that mission soon to be assumed by yet another new headquarters to be called CYBERCOM.

Inside the Washington Beltway, none of this qualifies as controversial. Beyond the Beltway, the Pentagon's global posture generates far less interest than the latest doings of Hollywood celebrities.

Call it habit or conditioning or socialization: The citizens of the United States have essentially forfeited any capacity to ask first-order questions about the fundamentals of national security policy. To cast doubts on the principles of global presence, power projection, and interventionism, as Ron Paul and Dennis Kucinich did during the 2008 presidential primaries, is to mark oneself as an oddball or eccentric, either badly informed or less than fully reliable; certainly not someone suitable for holding national office.

Because these concepts are so deeply entrenched, what passes for a "debate" over national security policy seldom rises above technical issues. Bureaucratic process—the never-ending review of and wrangling over budgetary priorities—becomes a mechanism for perpetuating the status quo and for distracting attention from the extent to which the Washington rules—the American credo of global leadership and the sacred trinity of U.S. military practice—commit the United States to what is in effect a condition of permanent national security crisis.

James Forrestal, the first person to serve as secretary of defense, coined a term to describe this permanent crisis. He called it *semiwar*.[16] Conceived by Forrestal at the beginning of the Cold War, and reflecting his own anticommunist obsessions, *semiwar* defines a condition in which great

dangers always threaten the United States and will continue doing so into the indefinite future. When not actively
engaged in hostilities, the nation faces the prospect of hostilities beginning at any moment, with little or no warning.
In the setting of national priorities, readiness to act becomes
a supreme value.

Semiwarriors created the Washington rules. Semiwarriors uphold them. Semiwarriors benefit from their persistence.

Regardless of what threats actually exist, semiwarriors,
some in uniform, others wearing suits, concur in the need
to sustain high levels of military spending. Even as they
sometimes make a show of bemoaning a stupendously prof-
ligate military-industrial complex, they routinely write off
tens of billions of wasted taxpayer dollars. Professing alarm
at the prospect of any would-be adversary gaining an edge
anywhere in anything, they devote huge sums not just to
enhancing existing U.S. capabilities, but to developing
entirely new ones—weapons systems sometimes set decades
into the future and blue-sky technologies that sound like
material for science-fiction novels. Although careful to genu-
flect before the historic achievements of the citizen-soldier,
they also nurture a warrior class largely divorced from the
society it serves. Never missing an opportunity to proclaim
their undying devotion to peace, these semiwarriors insist
that nothing should impede U.S. preparations for war.

Amid this constant clatter of sabers being honed, rattled,
drawn, and thrust, fundamental questions about efficacy
go unasked. The commonplace assertion that an ever-
quickening pace of change confronts the United States with
ever more complex problems reinforces this tendency. If
the challenges of the present are without precedent, then

the past has little of relevance to offer. So habits become entrenched. Contradictions go unnoticed. Above all, what gets lost along the way is accountability.

The scathing complaint of foreign policy critic Roger Morris, registered some thirty years ago, remains apt today. Average Americans, he wrote then, their attention absorbed by the problems of daily life at home, "give the rest of the planet only a distracted, fleeting glance." Easily persuaded that the United States is called upon to lead, they leave it to others to work out the details. As a result, ordinary citizens remain "heedless of the people and closed politics," cloaked in secrecy, that formulate policies advertised as essential to the nation's safety and well-being. From time to time, "dour, mostly anonymous men" emerge from behind closed doors "to announce discreetly some fresh disaster." Although inquiries and investigations inevitably ensue, the net effect is not to fix responsibility but to disperse it. Then the game continues, the terms of reference all but unaffected, the cast of characters largely unchanged, with Republican and Democratic insiders simply exchanging portfolios at periodic intervals.

"Aside from shedding a handful of figures too badly stained by Vietnam"—Morris was writing in 1980; today we might substitute the Greater Middle East—"no other field of American endeavor over the past two decades has been so little revived by fresh energy, talent, and perspective as our in-grown national security establishment." The burden of paying for the disasters concocted by this establishment, he continued,

> fall[s] most savagely on the majority of Americans with incomes under $20,000, the people whose pocketbooks

do the paying and whose sons tend to do the dying
for foreign policy but whose voices are largely absent
in its making.

Morris unleashed his salvo in the wake of the Soviet invasion of Afghanistan with the drama surrounding the Iran
hostage crisis still unfolding. This book appears, in the wake
of George W. Bush's Iraq War, in the midst of what has
become Barack Obama's Afghanistan War. Yet Morris's
central complaint still pertains.

> The lethal fault of American foreign policy is a mat-
> ter of neither left nor right, neither liberal cowardice
> nor conservative conspiracy, but rather a relatively
> banal bipartisan mediocrity. . . . A loss of compe-
> tence more than a loss of nerve, it is not different
> from nepotism and misrule in one's county com-
> mission or school board, a decrepit commuter rail-
> road or an expiring automobile manufacturer like
> Chrysler.[17]

To restore accountability requires first understanding how
we got where we are. How exactly did such principles come
to be enshrined as central to our national security consensus? Answering this question requires reassessing—and
reframing—the narrative of contemporary U.S. history.

The standard story line, promulgated by journalists and
indulged by scholars, depicts that history as a succession
of presidential administrations. The occupant of the White
House defines the age. The inauguration of a new chief
executive wipes the slate clean. Each new president starts
anew and puts his personal stamp on all that follows. So
the period from 1945 to 1952 becomes the Truman era. The
Eisenhower era follows, and in Eisenhower's wake comes

John F. Kennedy's abbreviated yet perpetually mourned age of Camelot. And so on down the line until the age of Obama, informed by the conviction, proclaimed even before the last ballot had been counted, that "tonight . . . change has come to America."

When it comes to justifying the erection of ever more lavish, self-referential postpresidential libraries, this reliance on the presidency as a vehicle for organizing U.S. history has proven eminently useful. Yet when it comes to assessing reality, slicing the past into neat four- or eight-year-long intervals conceals and distorts at least as much as it illuminates. The fact of the matter is: No president starts with a clean slate. Upon entering the Oval Office each confronts an imposing and often problematic inheritance. Constraints, some foreign, others domestic, limit his freedom of action. Struggling to control (or even to understand) that inheritance and to elude those constraints, presidents fail at least as often as they succeed.

Pretending to the role of Decider, a president all too often becomes little more than the medium through which power is exercised. Especially on matters related to national security, others manufacture or manipulate situations to which presidents then react. Only in the most nominal sense did Harry Truman decide to bomb Hiroshima. By the summer of 1945 the momentum dictating that the atomic bomb should be used had become all but irresistible. Much the same can be said about John F. Kennedy's 1961 decision to launch the Bay of Pigs operation, Lyndon Johnson's 1965 decision to commit U.S. combat troops to Vietnam, or even George W. Bush's decision to invade Iraq in 2003. In each case, the erstwhile commander in chief did little more than ratify a verdict that others had already rendered. Yet with rare exceptions, all presidents—even those held responsible for astonishing blunders—maintain the fiction of having remained fully in charge from start to finish. Thus do they sustain the cult of the modern presidency.

Dwight D. Eisenhower's justly famous "Farewell Address" stands out as one of those rare exceptions.[18] On the eve of leaving office—although not before—Eisenhower offered the American people a glimpse of powerful forces that lay behind and beyond presidential control. He honestly, accurately, and courageously (if belatedly) let his fellow citizens in on the secret that, in Washington, appearances were profoundly deceptive. In describing and decrying what he called the "military-industrial complex," Ike provided a sobering tutorial in political reality, disabusing Americans of civics book notions of a political apparatus purposefully committed to advancing some collective vision of the common good.

What Americans mistook for politics—the putative rivalry that pitted Democrats against Republicans, the wrangling between Congress and the White House—actually amounted to little more than theater, he implied. Behind the curtain, a consensus forged of ambition, access, money, fevered imaginations, and narrow institutional interests determined the nation's actual priorities. Although Eisenhower was about to surrender his office to a handsome young successor who promised dramatic change—neither the first nor last president to make such a commitment—he knew that John Kennedy's personal qualities, however attractive, counted for little given the forces arrayed against him. "The potential for the disastrous rise of misplaced power exists and will persist," the outgoing president warned. "We should take nothing for granted."

Eisenhower's unvarnished warning reflected his own

appreciation of a troubling new reality. The nation's "immense military establishment" married to a "permanent armaments industry of vast proportions" wielded influence— "economic, political, even spiritual"—that reached into "every city, every Statehouse, every office of the Federal government." In effect, by 1961, semiwarriors—those who derived their power and influence by perpetuating an atmosphere of national security crisis—had gained de facto control of the U.S. government.

Eisenhower chose not to acknowledge that he himself had served as their ally and enabler. Nor did he explain why he had waited until the eve of his return to private life to expose the existence of this misplaced power. Still, given the source, Ike's admission was nothing less than revelatory: Initiatives undertaken to ensure national security had given rise to new institutions and habits deeply antithetical to traditional American values.

These new forces had yielded unwelcome consequences that Eisenhower himself, whether as general or as president, had neither intended nor anticipated, threatening American democracy. To expect that Washington would remedy a problem that Washington itself had created was, as Eisenhower understood, a delusion. "Only an alert and knowledgeable citizenry," he insisted, could keep semiwarriors on a sufficiently short leash "so that security and liberty may prosper together." The outgoing president urged ordinary Americans to wake up, pay attention, and reclaim their democracy.

In 1961, Eisenhower's warning fell on deaf ears. Beguiled by Kennedy's wit, vigor, and apparent sophistication, dazzled by the credentials of those who signed on to chart the New Frontier, Americans ignored Ike's counsel, to their considerable misfortune. With the passage of time, that warning has only taken on increased urgency.

EMPIRE BUILDERS

The triad of global presence, power projection, and interventionism, fully enshrined by the time Ike bid the nation farewell, had many fathers, General and President Eisenhower not least among them. Still, the contributions of two figures stand out. If historical standing were a function of enduring legacy, then Allen Dulles and Curtis LeMay, both all but forgotten today, would each rate a memorial on the Mall in Washington. Were lasting impact the measure of merit, then Dulles and LeMay—semiwarriors par excellence—would certainly rank as more deserving of recognition than several recent presidents whose names adorn marble-sheathed libraries, museums, and public policy schools.

Dulles and LeMay were the antithesis of individualists. They were men who found personal fulfillment in the building of institutions. During the pivotal decade of the 1950s, they raised to prominence two organizations that helped define the maxims by which Washington came to operate and went a long way toward enforcing them as well: in Dulles's case the Central Intelligence Agency (CIA), in LeMay's, the Strategic Air Command (SAC). Important in their own right, these institutions wielded influence well beyond their formal mandate. The CIA and SAC promulgated a set of precepts that left a deep and lasting imprint on the entire National Security State, much as, say, the *New York Times* once imparted to the news business standards and expectations to which journalists elsewhere reflexively sought to adhere.

Dulles served as director of central intelligence from

1953 to 1961; no other DCI has matched his staying power. He stands in relation to the Agency as Bill Gates does to Microsoft. Like Gates, Dulles forged a juggernaut possessing enormous reach and inspiring a mix of fear and grudging respect. As with Gates, the empire that Dulles created expressed his own worldview, ambitions, and values. Just as Gates imparted to Microsoft a culture that proved a model for other tech-savvy entrepreneurs, so Dulles inculcated in the CIA a culture that became a model for the entire national security apparatus. The so-called Information Age was rich in opportunities to make money. In Silicon Valley, Microsoft provided a template for how to tap those opportunities. So, too, the age of the National Security State that dawned in the wake of World War II was rich in opportunities to amass and wield power. During the early years of the Cold War, Dulles's CIA showed the rest of Washington how to capitalize on those opportunities.

LeMay, too, was an empire builder, his accomplishments, if anything, outstripping those of Dulles. From 1948 to 1957—in contemporary military practice, an unusually long tenure—the four-star air force general commanded Strategic Air Command, the principal U.S. nuclear strike force and chief instrument for waging World War III.

When LeMay assumed command, SAC's ability to perform its core mission—to launch a nuclear attack against the Soviet Union—was questionable at best. Capabilities were limited, readiness poor. LeMay took it upon himself to change all that. Acquiring enormous fleets of aircraft that flew faster and farther and could carry heavier bomb loads, exploiting a rapidly growing U.S. capacity to produce nuclear weapons, and honing the skills needed to implement a war plan of ever broader scope and complexity, LeMay transformed SAC into a force held at instant readiness and capable of destroying not only the Soviet Union but the entire communist world many times over. Rightly remembered as the "Father of SAC," LeMay was also the father of Overkill.

In terms of background and upbringing, Dulles and LeMay came from different worlds. Each cultivated a distinctive operating style. Yet their similarities outweighed those differences and explain their influence.

THE GREAT WHITE CASE OFFICER

A cool, urbane, Princeton-educated patrician, Allen Dulles was born into a family with a strong tradition of public service. His grandfather John Foster and uncle Robert Lansing had each served as secretary of state, as would his older brother, John, in the Eisenhower years. Allen had spent his early career first as a diplomat, serving in 1919 as a member of the U.S. delegation to the Paris Peace Conference that ended World War I and then as a corporate lawyer with the prominent New York City firm of Sullivan & Cromwell.[19] Yet he entertained ambitions that success in the private sector could never satisfy.

In that regard, World War II came as a godsend. During the war, Dulles left Wall Street and became a leading figure in the Office of Strategic Services, the precursor to the CIA, heading up the large OSS operation in Bern, Switzerland. There, he developed an acute fascination with and demonstrated a pronounced knack for intelligence work. After the war, Dulles was prominent among those urging the creation of a permanent intelligence service. Soon after Congress created the CIA in 1947, he joined its ranks, managing the Agency's embryonic clandestine service before accepting Eisenhower's invitation to become director.

Dulles presided over the CIA's "golden years," when the

Agency's autonomy, prestige, and reputation reached their height.[20] Allowing its agents to operate on a very long leash, Eisenhower tacitly indulged Dulles's belief that covert action offered a way for the United States to take the offensive against the Soviet Union. That Allen's brother, John Foster, was serving as the president's trusted chief diplomatist elevated his standing even further. With the family business encompassing both the overt and covert aspects of U.S. policy (sister Eleanor was also an influential State Department official), the Dulles franchise in 1950s Washington glittered.

Breeding and education seemingly fitted Dulles for his sensitive post. If the United States was going to dirty its hands in the spy business, at least there was a gentleman in charge. In his dealings with people from outside the Agency, he exuded a combination of worldliness, sophistication, and refinement. In a fawning 1953 profile, the *New York Times* took note of his "intellectual forehead surmounted by a tidy thatch of sparse gray hair," wrote approvingly of his "close cropped gray mustache," and admired his suits with their "expensively casual look of Savile Row." His teeth "clenched around the stem of a thick briar pipe," he evinced "the composure as well as the look of a headmaster of an English boys' school." With his "cultured tastes and cosmopolitan interests," Dulles was someone Americans could trust.[21]

Other observers agreed. In August of that year, *Time* made Dulles the subject of a flattering cover story. Describing him as a "scholarly, hearty, pipe-smoking lawyer" with "the cheery, manly manner of a New England prep-school headmaster," the magazine credited the CIA director with shouldering "the most important mission in the long, sordid, heroic and colorful history of the intelligence services." Dulles was "uniquely qualified" to head the Agency and had already demonstrated the ability to run it "smoothly and with apparently inexhaustible energy." There was always room for improvement, but *Time* left no room for doubt that the CIA was in good hands.[22]

For its part, Congress was happy to shovel money at Allen Dulles's CIA with few questions asked. Most members of the press viewed it as their patriotic duty either to keep mum or lend a hand. Among a host of projects initiated at Dulles's direction, two in particular served to demonstrate the Agency's claim to perspicacity, daring, and competence: Operation TPAJAX, which in 1953 overthrew the democratically elected government of Mohammad Mossadegh and reinstalled the Shah on Iran's Peacock Throne; and Operation PBSUCCESS, a CIA-instigated coup that, in 1954, removed from office Jacobo Árbenz Guzmán, the democratically elected leftist president of Guatemala, effectively handing control of that country to the army. Both operations seemingly demonstrated that if allowed sufficient latitude, the CIA could be counted on to achieve a lot while spending very little—a judgment that became ever more difficult to sustain.

When he became director in 1953, according to one biographer, "Dulles had already decided the CIA must reach into every corner of the world."[23] By the end of the decade, he had achieved that aim, establishing a network of stations embedded in U.S. diplomatic missions that spanned the planet. (The Agency also maintained offices in several major American cities.) Persuaded that "covert operations should be increased in intensity and number," the director filled the Agency's upper ranks with people who shared his view as well as his fascination with tradecraft and his appetite for risk taking. Within the Agency itself, Dulles's intense personal interest in all aspects of clandestine activity earned him this nickname: the Great White Case Officer.[24]

When it came to choosing subordinates, Dulles prized zeal rather than balance. Those he placed in top jobs possessed impressive talents and flawed personalities: Frank Wisner, his deputy director for covert operations and then station chief in London, succumbed to madness and committed suicide; James Jesus Angleton, the alcoholic chief of CIA counterintelligence, famously descended into paranoia; William K. Harvey, station chief in Berlin, toted pearl-handled pistols, consumed a daily pitcher of martinis with lunch, and bragged incessantly of his sexual exploits; and Tracy Barnes, a compulsive adventurer, combined extraordinary bravery with a complete absence of common sense. Dulles himself was an inveterate womanizer and indifferent father.

Whatever their personal flaws, Dulles's men shared their chief's profound sense of duty. Without hesitation or question, they would literally do anything the Agency asked of them. By their own lights they were honorable men, unswervingly committed to a righteous anticommunist crusade. William Colby, one of Dulles's eventual successors, likened the ethos of the early CIA to "an order of Knights Templar," out "to save Western freedom from Communist darkness."[25]

Dulles's CIA pursued vast ambitions informed by equally vast doses of self-confidence, unencumbered by the slightest inclination toward introspection. Dulles and his chief lieutenants were literally too busy to think. Although addictions to alcohol and tobacco were commonplace, adrenaline was their true drug of choice.

Dulles and other senior CIA officials existed in a state of permanent auto-intoxication. Theirs was a life of crowded hours: secret White House briefings, Georgetown parties with Washington's smart set extending late into the night, whirlwind trips abroad to consult with allies or green-light some new scheme. They were in the thick of things. They knew the secrets. And anyone who was anyone knew that they knew, endowing them with a status that ranked several notches above mere celebrity.

When CIA officers spoke of waging the Cold War, it was the noun not the adjective that they emphasized. Of the Soviet bloc Dulles wrote, "[W]e are not really 'at peace' with them, and we have not been since Communism declared its own war on our system of government and life."[26] Americans may remember the 1950s as an interval of relative quiet before the storms of the following decade broke. For Dulles and the CIA, the Eisenhower era was the opposite of quiet. The Agency was actively engaged in all-out, no-holds-barred conflict.

The stakes in that conflict could not have been higher. To Dulles, persuaded that the Kremlin had launched "a master plan to shatter the societies of Asia and Europe and isolate the United States, and eventually take over the entire world," thwarting that plan required intense and continuous action. The second-order implications were plain: "The whole world is the arena of our conflict." Given that "our vital interests are subject to attack in almost every quarter of the globe at any time," it had become essential "to maintain a constant watch in every part of the world, no matter what may at the moment be occupying the main attention of diplomats and military men."[27]

As in any war, what mattered were results, the more immediate and tangible the better. For Dulles and his deputies, all other considerations were secondary. Their world presented itself as a series of problems to be solved and opportunities to be exploited. They had little time to spare for contemplating long-term effects. Their preferred measure of effectiveness was straightforward: Did the operation succeed or fail? According to this narrow standard, Iran and Guatemala showed the Agency at its scintillating best.

Dulles waged his clandestine war wrapped in an armor of moral certitude. The cause required actions that might ordinarily have appeared distasteful—disseminating false information, suborning foreign officials, planning acts of sabotage, overthrowing governments, and ordering assassinations. Yet the implications of failure—the Soviets over-running the Free World—seemed so dire as to justify acts that might otherwise have been considered beyond the pale. Indeed, for Dulles and his lieutenants, to do what others might shrink from doing became a symbol of rectitude. As Evan Thomas has written in his study of the early CIA, "The ability to swallow one's qualms, to do the harder thing for the greater good, was regarded as a sign of moral strength."[28] In this sense, the cause itself cleansed such acts of any taint of iniquity. However paradoxical, the pursuit of fixed and permanent universal values went hand in hand with the embrace of highly flexible moral standards.

Not surprisingly, devotion to the mission and to the Agency were inextricably linked. When, in 1953, a senior automobile executive nominated to the post of secretary of defense testified to his conviction that "what was good for the country was good for General Motors and vice versa," he was roundly derided. Yet Charles E. Wilson was merely expressing a sentiment shared by other movers and shakers of the day. Wall Street bankers, university presidents, big-city newspaper publishers, cardinal archbishops, and senior military officers all agreed: For the country to flourish, the institutions for which they bore responsibility had to flourish. To promote institutional interests was, therefore, to promote the common good. Generally left unsaid but

understood was this: To promote institutional interests was
also to elevate the personal standing of the individuals who
sat atop such institutions. For those occupying the executive
suite, institutional clout translated into personal influence
and frequently into more material benefits as well.

Dulles was an authentic patriot, who viewed the Cold
War as a righteous cause. No reason exists to question the
sincerity of that conviction. Yet the atmosphere of permanent crisis he encouraged created large opportunities both
to advance the well-being of the Agency and to satisfy his
own personal ambitions. To ignore this neat correlation
would be naïve. To put it another way, Dulles (and the CIA)
had everything to gain by hyping the Red menace and much
to lose should the suspicion take hold that the Russians might
not actually pose such a dire threat after all. To refine the
point that Charles Wilson made: In Dulles's eyes, whatever
threatened to harm the CIA endangered the country. And
anything that threatened the CIA threatened him personally.

No more dangerous threat existed, however, than the
possibility that outsiders—not Russians, but Americans—
might gain access to the secret world over which the CIA
exercised something like a near monopoly. Perpetuating
the Agency's (and the director's) hold on power demanded
the preservation of that monopoly. The prying eyes that
caused Dulles most concern belonged not to the president,
Congress, or the press—all of whom, if for different reasons, tended to defer to the CIA—but to the American
people.

Dulles was determined to refute the proposition that
allowing powerful agencies to operate without effective
oversight might be at odds with democratic practice. "It is not
our intelligence organization which threatens our liberties,"

he wrote. "The danger is rather that we will not be adequately informed of the perils which face us." Therefore,
"the last thing we can afford to do today is to put our intelligence in chains."[29] Keeping the CIA unchained implied
allowing the Agency to decide how much information to
dole out and what information to conceal. Protracted crisis
required that the standard rules of accountability and a
well-established American wariness of government bureaucracies be waived. Self-policing, based on the presumption
of good intentions, was deemed sufficient.

By the end of the 1950s, Dulles's CIA had established a
presence just about everywhere, or at least everywhere that
mattered to Washington. With its clandestine service the
Agency had acquired the capacity to project American power
into trouble spots around the world. And by undertaking
operations from Latin America and the Middle East to Western Europe and Southeast Asia, the Agency had placed itself
on the very front lines of the Cold War.[30] Thus had the CIA
become a favored instrument for making good the mandate
of the Washington consensus.

OLD IRON ASS

No less than Allen Dulles, Curtis LeMay was a master of his
calling.[31] For Dulles, that calling emphasized guile and
trickery. For LeMay, it centered on brute force: developing
and holding in readiness the means to destroy entire societies through long-range aerial attack. In this regard, he possessed unequaled genius.

In style and personality, the two men differed markedly.
Dulles was unreadable. LeMay was an open book. Whereas
the pipe-smoking CIA director projected a captivating

combination of cunning and refinement, LeMay, a cigar perpetually jammed in his mouth, cultivated a gruff, no-nonsense, coarse persona. No son of privilege, he entered the ranks of the military elite through the back door, working his way through Ohio State University, earning a commission in the army reserve, and then serving a long apprenticeship in the prewar army air corps. During World War II, LeMay came into his own. In England, he commanded first a bombardment group and then a division, playing a leading role in the Anglo-American Combined Bomber Offensive against Germany.

In July 1944, the War Department reassigned LeMay to the Pacific. There he assumed responsibility for strategic attacks against the Japanese home islands, presiding over the firebombing of Tokyo and other major Japanese cities and then directing the atomic attacks on Hiroshima and Nagasaki that ushered in the nuclear era. If obliteration bombing qualifies as an art, then LeMay, by war's end an upwardly mobile thirty-nine-year-old major general, had established a well-earned reputation as the world's foremost practitioner. When it came to "dehousing" civilian populations, the Luftwaffe's Hermann Göring and the Royal Air Force's "Bomber" Harris weren't even in the same league. When it came to burning cities, William Tecumseh Sherman, who terrorized the citizens of the Confederacy during the Civil War, was a tyro.

In the immediate postwar period, LeMay was assigned to command U.S. air forces in Europe. During the Berlin Blockade of 1948–1949, he engineered the heroic airlift that kept that city alive and yielded the West's first great victory in the Cold War.

The same qualities that had enabled LeMay to incinerate Tokyo explained his success in preserving Berlin: single-mindedness, tenacity, a ruthless demand for results, and a remarkable capacity for getting the utmost out of those who worked for him. In any outfit he commanded, LeMay made a point of establishing himself as the best pilot, the best navigator, and the best bombardier around. (By the time he left active duty in 1965, he had been checked out to fly seventy-five different types of military aircraft.)[32] Yet to classify LeMay as primarily an aviator is to sell him short; he was an innovator, a planner, a skillful bureaucratic infighter, and a political sophisticate.

LeMay's greatest gift was for orchestration. The effective conduct of large-scale air operations involved a multiplicity of factors: airfields, aircraft, ordnance, trained crews, mechanics, spare parts, fuel and lubricants, accurate weather forecasts, effective communications, up-to-date intelligence, base support, replacements, and on and on. Success required the synchronization of all these disparate parts to produce a harmonious result today, tomorrow, and for as long as the mission required.

When LeMay took over Strategic Air Command in October 1948, that organization was floundering. Located in Roswell, New Mexico, SAC's entire strike force consisted of some thirty modified World War II B-29s. A grand total of six air crews had completed the training needed to fly a mission. The entire U.S. nuclear arsenal numbered perhaps fifty Nagasaki-type bombs, each of which required elaborate preparation before employment. Assembling a single bomb took a team of thirty-nine technicians days to complete. Despite a widespread belief that the American nuclear monopoly had elevated the United States to a position of unquestioned military dominance, SAC's ability to deliver even a single bomb against a single target in the Soviet Union was iffy at best.[33]

Shortly after the destruction of Hiroshima and Nagasaki had brought Japan to its knees, LeMay told a Pentagon board: "Our only defense is a striking-power-in-being of such size that it is capable of delivering a stronger blow than any of our potential enemies."[34] He now set out to create just such a force.

A set of fortuitous circumstances helped. When the Soviets tested their own bomb in August 1949, they shattered Washington's nuclear complacency. In June 1950, the North Korean invasion of South Korea removed the postwar cap on military spending. Defense dollars became available in abundance. At about the same time, the United States developed the capability to mass-produce nuclear weapons. As an age of nuclear scarcity gave way to an era of atomic plenty, the supply of bombs no longer constrained SAC's development.

Dwight D. Eisenhower's election to the presidency in 1952 proved a boon for LeMay and SAC. The concept of "massive retaliation" now emerged as the centerpiece of Cold War strategy. Elected in part because of popular dissatisfaction with a costly, inconclusive war in Korea, Ike had no intention of being drawn into anything even remotely similar. Massive retaliation promised that Soviet aggression anywhere would elicit an all-out nuclear response. Ensuring the "credibility" and responsiveness of the nuclear strike force therefore became the Pentagon's highest priority.

Meanwhile, the rapid pace of innovation in aircraft and weapons design, jet engines, rocketry, and communications presented a dazzling array of ever-improving capabilities for LeMay to purchase. He wasted no time in exploiting these opportunities. His achievement was threefold.

First, he expanded SAC by several orders of magnitude,

acquiring people, aircraft, weapons, and real estate at a prodigious rate. By the mid-1950s, LeMay's command oversaw
some 200,000 personnel operating from 55 bases. As one
historian has put it, SAC became "an air force within an air
force," a personal fiefdom over which LeMay ruled as completely as Dulles ruled the CIA.[35]

Second, in place of the lackadaisical standards existing
in 1948, LeMay imbued his command with a culture of
maximum readiness. In effect, as Dulles did with the CIA,
he put SAC on a war footing, converting it into a "cocked
weapon." The phrase was no mere metaphor.

Third, LeMay inaugurated a program of continuous
modernization, illustrated by the fielding of successive new
bombers, each built in large numbers: nearly four hundred
Convair B-36s entering service in 1948; some two thousand
Boeing B-47s, first fielded in 1951; and over seven hundred
Boeing B-52s, the first of which flew in 1954. Along with the
bombers came five hundred Boeing KC-135 in-flight refuel-
ing aircraft, and well-funded programs aimed at developing
supersonic long-range bombers and ballistic missiles of intercontinental reach. As far as members of Congress were concerned, SAC served as an institutionalized economic stimulus
program, which made its commander a welcome figure on
Capitol Hill. (An appreciative LeMay described his congressional supporters as "keen and knowledgeable, yet pliant.")[36]

Like the CIA, SAC became its own self-contained world.
LeMay was an unsparing taskmaster, who drove his subordinates (and himself) hard. Duty in SAC was intense and
demanding, with eighty-hour workweeks not uncommon.
To maintain this complex organization at hair-trigger alert,
it was not enough to view war as a distant theoretical possibility. LeMay inculcated into SAC a single conviction, "We

are at war now," a sentiment that could just as easily been
etched above the entrance to the new CIA headquarters
erected in 1962 at Langley, Virginia.[37]

Although the prospect of delivering the ultimate weapon
in what would be history's ultimate war did not prove
conducive to introspection, the gravity of that responsibility did foster an inflated sense of self-importance. SAC's
bomber crews and Dulles's covert agents presented opposite faces of the same coin: They went about their tasks certain that they were inhabiting the very center of the universe
and doing the nation's most vital work.

LeMay's achievements garnered considerable public
acclaim. His assertion that SAC was all that stood between
the American people and Armageddon met with widespread
acceptance. In an "exclusive," "first account ever published"
of life on the SAC flight line, *Reader's Digest* declared in 1953
that "the free world may well stand hat in hand before our
superbly trained atom-bomber crews." The writer Francis V.
Drake continued:

> They stand guard for all of us 24 hours a day, 365 days
> a year, ready to obey a flash message from the White
> House that might order them to retaliate against an
> aggressor before the United States could be destroyed.

According to Drake, SAC was "the one force that has pre-
vented the outbreak of World War III."[38] The *New York Times*
agreed: "The SAC crew in a SAC plane is the West's Number
One deterrent to the Kremlin."[39]

Harper's magazine went even further. SAC's bomber
crews "have personally assumed the burden of America's
international commitments. While living in the midst of a

largely indifferent, peaceful society, they are daily fighting and refighting a deadly mock war." Although overworked and underpaid, SAC airmen derived satisfaction from "the pride of belonging to an elite" and from "the awesome responsibility they have accepted—if the worst should occur—to obliterate a city at one blow."

> For this mission everything human and therefore fallible must be dispensed with, must be trained out of them. Systematically the Strategic Air Command seeks to perfect its men, in the hope of honing out human error, doubt, and frailty.[40]

U.S. News & World Report concurred. SAC was "the bastion of the West" and "the only force in the world that restrains the Kremlin from nuclear conquest." With "more than 2,000 bombing planes and nearly 230,000 men deployed about the world," and with a highly classified number of armed bombers always on airborne alert, the magazine assured its readers, "SAC's purpose is peace."[41]

LeMay became a sort of rough-and-ready, straight-talking folk hero in the tradition of generals Andrew Jackson and Ulysses S. Grant. The press gushed as much over him as his command. Newspaper and magazines articles inevitably featured a photograph of LeMay scowling as he chewed on or wielded his thick cigar. To *Time*, he was "the indispensable man in the Air Force's top field command."[42] *Life* magazine dubbed him the "toughest cop in the Western world." During World War II, *Life* continued, LeMay knew that when he committed his bombers against Japanese cities "a lot of innocent and helpless men, women, and babies were also going to be burned up."

This fact did not deter LeMay. He is a thoroughgoing
professional soldier. To him warfare reduces itself to
a simple alternative: kill or be killed. He would not
hesitate for a moment—indeed he would not consider
any moral problems to be involved at all—in unleashing the terrible power that now lies in his hands. ...
LeMay is a tough man: the kind of man the Russians
respect.[43]

Yet as with Dulles's CIA, this golden age of the Strategic Air
Command carried with it implications that largely escaped
notice.

In the eyes of the press and of Congress, the SAC
commander—not the president or the secretary of defense—
became the ultimate judge of whether the American air
arsenal was sufficiently robust. For LeMay to express the
slightest doubt about the relative adequacy of American
power was to induce something resembling panic in Washington.

In May 1956, appearing before a Senate subcommittee,
LeMay testified that Soviet aircraft production was outpac-
ing that of the United States—the Communists were making more warplanes and better ones. In a showdown, the
United States could still prevail, he said, but not "without
this country receiving very severe damage." The reaction
was immediate. Senators professed indignation and called
for investigations. *Life* weighed in with a pugnacious article
entitled "Second Best in Air Is Not Good Enough." Adorn-
ing the essay were side-by-side photographs comparing
U.S. and Soviet military aircraft. The captions declared "Air
Force Trails Russia in Most Combat Planes" and "Soviet Lead
over U.S. Will Be Even Greater in 1958." The only problem
with this flap: Both qualitatively and quantitatively, Soviet

air capabilities lagged well behind those of the United States—which LeMay almost certainly knew.[44] Still, he had created a stir that worked to SAC's advantage.

Yet the real key to LeMay's success lay not in his ability to set the political agenda but in his absolute control over war planning. As SAC commander, he guarded the secrets pertaining to nuclear war as carefully as Dulles guarded the secrets pertaining to clandestine operations. Like his CIA counterpart, LeMay enjoyed almost unlimited autonomy. Here lay the ultimate source of his personal power.

LeMay—not the president, the secretary of defense, or the Joint Chiefs of Staff—calculated the capacity for inflicting damage on the Soviet Union that would suffice to deter aggression or win a nuclear war if deterrence failed. LeMay's approach to fighting such a war held nothing back. During World War II, he wrote, the idea had been to "bomb and burn them until they quit. That was our theory, and history has proved we were right."[45] With the advent of nuclear weapons came a further refinement of that theory: to deliver a knock-out blow in one concentrated spasm of destruction.

At SAC headquarters in Omaha, Nebraska, far from Washington's prying eyes, preparations for delivering that blow were literally ceaseless. With each successive revision of the war plan, the list of essential targets grew more extensive. This, not incidentally, generated a plethora of requirements for additional weapons, bases, aircraft, and supporting equipment.

Early versions of SAC's war plan had envisioned dropping bombs on a few dozen Soviet cities. Once LeMay took command, that changed. The planning process took on greater rigor and, counterintuitively, SAC's target list began to grow like Topsy. By 1957, LeMay's last year at SAC, plans for war with the Soviet Union envisioned attacks on more than 3,200 targets, each requiring multiple nuclear bombs to guarantee "assured destruction," not to mention countless millions of casualties. Aware that SAC had effectively seized control of war planning, President Eisenhower complained that "[t]hey are trying to get themselves into an incredible position of having enough to destroy every conceivable target all over the world, plus a three-fold reserve."

Such complaints were to no avail. Under LeMay's successors at SAC, the process continued. By 1963, the war plan included 8,400 targets across the communist bloc. By 1970, that number exceeded 10,000.[46] In many respects this qualifies as LeMay's most tangible achievement. Whether capabilities were driving requirements or vice versa became impossible to discern; the two worked in tandem. This much was indisputable: The war plan devised by SAC provided it with essentially unlimited drawing rights on the U.S. Treasury, with the army and navy left to fight over whatever scraps remained.

Like Dulles, LeMay loved his country and made considerable sacrifices on its behalf. Yet as with Dulles, LeMay's concern for the well-being of the United States blended seamlessly with his devotion to the well-being of the institution he led. LeMay was blind to the possibility that the infatuation with nuclear weapons he had done so much to encourage and that, during the 1950s, raised SAC (and himself) to such prominence might produce adverse consequences for the United States, particularly as other nations acquired or sought their own nuclear capabilities. That the production, testing, and use of nuclear weapons might have negative political, strategic, or environmental implications lay beyond his ability (or willingness) to consider. Short-term interests swept aside longer-term considerations. Thus were the true costs of a strategic paradigm that relied so heavily on such weapons concealed.

Henry Adams once observed that "men invariably follow interests in deciding morals."[47] This maxim applies to LeMay as much as it does to Allen Dulles. His interests (and those of SAC) required the removal of any moral impediment to waging a war of annihilation. To accomplish this, LeMay, like Dulles, declared in effect that the ends justified the means. As LeMay saw it, once war had begun the supreme imperative was to end that war as expeditiously as possible. As a staunch advocate of strategic bombing, he believed that the quickest way to do so was by inflicting the greatest amount of destruction possible, until the enemy lost either the will or the ability to continue the fight. Viewed from this perspective, it made little sense to discriminate between combatants and noncombatants. To bow to the sensibilities of the "writers, clergymen, savants, . . . self-appointed philosophers, and . . . beatniks" who sought to make such distinctions— LeMay dismissed them all as "mooncalves"—would simply prolong conflict.[48] This in his eyes violated a fundamental obligation.

LeMay and Dulles resembled each other in one other way as well. Even as each testified to his hopes of averting a showdown with the Soviet Union, each promoted patterns of behavior that increased the risks of such a confrontation. Just as Dulles relied on covert action to discomfit and harass, so LeMay employed SAC to poke, probe, prod, and remind the Soviet leadership of just how vulnerable they were to nuclear assault. SAC reconnaissance aircraft regularly penetrated Soviet airspace. SAC bombers made passes over Soviet coastal cities, such as Vladivostok.[49]

Strategic Air Command's nominal mission was one of

deterrence. "Peace is our profession" read its official motto. Yet LeMay's conception of deterrence implied an element of outright intimidation. Whereas the CIA was all about accepting risk—pushing the envelope, the bolder and more unconventional the better—SAC was all about the pursuit of absolute certainty, providing an iron-clad guarantee of unleashing the furies of nuclear destruction whenever and wherever required. Unlike Dulles, who indulged mistakes— Agency attempts to infiltrate agents behind the Iron and Bamboo Curtains repeatedly failed at great human cost— LeMay refused to tolerate free thinking, sloppiness, or lapses in judgment. Dulles valued daring. LeMay deman- ded conformity—strict adherence to procedures that SAC spelled out in great detail.

LeMay's aim was to secure the peace by demonstrating SAC's unquestioned and overwhelming dominance, creat- ing, in the jargon of nuclear strategy, a first-strike capability. "The main thing," LeMay later reflected, "was that this force was not built simply for retaliation. . . . It was built for people to see, and looking at it, nobody would want to tackle it. That was our main objective."[50] Dulles employed secret means to achieve observable results; LeMay wanted Ameri- ca's adversaries to contemplate the unimaginable—which meant displaying at all times for all to see the means of destruction at hand.

In practical terms, providing absolute assurance that "nobody would want to tackle it" was mission impossible— whatever payload, range, or standard of accuracy might seem adequate today would surely be inadequate tomor- row. Yet from an institutional point of view mission impos- sible was mission perfect.

Since LeMay and his commanders knew—or at least professed to believe—that the United States had no intention of ever implementing a policy of preventive war, they viewed their relentless pursuit of nuclear dominance as a source of stability. That the Soviets might interpret U.S. intentions and capabilities differently was not a matter to which they devoted any significant attention. Yet were intimidation to fail—were the Soviets to miscalculate or panic or mount some ill-advised response to SAC's goading—well, that too was all right. If the showdown had come, in the 1950s at least, LeMay was supremely confident of the outcome: "There was definitely a time when we could have destroyed all of Russia," he bragged in his memoirs, "without losing a man to their defenses."[51]

YIN AND YANG

To avert the outbreak of cataclysmic war, Strategic Air Command threatened destruction on a scale never before seen, with LeMay giving every indication that he was more than willing to make good on that threat. To ensure the survival of freedom, democracy, and liberal values, the Central Intelligence Agency engaged in activities that in our own day would satisfy the definition of state-sponsored terrorism, with Allen Dulles giving every indication that even the dirtiest of dirty tricks were acceptable as long as they were perpetrated by the honorable men of the CIA.

In the 1950s, Americans spent little time contemplating such ironies. In the midst of a never-ending national security crisis, the preference was for accepting at face value the self-image projected by institutions entrusted with ensuring the nation's safety. The tendency was to defer to those with inside knowledge and ask few questions. The CIA and SAC numbered at the very top of the organizations that benefited from this inclination. In this regard, Dulles and

LeMay, the emblematic semiwarriors of the early Cold War, accurately sized up the zeitgeist of the era and skillfully turned it to their advantage.

The anxieties and insecurities of 1950s America derived from many sources. In culture and religion, at the workplace and in the home, the acids of modernity were dissolving much that Americans once had found reassuring and familiar. By pointing to communism as the essence of the problem, the semiwarriors convinced their fellow citizens that whatever uncertainties the country might be facing at home, dealing with external threats had to come first— indeed, facing down the danger "out there" just might provide the surest route to dealing with problems back here. Persuading Americans that nothing was more important than national security qualified as a formidable achievement.

Nominally, these two men and the institutions they led were competitors. Intent on controlling all reconnaissance missions over the USSR, LeMay, for example, waged a fierce, ultimately unsuccessful campaign to have control of the CIA's U-2 "spy plane" transferred to SAC. In a deeper sense, however, the CIA and SAC enjoyed a reciprocal relationship, the existence and actions of one justifying the existence and actions of the other.

During the early, formative days of the Cold War, the CIA and SAC elevated a cult of global activism to a national first principle and so laid the foundation for what became the Washington consensus. Dulles's CIA waged World War III in the shadows. LeMay's SAC waged it through ostentatious saber rattling. Yet each complemented the other.

Ted Shackley, a longtime Dulles protégé, made the point explicitly, describing clandestine warfare as "the stitch in time that eliminates bloodier and more costly alternatives."

As Shackley saw it, the CIA saved the world from SAC. Through its brave day-in, day-out campaign in the shadow world of espionage and covert action, the Agency kept the Russians off-balance and on the defensive, thereby averting the possibility of "a nuclear confrontation between the Soviet Union, controlling much of the world, and an isolated, embattled United States, turning to its nuclear arsenal in convulsive desperation."[52]

For his part, LeMay might well have claimed that SAC was insulating the United States from any backlash triggered by CIA mischief making. A massive nuclear arsenal was held at the ready, giving pause to anyone inclined to retaliate against Agency operations that not infrequently went awry or produced unintended consequences. As much or more than the Soviet Union itself, in other words, the CIA and SAC each provided a raison d'être on which the other drew. Together they left an indelible mark on our age.

By the end of the Eisenhower era, all the elements of the Washington rules were firmly in place. Principles and practices established by the CIA and SAC—by now the yin and yang of the new National Security State—had become sacrosanct. All that seemingly remained was for the rest of the national security apparatus to come into conformity with them.

One particular institution lagged notably behind: the U.S. Army. Accustomed to making sharp distinctions between peace and war, army officers struggled to accommodate their service to the requirements of semiwar, a struggle further complicated by the citizen-draftees filling its ranks. A reliance on short-service soldiers was at odds with the demands of long-term struggle. The army of the 1950s was simply not well suited for inconclusive, open-ended quasi-hostilities.

Outflanked on the one side by SAC and on the other by

the CIA, the army by the dawn of the 1960s had become the unloved stepchild of the national security establishment. Soon thereafter, however, a makeover endowed the service with heightened allure. Offered a fresh chance to secure a niche within the Washington consensus, the army jumped at the opportunity, with disastrous implications for itself and the country.

2

ILLUSIONS OF FLEXIBILITY AND CONTROL

WITHIN TWENTY-FOUR HOURS OF HIS ELECTION AS PRESIdent on November 8, 1960, John F. Kennedy announced his intention to retain Allen Dulles as CIA director. When the new president took office on January 20, 1961, Curtis LeMay, no longer commanding SAC, was serving as the air force's vice chief of staff, the number two uniformed position in that service. Soon thereafter, with the current chief of staff due to retire, Kennedy nominated LeMay as his replacement.

Through such appointments, Kennedy signaled his administration's commitment to the prevailing national security paradigm and to the bipartisan consensus from which it derived its legitimacy. To those who questioned whether the young president possessed the requisite experience and toughness to take on the Soviets, keeping old hands like Dulles and LeMay on board (along with FBI director J. Edgar Hoover) provided a suitable response. Although the New Frontier, as the incoming administration branded its program, promised vigor and fresh thinking, those who had been at the forefront in waging the Cold War were keeping their seats at the table.

This reassuring picture with its emphasis on continuity concealed an intensifying behind-the-scenes struggle, simultaneously masked by, and captured in, the phrase *flexible response*. The national security policies devised during the Truman and Eisenhower eras had created winners and losers. Chief among the losers had been the U.S. Army. The heyday of massive retaliation and the golden age of covert operations rendered the army all but irrelevant.

Other than serving as a "tripwire"—plainly visible in West Germany and postarmistice South Korea to warn away would-be intruders lest they trigger a nuclear war—the army found itself largely cut out of the action. The clearest expression of this exclusion came in the form of the Pentagon budget share. By 1959, the army claimed but 23 percent of defense dollars while the navy received 28 percent, and the dominant air force scooped up the remaining 46 percent. Army leaders of the 1950s, preeminently Gen. Maxwell D. Taylor, another now-forgotten figure who left in his wake a wide swath of calamity, viewed this as intolerable.[1]

Flexible response, General Taylor's brainchild, grew out of the army's determination to reclaim a greater role in implementing the sacred trinity. Jockeying by have-nots to improve their position has long figured as a commonplace expression of bureaucratic politics, those with an ax to grind typically attributing to their parochial concerns cosmic significance. As Taylor saw it, by putting the army on half-rations, the Eisenhower administration was endangering the country. A minimally adequate national security posture meant not just being able to wage nuclear war and conduct covert operations, but standing ready to do everything

else in between—"everything else," of course, encompassing tasks typically falling under the army's purview.

During his tenure as army chief of staff from 1955 to
1959, Taylor's efforts to win greater respect (and budget
share) for his service met with little sympathy within the
confines of the Joint Chiefs of Staff or at the Eisenhower
White House. On leaving active duty, the frustrated Taylor
wasted no time in repackaging his argument as a short book,
which in the spring of 1960 appeared to considerable acclaim.
A stinging critique of Eisenhower-era policies as well as a
blueprint for reform, *The Uncertain Trumpet* enjoyed a seven-
week run on the *New York Times* bestseller list and found particular favor among Democrats, delighted to have a highly
decorated and reputedly cerebral four-star general publicly
lambasting a Republican administration headed by a highly
decorated and exceedingly popular five-star general.

Taylor's message was nothing if not straightforward. A
perception that the nation was "faced with declining military strength at a time of increasing political tension" compelled him to go public. Counting on nuclear weapons to
avert war, he wrote, was a "Great Fallacy." Eisenhower's
strategy of massive retaliation, which offered "only two
choices, the initiation of general nuclear war or compromise
and retreat," had "reached a dead end" and needed to be
scrapped. True security demanded that the United States
acquire the means "to react across the entire spectrum of
possible challenge." A new, more diverse mix of capabilities
that would enable the United States "to respond anywhere,
any time, with weapons and forces appropriate to the situation" defined the essence of flexible response. Diversifying
U.S. military capabilities would inter alia boost the army's
claim on resources, a point that Taylor did not bother to

make explicitly, but one not lost on even the casual student of interservice politics.[2]

The contest to choose Eisenhower's successor transformed Taylor's critique from an unhappy general's complaint into a full-fledged Idea Whose Time Had Come. While campaigning for the presidency Senator Kennedy echoed the notes sounded by Taylor's *Trumpet*, depicting Eisenhower-era national security policy as stodgy, stale, complacent, and completely inadequate. His language was unsparing. "[N]o amount of oratory," he told the American Legion,

> no extravagant claims or vociferous braggadocio, no unjustified charges, can hide the harsh fact that behind the rhetoric, behind the soothing words and the confusing figures, American strength relative to that of the Soviet Union has been slipping, and communism has been advancing steadily in every area of the world.[3]

If elected, Kennedy vowed to reverse this "decline" and make the United States "first in military power across the board." This implied, among other things, "expanding and modernizing our conventional forces," while endowing them with greater "versatility and mobility." Kennedy was by no means averse to nuclear weapons—indeed, promising everything for every service, he vowed to enlarge the strategic arsenal as well. Like Taylor, he merely insisted that it was also necessary to develop robust non-nuclear intervention capabilities, enabling U.S. forces to "put out a brushfire war before it becomes a conflagration."[4]

Kennedy took power amid expectations that he would vanquish the uncertainties that had so worried Taylor. In his inaugural address, the new president announced that

"the trumpet summons us again" and made plain his eager-
ness to answer that summons with unflinching resolve. Soon
thereafter Kennedy appropriated the phrase Taylor had
coined and *flexible response* became the official label attached
to the new administration's program for military reform.

Yet the purposes animating Kennedy's defense initiative
extended well beyond the narrow aims that had inspired
Taylor to speak out. This was no simple attempt to restore
the army's relevance. The president and his advisers intended
to devise new and creative ways of making force useful.
Keen to reinvigorate U.S. global leadership, they wanted to
expand the range of options available to policy makers.
Whereas Eisenhower had counted on the prospect of nuclear
cataclysm to forestall the actual event, Kennedy's "action
intellectuals" believed that keeping World War III at bay
required a forward-leaning posture: The United States
needed to demonstrate its willingness to fight non-nuclear
wars. With all the certainty of men unacquainted with the
actual use of power, they did not doubt their ability to compel war to do their bidding. Not for the last time, an enthusiasm for limited war served chiefly to open the door to
unlimited military expenditures.

That flexible response was going to cost money was
never a concern. So the lid Eisenhower had struggled to
impose on Pentagon spending now came off. During Kennedy's first year in office, military outlays rose 15 percent.[5]
To close a nonexistent "missile gap" that had figured as a
prominent campaign issue, the administration doubled the
production rate of land-based intercontinental ballistic missiles from thirty to sixty per month and boosted the planned
fleet of Polaris nuclear submarines—each of which carried
sixteen nuclear-tipped missiles—from twenty-nine to forty-
one. The effect of this urgently promoted buildup was to

increase the actual "missile gap" that already favored the
United States by a considerable margin. In this sense,
although spooking the Kremlin, Kennedy gave the air force
and navy little cause for complaint.

Much as Taylor had intended, however, the primary beneficiary of flexible response was the army. Between 1961 and
1962, its budget shot up, as the service added 207,000 more
soldiers to its rolls. The number of active-duty divisions
increased from eleven to sixteen. To bolster the U.S. commitment to NATO, Kennedy dispatched additional ground
troops to West Germany. He also more than doubled the
army's Special Forces and expressed intense personal interest in the development of counterinsurgency doctrine and
techniques—these, Kennedy believed, held the key to rolling back the Red tide threatening to inundate the Third
World.[6] Readiness, mobility, and deployability became the
new watchwords: Kennedy's army existed not to serve as a
nuclear tripwire, but to engage the enemy—with particular
attention to applying force on a limited scale for limited
aims while minimizing the risk of events mushrooming out
of control.

An editorial published in *Life* on the eve of Kennedy's
inauguration conveyed the spirit of the moment. Along the
"long frontier between the Communist and free worlds," it
claimed, the United States and its allies were likely to face
"the necessity of resisting aggression" in any number of
places. Existing capabilities did not suffice for what *Life*
called the "brush-fire wars" now looming on the horizon. In
fighting such wars, the overriding aim was to put out the fire,
not blow up the world. In that regard, "a tailored response is
the best way to minimize the risk of 'escalation.'" The magazine left it to a then obscure Harvard professor named
Henry Kissinger to spell out the implications. "[T]he secu-

rity of the free world," he opined, required that the United
States have "military units capable of checking Soviet aggression *at any scale of violence.*" The editors of *Life* agreed wholeheartedly. And that meant the United States was going to
need many more "foot soldiers than are now in uniform"—a
view that comported precisely with the thinking of the new
administration about to assume power in Washington.[7]

So the years of neglect that Taylor had called the army's
"Babylonian captivity" came to an end.[8] No longer would
the United States have to rely on SAC and the CIA as its sole
instruments of power projection with the range of alternatives confined to all-out nuclear attack or covert "dirty tricks."
Conventional war fighting and unconventional counterinsurgency forces now formed part of the mix.

The intent, recalled Robert McNamara, the Ford Motor
Company executive recruited to become Kennedy's secretary
of defense, was "to broaden the range of options by strengthening and modernizing the military's ability to fight a non-
nuclear war."[9] In the lexicon of the New Frontier, *options*
ranked as a favored word. Flexible response was all about
creating options.

Kennedy's acolytes portrayed this as a dramatic departure from the past. In truth, it was anything but. Rather than
overturning the national security paradigm of the 1950s, flexible response actually served to affirm it, even while incorporating into the Washington consensus those who had felt
excluded.

During the Eisenhower era, there had never been enough
money to go around. Flexible response promised more
money more evenly distributed. Henceforth, every part of
the national security establishment was going to have a part
to play. In this sense, the administration's real achievement
was to eliminate the last remnants of internal resistance:

Obstreperous army generals were now on board. Kennedy had renewed and enriched the U.S. global military presence, its power projection capabilities, and—as events quickly demonstrated—its penchant for intervention as well.

WHO'S IN CHARGE?

Largely concealed from the American public, but clearly evident within Washington, flexible response also raised key questions of control. Who exactly was to exercise the options that the administration's defense reforms were making available? For Kennedy and his lieutenants the answer to that question was quite clear: They were intent on restoring to the White House the authority over national security issues that, in their view, had been severely compromised during the Eisenhower era. Reasserting presidential primacy necessarily implied bringing the CIA and SAC to heel.

In a sense, this effort had already begun. In December 1960, Eisenhower himself had taken a first step toward chipping away at SAC's monopoly over nuclear war planning. The outgoing president ordered the Pentagon to draft a comprehensive new blueprint for nuclear war, a plan incorporating guidance issued from Washington, rather than simply reflecting SAC's own preferences.[10]

In its first iteration, the resulting Single Integrated Operational Plan (SIOP) was more symbolic than real. The struggle for control of the nation's nuclear arsenal was only beginning, that struggle now pitting Secretary of Defense McNamara, an exceedingly smart man who, in his own words, saw "quantification as a language to add precision to reasoning," against LeMay, who tended to go with his gut and knew that he had forgotten more about warfare than even the smartest civilian could learn, whatever the analytical tools applied. The McNamara who, at age forty-four, took office in January 1961 "had no patience with the myth that the Department of Defense could not be managed."[11] Dispelling that myth meant among other things showing Curtis LeMay who was boss.

McNamara's arrival at the Pentagon marked the resumption of a relationship with LeMay that dated back to World War II. The two men had their own rich history. If by the 1960s their thinking about war had diverged, they had once been close collaborators. During the latter stages of World War II, McNamara, then a young army air corps staff officer, worked for LeMay, serving as (in McNamara's words) "part of a mechanism" that proffered advice on how to inflict the greatest amount of damage on Japanese cities with the greatest efficiency.[12] McNamara's considerable analytical prowess had facilitated the killing of several hundred thousand noncombatants. Whether the result qualified as harsh but necessary or as a war crime—late in life, McNamara inclined toward the latter—the new defense secretary's fingerprints were all over the bombing campaign that had reduced Japan's cities to ashes and that LeMay viewed as the model for how to wage war against the Soviet Union.

The ensuing contest between the two centered on the composition, size, and anticipated employment of America's nuclear strike force, with its stockpile of existing weapons now exceeding eighteen thousand. During the previous decade, LeMay had played a dominant role in determining these matters. In the new decade, McNamara intended that he, acting as the president's agent, would do so.

When it came to the composition of the force, the contest centered on the future of the B-70 Valkyrie, a supersonic, long-range bomber then under development. LeMay viewed the Valkyrie as essential to ensuring SAC's ability to penetrate

Soviet air space. Fielding the B-70 was his—and therefore, the air force's—top priority.

Given the growing capabilities of land-based and submarine-launched ballistic missiles, McNamara was not persuaded, especially with the subsonic B-52 less than a decade old and the B-70 expected to cost $20 billion over ten years. Concluding that the United States really didn't need the Valkyrie, McNamara decided to kill it, sending LeMay into a rage. The air force general found especially intolerable "the Secretary's saying 'No' to something the military wished to do and giving *a military reason* for his action." While devaluing genuinely professional advice, "he and his coterie were setting themselves up as military experts."[13] LeMay dialed up his friends on Capitol Hill and persuaded them to appropriate enough funds to keep the B-70 program alive. McNamara simply refused to spend the money: The B-70 was dead. McNamara had seemingly won the first round on points.[14]

McNamara and LeMay next locked horns over the size of the U.S. strategic arsenal: How much was enough? The ability of the United States to produce nuclear weapons along with the means to deliver them had become essentially limitless. When it came to the silo-based Minuteman ICBM, Gen. Thomas Power, LeMay's successor at SAC, was pressing for a force of ten thousand missiles. The air force was formally requesting three thousand. McNamara's analysis persuaded him that even Eisenhower's planned force of six hundred ICBMs was probably too large; a few hundred missiles should suffice. Yet with Kennedy having vowed to close an ostensibly dangerous, but actually nonexistent "missile gap" invented by his campaign and with Congress unhappy with the defense secretary's highhanded disposition of the B-70, analytical rigor took a backseat to politics.

McNamara arbitrarily declared that the nation's security required 1,200 Minutemen, giving the air force less than it wanted, but enough to keep its supporters happy.[15] Score round two for LeMay.

Finally, there was the matter of thinking the unthinkable: envisioning how to wage actual nuclear war. Here, McNamara managed to tie himself in knots while essentially affirming the status quo. SIOP-61 reflected LeMay's preference for an all-out nuclear attack on the Soviet Union, the People's Republic of China, and most of the communist world. McNamara recoiled from the prospect of cold-blooded slaughter on such a scale. He sought an approach to nuclear war offering the president (and himself) choice, flexibility, and the ability to discriminate. McNamara wanted options. And as the forces under his direction refined their plans for blowing up the world, he wanted the conscience-salving assurance that the United States had not entirely disregarded the moral implications involved.

For assistance in this quest, McNamara turned not to the uniformed military, whose creative capacity he doubted, but to the fraternity of nuclear strategists. By the 1960s, these well-credentialed political scientists, economists, and mathematicians, installed in leading universities or at think tanks such as RAND, had carved out for themselves a comfortable niche as influential interpreters of the Washington consensus. Trafficking in jargon tricked out as profundities, these self-described policy intellectuals purported to bring to the study of nuclear warfare greater rigor than the likes of LeMay deemed either feasible or necessary.

Intent on investing the U.S. nuclear posture with greater "credibility" without being excessively provocative, they generated a dizzying array of obfuscating twaddle: finite deterrence, graduated response, controlled response, counterforce, counter-cities, counterforce no-cities, damage limitation, full first strike, decapitation, second strike, assured second strike, and assured destruction. Never, however, did this endeavor yield any definitive conclusions, ostensibly brilliant strategic insights becoming obsolete more quickly than the aircraft comprising SAC's bomber force. To model nuclear war, they conjured up absurdly complex scenarios— Herman Kahn's "escalation ladder" had forty-four rungs beginning with "Ostensible Crisis" and culminating with "Spasm or Insensate War."[16] They pondered such imponderables as how to create space for negotiating pauses in the middle of a nuclear exchange.

Intent on basing nuclear strategy on something other than the naked threat to obliterate large segments of humankind, McNamara waded into this murky thicket, almost immediately lost his bearings, and eventually emerged pretty much where he had entered. Whichever way he turned, McNamara ran up against the same conclusions: In *any* nuclear crisis, there was no way to guarantee that the other side would understand, agree with, or conform to whatever logic happened to inform U.S. actions.

The very notion of exercising carefully calibrated "options" to maintain "control" in a war gone nuclear was a mirage. Barring the absolutely certain and complete elimination of an adversary's retaliatory capability, *any* use of a nuclear weapon against another nuclear weapons state would pose unacceptable risks to the attacker; victory, that is, was a chimera. Finally, *any* use of nuclear weapons would result in devastation on a scale impossible to justify; humanely waged nuclear war was an oxymoron.

Regarding massive retaliation as crude and brutal, while unable to imagine himself ordering such an extreme response, McNamara felt the Eisenhower approach lacked credibility. It was, therefore, "useless" as a basis for a strategy of deterrence.[17] He pursued what he fancied to be a more rigorously analytical approach. His conclusion was this: Confronting the Kremlin with the prospect of assured destruction of one-quarter to one-third of the Soviet population and two-thirds of Soviet industry would prevent the Cold War from turning hot. He calculated further that the delivery of four hundred megatons of nuclear weapons—equivalent in destructive power to 26,600 Hiroshima-type bombs—would suffice to inflict that level of damage.[18]

As it happened, the U.S. nuclear arsenal had long since passed that plateau. The strategic forces being expanded at McNamara's behest already had many thousands of megatons at their disposal. To bring his revised strategy into alignment with these already existing capabilities (and undoubtedly with an eye to satisfying various political and bureaucratic interests), McNamara declared that *each* of the three major components of the U.S. strategic strike force—the long-range bombers, the land-based ICBMs, and the submarine-launched ballistic missiles—needed to be *independently* capable of inflicting the requisite level of assured destruction. Whether such an attack implied killing the entire Soviet population or one-third of the population three times over was not clear. McNamara had plainly decided that credibility required considerable redundancy.

This "strategic triad," too, now became enshrined as an essential component of U.S. policy. The net effect was to render permanent the oversized, multidimensional nuclear strike force that the Kennedy administration had declared an urgent necessity. Even today, nearly fifty years after its creation, twenty years after the end of the Cold War, the triad, although modified and updated many times, survives.

Here lies McNamara's most enduring contribution to nuclear policy.

McNamara's search for options and flexibility, not to mention his attempt to inject moral considerations into nuclear war planning, produced negligible results. No matter how hard McNamara tried to rationalize nuclear strategy, it remained stubbornly irrational. As in the 1950s, so too in the 1960s, nuclear war meant nuclear holocaust. The real winner of the contest was the Washington consensus, which emerged from this supposed battle of the titans reaffirmed and stronger than ever.

When the dust of McNamara's strategic reassessment had settled, the outcome did not especially discomfit senior military officers like LeMay, defense contractors, or their congressional supporters. They got most of what they wanted and could live comfortably with the results. For their part, the Soviets must have wondered what all the fuss was about. The label attached to U.S. strategy might have changed, but as one historian has aptly observed, "assured destruction was surely massive retaliation by another name."[19]

DUMB AND DUMBER

Meanwhile, a covert operation gone badly awry provided Kennedy with a tutorial regarding the risks involved in allowing agencies other than the White House to determine the course of national security policy.

Eisenhower was hardly the first and would not be the last president to bequeath his successor a poison pill. In Kennedy's case, the inheritance bore the label Operation Zapata, a scheme concocted by the CIA, albeit with Eisenhower's assent, that aimed to repeat in Cuba the successes the Agency had ostensibly achieved in Iran and Guatemala.

Just as the CIA had overthrown Mossadegh and Árbenz, it now set out to overthrow Cuban leader Fidel Castro, raising a small force of 1,400 Cuban exiles to invade their homeland with expectations of triggering a popular uprising.

The ensuing failure is too well known to require a detailed accounting here. Suffice it to say that Kennedy, sensing the enterprise was a dubious one, stalled for time, sent subordinates back to take a second look, and tinkered with operational details before reluctantly allowing it to proceed. When giving the final go-ahead, the president insisted that the operation succeed or fail on its own: Under no circumstances was he going to send in U.S. forces if the CIA-trained proxies got into more trouble than they could handle.[20]

Even before the first Cuban exile hit the beach at the Bay of Pigs on April 17, 1961, everything had begun to go wrong. With disaster looming, the CIA made an eleventh-hour appeal, entreating Kennedy (through Secretary of State Dean Rusk) to order direct military intervention. The president denied that request. When the operation soon thereafter collapsed, leakers wasted no time in blaming the White House: Kennedy's timidity in refusing to commit American muscle, they claimed, had doomed the enterprise.

For our purposes, the real significance of the Bay of Pigs lies in what next ensued. Kennedy's response to his first foreign policy crisis produced results—almost all of them negative—that went far beyond what the president himself could possibly have envisioned. In that sense, the Bay of Pigs stands in relation to the Kennedy presidency as the 1964 Gulf of Tonkin incident would to the presidency of Lyndon Johnson or the 1979 takeover of the U.S. embassy in Tehran to the presidency of Jimmy Carter. As a turning point, the Bay of Pigs deserves comparison with 9/11—a moment that created an opening to pose first-order questions, but elicited instead an ill-conceived, reflexive response. As would John-son, Carter, and George W. Bush, Kennedy in 1961 squandered an opportunity to rethink and reorient U.S. policy, with fate-ful implications.

Less than a hundred days into his presidency, Kennedy found himself obliged to take personal responsibility for the most humiliating foreign-policy failure the nation had experienced in decades. He was adamant that this would never happen again.

In Washington, large-scale failure or scandal inevitably produces demands for explanations. More often than not, however, the ensuing investigation undertaken by some congressional committee or blue-ribbon commission devotes less attention to uncovering truth or probing for underlying causes than to limiting political fallout.

So in the wake of the Bay of Pigs, the president turned to Maxwell Taylor, recruiting him to head up an in-house inquiry into the causes of the debacle. As chair of the Cuba Study Group, the retired general presided over an investi-gation that gave the president what he wanted. Besides Tay-lor, the group consisted of chief of naval operations Adm. Arleigh Burke, CIA director Allen Dulles (whose agency had, after all, planned, prepared, and overseen the debacle), and Attorney General Robert Kennedy—all of whom, albeit for different reasons, were more interested in damage con-trol than in pursuing the facts wherever they might happen to lead. Not surprisingly, Taylor and his colleagues focused almost exclusively on tactical and operational issues, while giving wide berth to anything touching even remotely on basic policy. It was the equivalent of investigating a bridge collapse without bothering to assess the structural integrity of the basic engineering design.

As Taylor interpreted his charge, he was to evaluate the

Bay of Pigs as one instance of U.S.-orchestrated "paramili-
tary, guerrilla, and anti-guerrilla activity . . . with a view to
strengthening our work in this area."[21] What mattered most
was to get on with business. When it came to identifying
the "proximate cause" of Operation Zapata's failure, therefore, Taylor's group concluded that the core problem was a
"shortage of ammunition." That the Cuban exile air force—a
ramshackle collection of obsolete aircraft, largely crewed by
CIA contractors—had performed poorly also emerged as a
matter of concern. Finally, there was the fact that the executive branch "was not organizationally prepared to cope
with this kind of military operation." A rejiggering of the
organizational charts, allowing for more effective presidential control, was clearly in order.[22]

Exactly how Cuba threatened U.S. interests, thereby neces-
sitating Castro's removal, and whether or not covert action
offered a plausible way to achieve that aim: These were matters the Cuba Study Group did not take up. In reporting their
findings to the president, Taylor and his associates were content to note: "They had been struck with the general feeling
that there can be no long-term living with Castro as a neigh-
bor." The basis of this general feeling remained unexplored
and unexplained.

The members of the study group—who engaged in little
actual study—deemed it sufficient to assert that Castro's
"continued presence within the hemispheric community as
a dangerously effective exponent of Communism and Anti-
Americanism constitutes a real menace." They urged Kennedy to have another go at the Cuban dictator, recommending
that "new guidance be provided for political, military, economic and propaganda action against Castro."[23] Kennedy
welcomed these findings, which conveniently coincided with
his own existing views.

The Bay of Pigs might have provided an opportunity for what we today call "a teachable moment." Taylor's management of the Cuba Study Group—its classified findings needless to say withheld from the public—ensured that nothing of importance would be taught or learned. Yet when he had finished his assignment, Taylor could rightly claim a threefold achievement. First, by confining his inquiry to tactical issues, he deflected criticism away from the existing national security consensus. Fundamental questions, whether, for example, relying on covert action to overthrow foreign governments was worth the risk and actually served the national interest, remained off-limits. Second, by suggesting that culpability within the White House extended no further than a few organizational deficiencies, he created an opportunity for Kennedy (working through trusted lieutenants) to assert greater oversight over high-priority covert operations. Exercising direct White House control over CIA activities would reduce the likelihood of Agency gaffes ever getting the president into a similar pickle.

Finally—perhaps as a reward for items one and two—Taylor managed to make his way back into a position of power. Kennedy's disenchantment with the Joint Chiefs of Staff for having failed to alert him to the risks posed by Zapata—whether the Chiefs were malicious, lazy, or just stupid was not clear—persuaded him to recall Taylor to active duty, first by inventing the post of Military Representative to the President, and then by appointing him as chairman of the Joint Chiefs.

The most immediate result of the Bay of Pigs debacle was to redouble the administration's determination to eliminate Castro. Although the Pentagon focused its attention on the possibility of direct military intervention, the White House remained wary of action that smacked of naked

imperialism. Instead, the Cuba Study Group's recommenda-
tion that the president issue "new guidance" regarding
action against the Cuban dictator found expression in Operation Mongoose, an aggressive program of covert action
that aimed to get rid of Castro and subvert his revolution. In
hopes of ensuring the program's success—and protect himself from being duped again—Kennedy fired Allen Dulles
along with other senior CIA officials who had concocted
Operation Zapata. He then assigned responsibility for Mongoose to his most trusted deputy: his brother Robert, the
attorney general, now doing double duty as the nation's
chief law enforcement officer and its principal impresario of
dirty tricks.

The younger Kennedy became chair of a newly created
anti-Castro steering group known as the Special Group
(Augmented), charged with coordinating the actions of all
government agencies conspiring to topple Castro. Bringing
to this task the energy for which he was well known, Robert
Kennedy declared his intention to "stir things up on [the]
island with espionage, sabotage, [and] general disorder,"
working through Cuban exiles. Direct military intervention
was to be a last resort.

The likelihood of such actions inducing unintended
consequences left the attorney general undaunted: "[W]e
have nothing to lose in my estimate."[24] The younger Kennedy wasted no time declaring that solving the Cuba
problem ranked as "the top priority in the United States
Government—all else is secondary—no time, money, effort,
or manpower is to be spared."[25]

Likewise not to be spared were the legal and moral
norms to which U.S. officials professed allegiance. With leg-
endary spook Maj. Gen. Edward Lansdale acting as Kennedy's chief of operations, all sorts of bizarre chicanery soon

followed, including collusion with the Mafia in plots to assassinate Castro, fantastical schemes aimed at inciting popular insurrection, and a program of sabotage directed at Cuba's food supply, power plants, oil refineries, and other economic assets—all of this together constituting one of the most infamous and profitless episodes in the history of American statecraft.

From the outset, Mongoose was bravado and swagger masquerading as policy. "We are in a combat situation—where we have been given full command," Lansdale announced in January 1962, adding that with "all the men, money, material, and spiritual assets of this most powerful nation on earth," failure was not an option.[26] At Robert Kennedy's urging, Lansdale cobbled together an ambitious program to "help the Cubans overthrow the Communist regime from within Cuba and institute a new government with which the United States can live in peace."

The resulting plan distributed among various executive departments and agencies thirty-two specific tasks, running the gamut from "inducing failures in food crops" and mounting sabotage attacks to recruiting defectors and devising "songs, symbols, [and] propaganda themes" to boost the morale of an all but nonexistent indigenous resistance. According to Lansdale, accomplishing this menu of tasks would culminate with Castro's overthrow. The target date for completion: October 1962.[27]

The manic activity that followed included a pronounced element of opéra bouffe. The slogan devised to inspire the Cuban opposition (task 27) was "Guasano Libre," loosely translated by one unimpressed State Department official as "worms of the world unite."[28] Concerted attempts by the Defense Department to induce Cuban exiles to enlist in the U.S. armed forces (task 32) yielded a meager total of 142 recruits. Hundreds more expressed interest only to be rejected on "moral and security grounds." The explanation for this puzzling problem? Most of the would-be warriors, reported Deputy Secretary of Defense Roswell Gilpatric, "were found unacceptable on the basis of admitted sexual deviations."[29]

Within weeks, it became evident that prospects for fomenting an uprising inside Cuba were remote. Sabotage, harassment, propagandizing, economic warfare, and assassination plots would not suffice to eliminate Castro. Disappointment did not, however, persuade the administration to reassess its objectives, nor is there evidence that it abandoned Lansdale's timetable. Instead, Mongoose underwent a metamorphosis. Rather than itself serving as the instrument of decision, it became an interim step, intended to pave the way for "the instantaneous commitment of sufficient armed forces to occupy the country, destroy the regime, free the people, and establish in Cuba a peaceful country."[30] As early as March 1962, therefore, Lansdale was asking the Pentagon to provide "a brief but precise description of pretexts which the JCS believes desirable" to justify "direct military intervention."[31]

From our present vantage point, with the passing of several decades during which nine of Kennedy's successors managed to coexist with Castro even as the Kennedy brothers achieved the status of secular saints, Operation Mongoose appears inexplicable. Suffice it to say that by the end of 1961, the Kennedy administration was fixating on Fidel Castro with the same feverish intensity as the Bush administration exactly forty years later was to fixate on Saddam Hussein—and with as little strategic logic.

In its determination to destroy the Cuban Revolution, the Kennedy administration heedlessly embarked upon what was, in effect, a program of state-sponsored terrorism. In substance if not in scope, the actions of the United States toward Cuba during the early 1960s bear comparison with Iranian and Syrian support for proxies engaging in terrorist activities against Israel since the 1980s. The principal difference is that, whereas Hamas and Hezbollah have achieved considerable success, at least in enhancing their political standing, the U.S. attempt to unseat Castro achieved none whatsoever. Apart from expending the lives of several dozen guileless exiles who, at the CIA's behest, attempted to infiltrate their home island, those efforts were stillborn. From a moral and legal point of view, Operation Mongoose was indefensible. From a practical point of view, it turned out to be arguably even more stupid than Operation Zapata.

How can we explain this? Why did an administration whose senior members fancied themselves to be pragmatic and analytical go off the deep end in its pursuit of a dictator governing a country that, in 1961, boasted a population of slightly less than six million, a per capita income one-fifth that of the United States, and negligible military power?[32]

No doubt domestic politics provides at least a partial explanation. In his handling of the Bay of Pigs, President Kennedy looked weak and vacillating, opening himself up to withering criticism from the Republican opposition as well as from elements of the permanent government, notably the military and the CIA, skilled at manipulating the popular fear of communism for their own political purposes. Reenergizing the campaign to get Castro offered a way of rebutting any charges that the young president lacked toughness and so could be circumvented or ignored. For Kennedy (and every president since), projecting an image of toughness became an essential part of the job description.

That said, the response to the Bay of Pigs also testified to the authority of the reigning precepts of national security. Even in the wake of a humiliating setback, they remained sacrosanct. After all, since the onset of the Cold War, covert action had established itself as the preferred instrument of power projection. As the most readily available means of satisfying Washington's appetite for global interventionism, it complemented a nuclear arsenal that was considered absolutely essential but difficult to use. The methods devised by Allen Dulles and the methods perfected by Curtis LeMay worked in tandem to create the aura of secrecy, prestige, and power that now allowed presidents to assert and exercise quasi-imperial prerogatives.

The Bay of Pigs fiasco had seemingly called into question the efficacy of covert operations. This Kennedy and his lieutenants, devoted to enhancing the authority of the presidency, were not prepared to accept. After all, the agenda being marketed under the banner of flexible response aimed not to reduce the options for projecting power but to enrich them, while ensuring that the president alone call the shots. Operation Mongoose's transformation from a program of subversion into a prelude to invasion hinted at where this search for more options pointed.

Not surprisingly, then, just as there was no serious effort to reevaluate the threat the Cuban Revolution posed to U.S. interests, so too there was no serious effort made to reassess the U.S. penchant for overthrowing governments not to its liking. To entertain either prospect would have required gifts of imagination (and, arguably, political courage) that neither Kennedy nor the other Cold Warriors of his inner circle possessed. The antidote to covert failure was—and this became a pattern in the future—to up the ante and devise overt alternatives.

Theodore Sorensen, special counsel to the president and

a loyal chronicler of Camelot, found it heartening that Kennedy had taken from the Bay of Pigs episode "so many major lessons," gained "at so relatively small and temporary a cost."[33] Soon thereafter, those lessons "helped save the world."[34] Arthur Schlesinger, the Democratic court historian then serving as one of the president's special assistants, concurred. "[N]o one can doubt," he wrote, "that failure in Cuba in 1961 contributed to success in Cuba in 1962."[35] To arrive at such exceedingly generous judgments, Sorensen and Schlesinger excluded from their accounts the post–Bay of Pigs vendetta against Castro that consumed the Kennedy brothers.

In fact, Kennedy and his advisers learned astonishingly little from the Bay of Pigs. In that action-oriented era, the tempo of CIA activity actually quickened. "Ike had undertaken 170 major covert CIA operations in eight years," writes Tim Weiner in his history of the CIA. "The Kennedys launched 163 major covert operations in less than three."[36] In short, the only thing that mattered to the president and his brother was how to get Operation Zapata right the next time.

The president memorialized by Sorensen and Schlesinger was a singular figure, standing apart from the notably dull and pedestrian Eisenhower and from Kennedy's own immediate successor, the boorish Lyndon Johnson. Keepers of the JFK legend could never bring themselves to acknowledge that Zapata and Mongoose situated their hero squarely within a dubious tradition that predated his presidency and survived his assassination. Peas need not be identical to come from the same pod.

To the Precipice

Intended to deflect threats to U.S. security, the pattern of behavior that produced Zapata and Mongoose served instead to create threats where none had existed. So it was in 1962. In mid-August, the CIA warned General Lansdale that Soviet leaders intent on "deter[ring] an anticipated US military intervention against Castro" might be tempted to "establish a medium-range missile base" in Cuba.[37] Neither Lansdale nor anyone else in a position of influence paid much attention to this prescient forecast.

The Kennedy administration's obsessive pursuit of Castro had accomplished only one thing: It removed any doubts the Cuban dictator may have entertained about the dangers facing his regime. To defend his revolution, Castro looked to the Soviet Union, with which Cuba had already established a "fraternal" relationship. In response to his insistent entreaties, Nikita Khrushchev, general secretary of the Communist Party of the USSR—resenting Soviet strategic inferiority and keen to preserve Marxism's sole foothold in the Western Hemisphere—now offered protection in the form of generous Soviet security assistance: more and better weapons along with more trainers. In April 1962 Castro readily accepted this offer.[38]

At first, the weapons were defensive—antiaircraft missiles, for example. In May, however, the Soviet presidium added surface-to-surface ballistic missiles and nuclear warheads to the list. Shrouded in secrecy, these along with contingents of Red Army regulars soon began making their way toward Havana. The two preferred means of projecting U.S. power—covert operations and strategic attack—were now on a collision course. Washington's enthusiasm for clandestine warfare had emerged in part from the belief that it offered a way to solve problems without undue risk of triggering all-out war. Now the Kennedy administration's insistence on using covert means to liquidate its Castro problem would bring the world to the brink of a nuclear exchange.

Americans habitually assign responsibility for the ensuing Cuban missile crisis to the Soviet Union. According to
the conventional story, Khrushchev, a boorish, blustering
gambler given to emotional outbursts, overreached. Exhibi-
ting coolness and sophistication, Kennedy then saved the
day, thereby averting World War III. This self-justifying
interpretation works only by confining the narrative to the
famous "thirteen days," excluding most of what went before
and much of what came after.

"Khrushchev should have realized," wrote Kennedy's
secretary of state, Dean Rusk, in his memoirs, "that deploying missiles in Cuba was too threatening and destabilizing
for the United States meekly to allow this to happen."[39] On
whether Kennedy should have realized that the Soviet Union
would not meekly allow Castro's overthrow, Rusk is silent.
Indeed, inside the administration the governing assumption was that the Soviets would remain passive in the face of
American provocations. An interagency "Plan for Cuba"
declared categorically that "the USSR will not intervene
militarily" to preserve the Cuban Revolution. Although the
Soviets might ratchet up the pressure in Berlin or other hot-
spots, they were sure to "stop short of a direct major confrontation with the U.S."[40]

Dismissing Operation Mongoose as "terribly ineffective"—
and by implication inconsequential—Secretary of Defense
McNamara found it hard to believe that either Cuba or the
Soviet Union took seriously U.S. efforts to subvert Castro.
After all, McNamara avowed long after the fact, prior to
October 1962 the United States "had no plan to invade Cuba."
When challenged on this point, he amended his statement:
"Okay, we had no intent." Yet the veracity of even that asser-
tion requires an exceedingly narrow definition of "we."[41]
In OPLAN 314-61, the military establishment over which

McNamara presided had developed a detailed invasion plan that senior U.S. commanders by the autumn of 1962 were fully prepared—even eager—to implement.[42]

Kennedy administration officials also rejected comparisons between the nuclear-tipped Jupiter missiles targeting the USSR from U.S.-controlled launch sites in Turkey and Italy and the subsequent Soviet decision to deploy nuclear-tipped missiles to Cuba. That a causal relationship might exist between the two, with U.S. actions inspiring or provoking a Soviet response, was not something they were prepared to consider. Kennedy's advisers deemed the Jupiters another part of the Eisenhower legacy, unworthy of anyone's serious attention. The U.S. missiles, wrote Sorensen, "had practically been forced on Italy and Turkey by an administration unable to find any worthwhile use for them." They were "obsolescent and of little military value."[43] That the Kremlin might see matters differently—that the Jupiter's very vulnerability might persuade the Soviets to see it as a first-strike weapon—was inconceivable.

Even as the administration sought to widen its edge over the Soviet Union in nuclear striking power and worked feverishly to subvert the Cuban Revolution, the men of Kennedy's inner circle remained certain of their good intentions. They abhorred war and yearned for permanent peace. If peace somehow remained elusive, the fault must necessarily lie with others—with the recklessness (or malevolence) of Fidel Castro and Nikita Khrushchev in the early 1960s, and Iran's Ayatollah Khomeini, Iraq's Saddam Hussein, and Al Qaeda's Osama bin Laden at a later date, all of whom maliciously misconstrued America's motives or stubbornly refused to endorse America's benign vision for world order.

When some event disrupts the American pursuit of peace—the missile crisis of 1962, the overthrow of the Shah of Iran in 1979, Saddam Hussein's assault on Kuwait in 1990, or the terrorist attacks of 9/11—those exercising power in Washington invariably depict the problem as appearing out of the blue, utterly devoid of historical context. The United States is either the victim or an innocent bystander, Washington's own past actions possessing no relevance to the matter at hand. Critics of the reigning national security consensus—skeptical scholars or political radicals—might suggest otherwise, but in the corridors of power such dissenters have no standing.

So although the dots connecting Zapata and Mongoose to the missile crisis were plainly evident, the Kennedy administration professed not to see them. In much the same way, the administration of George W. Bush would ignore the chain of events that paved the way for September 11, 2001: the overthrow of Iranian prime minister Mohammad Mossadegh and the fervent U.S. embrace of the shah in 1953, its deference to Israel since the 1960s, its marriage of convenience with Saddam in the 1980s, its support for jihadists in Soviet-occupied Afghanistan during that same decade, and its military occupation of the Persian Gulf after Operation Desert Storm in the 1990s—each one eminently justifiable according to the established precepts of national security policy, but together producing an explosive backlash. To acknowledge the relationship between these policy initiatives and 9/11 would be to call into question a national security tradition going back decades—this American leaders still refuse to consider.

To his enduring credit, in this moment of maximum peril, President Kennedy suspended that tradition, even if only briefly. For public consumption, the administration insisted—and never ceased to insist—that the surprise sprung by Cuba and the Soviet Union had come out of

nowhere and was utterly without justification. Privately, however, Kennedy was willing to acknowledge the causal relationship between past U.S. actions and the problem he now
confronted. Those on the other side had their own gripes, not
least of all the relentless U.S. campaign to destabilize Cuba
and the presence of U.S. nuclear-tipped missiles along the
perimeter of the Soviet Union. Castro and Khrushchev were
acting in ways that Kennedy himself would have acted, had
circumstances been reversed. Negotiating a peaceful resolution of the missile crisis, therefore, required that Kennedy
take their complaints into account.

In navigating a way out of a predicament that his own
intemperate actions had helped induce, Kennedy did exhibit
admirable coolness and sophistication. He ignored the goading of those, Maxwell Taylor and Curtis LeMay prominent
among them, who insisted that (in LeMay's words) "we don't
have any choice except direct military action." He opted
instead for indirect action, a naval blockade styled as a
"quarantine." In a Joint Chiefs of Staff meeting with the president, LeMay derided this decision as "almost as bad as the
appeasement at Munich."[44] In fact, LeMay knew only half
the story. In exchange for Khrushchev's promise to remove
Soviet nuclear weapons from Cuba, Kennedy was secretly
offering the Russian leader important concessions. These
included a pledge not to invade Cuba and a promise to quietly withdraw the Jupiters from Italy and Turkey. "Appeasement" by almost any definition of the term, this approach
worked, at least in defusing the immediate crisis.

OVER THE EDGE

What had Kennedy and his men learned from their brush
with Armageddon? The conventional view is that they

learned a lot, the chief evidence offered being a speech the
president gave at American University on June 10, 1963. In
this address, Kennedy vowed that the United States would
do its "part to build a world of peace where the weak are
safe and the strong are just." He invited Americans to
rethink the Cold War, quit blaming the Soviet Union for the
world's ills, and "help make the world safe for diversity." To
emphasize his administration's support for a proposed permanent global ban on the atmospheric testing of nuclear
weapons, he announced a unilateral suspension of further
atmospheric tests by the Pentagon.

> The United States, as the world knows, will never start
> a war. We do not want a war. We do not now expect a
> war. This generation of Americans has already had
> enough—more than enough—of war and hate and
> oppression.

As interpreted by his admirers, the president's remarks her-
alded a major policy shift, with the United States henceforth
oriented, in Kennedy's words, "not towards a strategy of
annihilation but towards a strategy of peace."[45] In fact, the
shift entailed far less than was advertised. Having barely
avoided war in the Caribbean, the United States was even
then hurtling toward war in Southeast Asia.

The previous October during secret White House delib-
erations while the United States stood eyeball-to-eyeball with
the Soviet Union, Maxwell Taylor had predicted that "if we
do not destroy the missiles and bombers, we will have to
change our entire military way of dealing with external
threats."[46] As the JCS chairman saw it, to give way over Cuba
would be tantamount to abandoning the essential premises
of national security policy.

Taylor need not have worried. Even though the United States did not destroy the Soviet missiles and bombers deployed to Cuba, the standard U.S. response to perceived external threats, emphasizing global military presence, power projection capabilities, and intervention, survived without a scratch. The peaceful resolution of the missile crisis in no way dampened the Kennedy administration's enthusiasm for flexible response or enriching the options available to the president for employing force. In this regard, the course of events in Vietnam testifies to the realities of U.S. policy far more accurately than does Kennedy's oft-cited speech at American University.

To be fair, Kennedy inherited a mess in Vietnam. Yet over the course of his brief tenure in office, he compounded that mess, passing to his successor a far more difficult situation. There is no evidence that any lessons drawn from his administration's Cuban encounters had a positive effect on the way it dealt with Vietnam.

Whenever the subject of Vietnam comes up, Kennedy's defenders invariably explain what the president would have done had he not been assassinated in November 1963. Once elected to a second term, they insist, he intended to pull the plug on the American commitment to South Vietnam. "I think it highly probable," wrote Robert McNamara in his memoir, "that, had President Kennedy lived, he would have pulled us out of Vietnam."[47]

Those less enamored with the martyred president might be tempted to quote the protagonist of Ernest Hemingway's great novel of the 1920s, *The Sun Also Rises*. The woman with whom Hemingway's protagonist Jake Barnes is in love suggests that, were it not for World War I, they might have lived happily ever after. "Yes," Jake replies. "Isn't it pretty to think so?"

In fact, Kennedy saw South Vietnam as the crucial test case of flexible response, an opportunity to demonstrate that counterinsurgency and nation-building techniques could defeat communist-inspired "wars of national liberation"— that when it came to projecting power, the United States had at hand tools other than those offered by the CIA and SAC.[48] With this in mind, the president

- increased the U.S. military presence in South Vietnam from nine hundred to nearly seventeen thousand "advisers."
- eased restrictions on U.S. military personnel, authorizing those advisers to engage in combat operations or in combat support operations like Operation Ranch Hand, in which U.S. Air Force aircraft dumped large quantities of defoliants such as Agent Orange on the Vietnamese countryside.[49]
- more than doubled the level of material support provided to the Army of the Republic of Vietnam (ARVN), including heavy equipment such as armored combat vehicles and field artillery along with more than three hundred military aircraft.[50]
- did nothing in his public representations to refute claims made by others in his administration—Taylor and McNamara in the forefront—that South Vietnam represented a vital U.S. national security interest.[51]
- permitted members of his inner circle to conspire with ARVN generals intent on toppling President Ngo Dinh Diem, installed by the United States as president of South Vietnam in 1955.[52]

In 1961 Vice President Lyndon Johnson had hailed Diem as the "Winston Churchill of Asia." Two years later, however, the South Vietnamese autocrat had become, in Washington's eyes, an intolerable impediment to U.S. efforts to defeat the communist insurgency, widely assumed to be directed by North Vietnam.

The coup, launched on November 1, 1963, with direct involvement of both the U.S. ambassador in Saigon, Henry Cabot Lodge, and the CIA, succeeded. The generals overthrew Diem and murdered him, choosing a U.S.-manufactured armored personnel carrier as the execution site. Washington had counted on Diem's removal to reenergize the war against the Viet Cong (VC). The generals who made the coup were expected to be more cooperative. In fact, operational success produced political catastrophe. In Saigon, the coup threw open the floodgates of instability and dysfunction. Three weeks later, with events in Vietnam careening out of control, Kennedy himself was dead.

Here was yet another debacle on a par with the Bay of Pigs, this time entirely of the administration's own making. American complicity in the coup again showed how little those around Kennedy had learned from the events that had occurred on their watch. Assumptions that decisions made in Washington were sure to shape and determine the course of events far afield remained firmly in place. Having concluded that Diem was obstructing their purposes in Vietnam, they acted with astonishingly little consideration for the downside risks.

Kennedy's assassination freed the president from being called to account for all that ensued. In fact, as U.S. involvement evolved into a national nightmare, it became all the more necessary to hold the martyred president sinless. Doing so sustained the comforting belief that, were it not for an assassin's bullet, the United States might have avoided a decade of trauma involving war, division, demoralization, domestic upheaval, and defeat. Had fate only allowed Kennedy to live, the high ideals and visionary aspirations that he was said to have represented might have achieved fulfillment.

In the popular imagination, none of the subsequent revelations about Kennedy's character have dented this wishful thinking. The problem with sacralizing his memory is not that it ignores his philandering, abuse of drugs, and concealment of chronic health problems, but that it creates an impression of discontinuity where none existed. The abrupt termination of Camelot did not ring down the curtain on some ambitious effort to reorient American statecraft. The Kennedy who embraced the strategy of overkill, sought to subvert the Cuban Revolution, and deepened the U.S. commitment to South Vietnam was continuing work that his predecessor had begun. When Lyndon Johnson replaced Kennedy in the Oval Office, the postwar tradition of American statecraft passed into the hands of yet another faithful steward.

Taylor and McNamara restore our appreciation of those continuities. When Kennedy went to his reward, they stayed on to serve his successor—Taylor accepting LBJ's appointment to become U.S. ambassador to Saigon in 1964 and McNamara remaining at his post in the Pentagon until 1968.

Taylor and McNamara did not see themselves as turncoats. They were not defiling Kennedy's memory. They were carrying on his work. The pursuit of options did not end with Kennedy's death.

FREEFALL

Well over forty years after his passing, the carefully burnished image of John F. Kennedy still glistens. Ngo Dinh

Diem, meanwhile, has all but vanished from collective memory. Yet to a far greater extent than Kennedy's murder at the hands of a deranged gunman, Diem's overthrow, engineered by the U.S. government, qualifies as a historical turning point.

Once Diem passed from the scene, the situation in South Vietnam quickly went from awful to far worse. For senior officials back in Washington, every available course of action now appeared unattractive. Devoted to the techniques inherent in the Washington consensus, however, and unable to conceive of an alternative approach to exercising "global leadership," they swallowed their doubts and plunged on. All of this happened to the accompaniment of considerable angst and hand wringing, with Taylor and McNamara playing pivotal roles. Making an equally important contribution was McGeorge Bundy, the bespectacled and buttoned-down former Harvard dean who had served as Kennedy's special assistant for national security affairs and who soldiered on in that capacity under Johnson.

At the urging of this unholy trio, Lyndon Johnson bet his presidency and his domestic vision of creating a "great society" on the proposition that the exceedingly unwelcome climes of Southeast Asia posed no barrier to the effective application of flexible response.

Again, the domestic political calendar dictated the tempo of decision making. In August 1964, the Tonkin Gulf incident—North Vietnamese gunboats allegedly launching unprovoked attacks against U.S. Navy warships—enabled Johnson to pocket a blank check for further war. Voting with near unanimity, a compliant Congress authorized him "to take all necessary measures to repeal any armed attack against the forces of the United States and to prevent any further aggression." Yet for the moment, Johnson, presenting himself in the 1964 presidential campaign as the candidate of peace and reason, temporized. Only after he had secured a full term as president did Vietnam claim his sustained attention. Then, with deteriorating conditions in Saigon permitting no further delay, the pace of events quickened. Between January and April 1965, the United States took full ownership of the Vietnam War.

As McNamara described it, throughout this brief interval, the administration fixated exclusively on the "question of what military course to follow."[53] That a viable military option might not exist or that nonmilitary alternatives deserved careful consideration were propositions that received scant attention.

A long January 6 cable from Ambassador Taylor to President Johnson set in motion the train of decisions that culminated in the full-fledged application of flexible response. The situation in Saigon looked bleak, Taylor reported.

> We are faced here with a seriously deteriorating situation characterized by continued political turmoil, irresponsibility, and division within the armed forces, lethargy in the pacification program, some anti-US feeling which could grow, signs of mounting terrorism by VC directly at US personnel and deepening discouragement and loss of morale throughout [South Vietnam].

Absent urgent and forceful action by Washington, Taylor foresaw the emergence in Saigon of a government likely to seek "accommodation with the National Liberation Front and Hanoi." Diem, it turned out, had been an irreplaceable figure. "I doubt that anyone appreciated the magnitude of the centrifugal political forces which had been kept under control by his iron rule."

Simply trying harder was unlikely to produce better results next week or next month. The advisory program—Taylor reported that there were now 23,700 U.S. military personnel in country—had "probably reached about the saturation point." The order of the day was to try something different. "The game needs to be opened up," Taylor advised, "and new opportunities offered for new breaks which hopefully may be in our favor."

In Taylor's view, opening up the game need not require the introduction of U.S. ground troops. Instead, the former army general and self-described skeptic regarding the efficacy of aerial bombardment pressed for a "program of graduated air attacks" directed against North Vietnam. Air power constituted "the most flexible weapon in our arsenal of military superiority," he wrote. Its skillful application would "bring pressure on the will" of those who governed in Hanoi.

"As practical men," Taylor continued, "they cannot wish to see the fruits of ten years of labor destroyed by slowly escalating air attacks (which they cannot prevent) without trying to find some accommodation which will exorcise the threat." In the meantime, this affirmation of America's commitment to South Vietnam was sure to "give the local morale a much needed shot in the arm," boosting flagging spirits and putting to rest suspicions that the United States might be looking for ways to cut its losses. Taylor concluded: "[W]e should look for an occasion to begin air operations just as soon as we have satisfactorily compromised the current political situation in Saigon."[54]

"Compromising" the political situation in Saigon implied

establishing some semblance of a stable and effective South
Vietnamese government. First, get the South on track politically, then hammer the North militarily: This was Taylor's
proposed sequence. Unfortunately for his plan, there was
little to suggest that further American coaching, chiding, or
conspiring was going to fix the political situation in Saigon.
As Taylor himself acknowledged, "No amount of persua-
sion or communication is going to make [the South Viet-
namese] other than what they are over the short term."[55]
Nonetheless, bombing the North—styled as "reprisals" to
convey the sense that the United States was responding
defensively to Viet Cong attacks in the South—now emerged
as the favored next step.

Johnson himself remained unconvinced. So the president's national security adviser and defense secretary now
weighed in, prodding their boss to act. The United States,
they argued, could no longer afford to wait for South Vietnam to get its act together. "Bob [McNamara] and I," wrote
Bundy in a memo to the president on January 27, "are persuaded that there is no real hope of success in this area
unless and until our own policy and priorities change." The
confidence of the South Vietnamese in their patron and
protector was, Bundy insisted, waning. Seeing "the enormous
power of the United States withheld," they now doubted the
depth of American seriousness.

By declaring that "we will not go further until there is a
stable government" in Saigon, the administration had shack-
led itself to "a policy of first aid to squabbling politicos and
passive reaction to events we do not try to control. . . . Bob
and I believe that the worst course of action is to continue in
this essentially passive role which can only lead to eventual
defeat and an invitation to get out under humiliating circumstances."

The United States needed to shed its shackles. *"We see two alternatives,"* Bundy added.

> The *first* is to use our military power in the Far East and to force a change in Communist policy. The *second* is to deploy all our resources along a track of negotiation, aimed at salvaging what little can be preserved with no major addition to our present military risks.[56]

Both he and McNamara, Bundy told the president, favored the first alternative. They could hardly do otherwise. To concede that American military power was inadequate to the task of making the North Vietnamese behave would nullify claims that flexible response was enhancing the utility of force while reducing the moral impediments to its employment—in other words, that it represented an improvement over the strategy of massive retaliation that they openly disdained.

Instead, McNamara and Bundy had neatly removed one of the major obstacles to Taylor's proposed coercive air campaign—the assumption that the United States needed first to establish a stable government in Saigon.[57] All that remained was to find a convenient excuse for launching such a campaign.

This the Viet Cong obligingly provided on February 6, 1965, when they attacked Camp Holloway, the U.S. air base at Pleiku, killing eight Americans, wounding dozens more, and destroying ten U.S. military aircraft.

"Pleikus are like streetcars," Bundy subsequently remarked. The key was to be ready to hop aboard when one came trundling along.[58] Visiting Taylor in Saigon at the time of the Pleiku attack, Bundy was ready for his streetcar.

Within twenty-four hours he was cabling Johnson that, absent a "policy of graduated and continuing reprisal," defeat in South Vietnam appeared "inevitable—probably not in a matter of weeks or perhaps even months, but within the next year or so." To attempt a negotiated settlement was folly, amounting to "surrender on the installment plan." Immediately at risk were not only "the international prestige of the United States" but also "a substantial part of our influence."[59] An opportunity to regain the initiative and turn things around was now presenting itself.

One point deserves particular emphasis here. For Bundy and others in the administration, the urge to act grew out of considerations unrelated to the crisis of the moment or even to Vietnam as such. The formal report rendered by the Bundy mission let the cat out of the bag. "We cannot assert that a policy of sustained reprisal will succeed in changing the course of the contest in Vietnam," that report acknowledged. *"What we can say is that even if it fails, the policy will be worth it."* The very act of bombing the North would demonstrate American will, "damp[ing] down the charge that we did not do all that we could have done." Pain inflicted on the North Vietnamese would "set a higher price for the future upon all adventures of guerrilla warfare," thereby increasing "our ability to deter such adventures." In effect, the United States needed to bomb North Vietnam to affirm its claims to global primacy and quash any doubts about American will. Somehow, in faraway Southeast Asia, the continued tenability of the Washington consensus was at stake.[60]

Clambering onto his streetcar, Bundy found plenty of company already aboard. Within the administration, his own efforts, reinforced by those of Taylor and McNamara, had forged a solid majority in favor of escalation. On February 8, back in Washington and presiding over a meeting of the National Security Council, Bundy polled those in attendance and found that "without dissent, all agreed to act, that we should apply force against the North." According to notes taken at the meeting, McNamara chimed in with the comment "that we should move forward and should keep going."[61] Soon thereafter, President Johnson gave his consent.

In this case, moving forward had a specific meaning. Declaring its determination to prevent further incidents like Pleiku, the Johnson administration decided to subject North Vietnam to a campaign of sustained aerial bombardment. In effect, self-defense provided a rationale—or pretext—for making a small war bigger, for loosening those shackles on American military might, and for going on the offensive.

Much the same thing, of course, occurred after September 11, 2001. Averting further terrorist attacks provided a rationale—or pretext—for launching a "global war on terror," for shedding any remaining constraints on the use of American power, and for invading Afghanistan and Iraq. In its own way, 9/11 was also a streetcar that members of the George W. Bush administration seized upon with the same alacrity that Bundy and his colleagues had seized upon Pleiku.

As in 2001 so in 1965, the underlying purpose was anything but defensive. In the wake of painful tragedy, U.S. officials preoccupied themselves not with protecting exposed American assets (whether Camp Holloway or Manhattan), but with doubling down on the existing approach to exercising global leadership. In both cases they rejected out of hand the possibility that such an approach might itself render the United States more vulnerable rather than more secure. For Washington, the essential response to setbacks, whether relatively modest as in February 1965 or calamitous as in September 2001, is not thoughtful reflection but energetic action, preemptively diverting attention away from the existing premises of national security.

On his way back from Saigon, Bundy made a special point of reassuring Johnson that "U.S. policy within Vietnam is mainly right and well-directed." Naysayers didn't know what they were talking about and could be ignored. "None of the special solutions or criticisms put forward with zeal by individual reformers in government or in the press is of major importance, and many of them are flatly wrong."[62]

In 1965 as in 2001, naysayers with access to the White House were few in number. In the wake of Pleiku, the role of lonely dissenter fell to Senator Mike Mansfield, the Democrat from Montana who was then Senate majority leader. In a city where esteem is the reward of well-regarded figures who don't wield much clout, Mansfield was said to be much esteemed.

Yet his critique of the Pleiku incident and its aftermath merits our attention. In a letter to President Johnson on February 8, Mansfield had the temerity to suggest that the Viet Cong had penetrated Camp Holloway because the Americans there had failed to properly defend themselves. The problem, he told the president, was one of "lax" security. The failure resembled another recent incident, in Bien Hoa, where "we were caught off guard." The solution to the problem was not to bomb North Vietnam. It was to do a better job of manning the perimeter.[63]

Much the same argument might have been made after 9/11: Nineteen jihadists armed with box cutters perpetrated the most devastating attack on the United States since the War of 1812 because security at American airports was lax.

To avert a recurrence, the United States might have attended to repairing its defenses. Instead, within twenty-four hours, senior officials in the Bush administration were pressing for an invasion of Iraq, a country not involved in the 9/11 conspiracy.

As in 2001 so too in 1965, defense—protecting Americans from harm—never figured as more than an afterthought. At stake was a thoroughly militarized conception of statecraft to which those at the center of power remained deeply wedded. Those adhering to that conception—officials like Bundy, McNamara, and Taylor in 1965 or Dick Cheney, Donald Rumsfeld, and Paul Wolfowitz in 2001—depicted the vigorous exercise of American leadership (by which they meant the vigorous application of hard power) as essential to peace. When leadership thus defined yielded not peace but war, questions naturally arose about the efficacy of that conception. Sustaining the Washington consensus—and preserving the status of those whose authority derived from their ostensible ability to interpret that consensus—meant suppressing such questions. In practice, this meant that the only permissible response to violence was more violence.

Mansfield's critique challenged that consensus. Deepening the U.S. involvement in the war would exacerbate rather than alleviate the nation's security problems, he told the president. Given existing commitments to some forty-two "countries or groups of countries scattered around the world," the United States was already facing the risk of overextension. Although Mansfield couldn't specify a solution to the particular predicament posed by South Vietnam, he felt certain that "the trend toward enlargement of the conflict . . . is not going to provide one."[64]

Mansfield may not have articulated an alternative to the

Washington rules, but he was implicitly questioning the principles on which they rested. He was, after all, inviting the president to consider reducing the U.S. global military presence. He was suggesting that, for all the money the country had invested in configuring its forces for power projection, the utility of those forces might be limited. When it came to intervention, he was suggesting that the United States ought to exercise greater self-restraint.

President Johnson assigned Bundy the task of rebutting this critique, which the national security adviser did in a long letter dated February 9, 1965. Bundy refused to give an inch. There was no need to reassess administration policy. Things were essentially on track. "[T]he vast majority of the Vietnamese people do not wish to fall under Communist domination," Bundy assured Mansfield. Recent events on the battlefield showed that ARVN soldiers "are tough and resilient fighters and that their morale remains high." For their part, American soldiers were learning "important lessons" from whatever setbacks they might be experiencing. "More generally," Bundy wrote,

> it does not appear to me that the power of the United States around the world is "stretched too thin." We have been able to keep our commitments around the world for a quarter of a century and our country has never been richer or more at ease.

That Americans were dying in South Vietnam "gives the President personal sorrow." Even so, Bundy continued, "we cannot say that the current level of sacrifice in Southeast Asia is unduly heavy." In short, there was no need for the Johnson administration to consider a different course in Vietnam, nor to reevaluate its posture globally.[65]

A day later, the senator fired back. In a second letter to the president, Mansfield predicted that U.S. air attacks against the North would succeed only in increasing the level of violence in the South. "They are not fools," he wrote in reference to the North Vietnamese leadership, "and they are not going to play the game as fools."

> They are going to continue to play their strength against our weakness. Our weakness is on the ground in Viet Nam, where isolated pockets of Americans are surrounded by, at best, an indifferent population and, more likely, by an increasingly hostile population.

Mansfield anticipated air strikes against the North producing a "tit-for-tat pattern" of mutual retaliation, putting U.S. installations in the South at ever greater risk. To ensure their security, "the outposts will have to be *vastly strengthened by American forces*." Air escalation, therefore, necessarily implied escalation on the ground. This Mansfield adamantly opposed, proposing instead that the United States launch a diplomatic initiative aimed at securing "a cease fire throughout Viet Nam and Indochina."[66]

Again, Bundy replied on the president's behalf, undertones of exasperation creeping into his response. "Let me try once again to comment," he began. Yes, "the Vietnamese Communists will try as hard as they can to show that they have more determination than we." Yet Bundy seemed unabashed at the prospect. Bring 'em on. As for Mansfield's proposed cease-fire initiative, this Bundy dismissed as akin to applying "equal standards to the cops and to the robbers." Negotiations were out of the question.[67]

With that, debate—such as it was—ended. That same day,

the U.S. bombing of North Vietnam began in earnest. Nominally in response to an attack on an American barracks at Qui Nhon, the retaliatory air strike of February 11 blended seamlessly into a comprehensive and continuing series of raids dubbed Operation Rolling Thunder. Although the Johnson administration styled the U.S. attacks as reprisals, this was but a useful fiction. Washington's objectives determined the tempo of air operations. Foremost among those objectives was relying on air power to coerce the North Vietnamese leadership into accepting the existence of South Vietnam as an independent nation aligned with the United States.

Rolling Thunder's leading proponents did not set out to destroy North Vietnam. Although Curtis LeMay was then still advocating a one-size-fits-all solution to the problem— "bomb them into the Stone Age"—they rejected this maximalist approach in favor of what they considered more nuanced and discriminating methods.[68] The object of the exercise was not to obliterate but to influence. Through a "measured, controlled sequence of actions," consistent with the spirit of flexible response, the United States intended to "persuade [North Vietnam] to stop its intervention in the South."[69]

Yet just as Mansfield had predicted, the air offensive against the North almost immediately generated demands for additional reinforcements in the South. By February 23, Gen. William C. Westmoreland, the senior commander in Saigon, was already pressing for a marine battalion to secure the American base at Da Nang, essential to U.S. air operations.[70] Four days later, President Johnson approved the commitment of not one, but two marine battalions, supplemented by a helicopter squadron.[71] On March 2, McNamara cabled Taylor with the news that he was sending army chief of staff Gen. Harold K. Johnson on a mission to Saigon "to examine . . . what more can be done within South Vietnam." In his consultations with General Johnson, McNamara advised Taylor to "assume no limitation on funds, equipment, or personnel."[72]

On March 10, Assistant Secretary of Defense John McNaughton, a key McNamara aide, produced a paper offering *"a massive US ground effort"* in South Vietnam as one possible way to regain the upper hand.[73] On March 14, General Johnson produced his "what more can be done" proposal, which floated the possibility of deploying four U.S. divisions across South Vietnam and Laos.[74] Within two days, Bundy was writing that the deployment of major U.S. ground forces "may soon be necessary for both military and political reasons."[75]

On March 18, Taylor signaled his support for sending a U.S. Army combat division to South Vietnam.[76] On March 20, the Joint Chiefs of Staff told McNamara that the commitment of major U.S. combat formations had become "imperative if defeat is to be avoided."[77] At an April 6 meeting of the National Security Council, President Johnson approved a major expansion of U.S. support personnel in South Vietnam, entailing an additional eighteen thousand to twenty thousand troops. He also revised the mission of the marines already in Da Nang "to permit their more active use."[78] Finally, on April 14, at a luncheon meeting with Bundy, McNamara, and the Joint Chiefs of Staff, the president agreed to the immediate deployment of the army's 173rd Airborne Brigade, to begin combat operations near Bien Hoa. The American war in Vietnam now began in earnest.

Just shy of one hundred days earlier Ambassador Taylor

had ventured to suggest that "the game" needed opening up. During the weeks that followed, he and his colleagues had done that and more; indeed, they had radically transformed the game. That they were able to do so reflected modifications to the Washington rules implemented under the auspices of flexible response.

Between 1961 and 1965 much had happened. No longer did observers wonder if CIA headquarters in Langley or SAC headquarters in Omaha had hijacked basic national security policy. From his perch in the Pentagon, McNamara was in charge of the military, including General LeMay. Indeed, McNamara's control of Operation Rolling Thunder extended to personally approving the list of targets to be hit.[79] At the White House, the president and his lieutenants were in charge of everything, including the Central Intelligence Agency.

By 1965, projecting American power no longer meant choosing between covert-style "dirty tricks" and all-out nuclear war. New concepts and capabilities abounded, providing a panoply of additional options: limited strategic bombing employed as a method of signaling or suasion; conventional combat emphasizing technologically enhanced firepower and mobility; theories of counterinsurgency, pacification, and nation building; and innovative new approaches to covert action, among them a secret program for liquidating Viet Cong cadres that came to be called Operation Phoenix.

Beginning that summer, U.S. forces flooded into South Vietnam, the American troop presence in that country eventually exceeding half a million. In the ensuing years, flexible response faced its most demanding test. It failed that test ignominiously.

No single factor can adequately explain why the event that Americans call the Vietnam War occurred. A profound ignorance of Vietnamese history and the legacy left by European colonialism; Washington's insistence on seeing communism as monolithic; the ostensible lessons of Munich and the influence of the so-called domino theory; the perverse political impact of domestic anticommunism; a civil-military relationship crippled by mistrust and dishonesty; the limited abilities of key advisers like Taylor compounded by the hubris of others like Bundy and McNamara; Johnson's fear of being the president who "lost" Vietnam, along with a host of other private insecurities besetting the president of the United States: All of these played a role.

Yet there was also this: In an obscure corner of Southeast Asia about which most Americans knew little and cared less, the survival of the Washington rules was seemingly at stake. By 1965, America's inability to impose its will on Vietnam threatened the underpinnings of U.S. global leadership. As viewed from Washington, American credibility was on the line. If Viet Cong insurgents and their North Vietnamese backers got away with defying the United States, then others might be similarly tempted. Enemies would be emboldened while nations in the habit of taking their marching orders from Washington might become less inclined to do so. With a strategy of global presence, power projection, and interventionism no longer guaranteeing success, alternative approaches to national security strategy might even gain a hearing at home, with basic strategy no longer taken as given. To those whose interests were served by preserving that strategy, this was an intolerable prospect. So among the explanations for the Vietnam War we can add this one: It was a war fought to sustain the Washington consensus.

In 1961, the "best and brightest" had assumed ownership of that consensus. Determined to remove any doubt as to who was in charge, they moved quickly to assert unquestioned control. Dissatisfied with the means available, they sought to devise new and more flexible instruments of power. Beginning in 1965, they put their handiwork to the test in Vietnam, the brush-fire war that, in their own minds, loomed large as a test of American global leadership. To their considerable dismay, they soon discovered that efforts to douse the fire produced the opposite effect. In attempting to snuff out a small war they produced instead a massive conflagration. Determined to demonstrate the efficacy of force employed on a limited scale, they created a fiasco over which they were incapable of exercising any control whatsoever.

3

THE CREDO RESTORED

FOR A TIME, THE VIETNAM WAR THREATENED TO DISCREDIT the Washington rules. Adherence to the American credo and the sacred trinity, as interpreted by Kennedy, Johnson, and their advisers, had produced unmitigated disaster. Washington itself seemingly hovered on the brink of sanctioning a serious debate over basic national security strategy. Heresy enjoyed a brief vogue.

That moment soon passed. Within Washington, doubt briefly flickered, only to be quickly snuffed out. Although the Vietnam War ended in monumental failure, the consensus that had given birth to that failure survived. The Washington rules emerged all but unscathed. Indeed, within a few years of the last American soldier leaving South Vietnam, the national security consensus had been fully restored, once again enjoying all but complete immunity. Explaining this remarkable sequence of events is the story to which we now turn.

Although nonconformists always exist, they rarely

matter—a dictum that applies to American statecraft no less than to theology or any other pursuit that rests on faith rather than empirical evidence. Yet as Lyndon Johnson sent U.S. troops in ever-increasing numbers to fight in Vietnam, he inadvertently created conditions in which heresy flourished and heretics gained a serious hearing.

The war triggered massive protest. At first, President Johnson (and his successor, Richard Nixon) sought to co-opt their critics, professing their own abhorrence of war and commitment to peace. When that didn't work, they tried to ignore the commotion in the streets. When that too fell short, they impugned the motives of those who opposed their policies and questioned the patriotism of those resisting the war. Still, the complaints voiced on the outside resonated with figures on the inside. Individuals who might normally have been counted on to defend the Washington rules now had the temerity to admit their own loss of faith. Beginning in the mid-1960s, the Vietnam War emboldened such insiders to express doubts about matters that hitherto had seemed sacrosanct. It was as if cardinal archbishops suddenly began questioning Rome on the fundamentals of Roman Catholic belief.

Among the prominent figures breaking ranks, two in particular still stand out: Sen. J. William Fulbright and Gen. David M. Shoup. Their perspectives differed as did their proposed remedies, but together they fashioned a sustained and probing critique of the American credo. That their attempt to displace that credo met with defeat does not detract from the gallantry of their efforts. That the record of their apostasy has all but vanished from public memory only testifies to the thoroughness with which the defenders of the party line were able to scrub clean the status quo.

An erudite and flinty Democrat from Arkansas, Fulbright served from 1959 to 1974 as chairman of the Senate

Foreign Relations Committee and in that position made himself a force to reckon with. As Lyndon Johnson Americanized the Vietnam War, the senator became increasingly vocal not only in opposing it but in questioning the assumptions that informed U.S. policy. Through a series of Senate hearings, speeches, and writings, he vented those concerns, most completely and compellingly in his widely read 1966 book *The Arrogance of Power*.

Fulbright's purpose in writing the book was to expose as defective Washington's existing approach to exercising global leadership and to offer an alternative. On all matters pertaining to foreign policy, Fulbright took for granted American good intentions. Problems occurred when good intentions were married to seemingly bottomless reserves of power. The result was self-delusion combined with a tendency to lose touch with reality. Power, Fulbright wrote,

> tends to confuse itself with virtue and a great nation is peculiarly susceptible to the idea that its power is a sign of God's favor, conferring upon it a special responsibility for other nations—to make them richer and happier and wiser, to remake them, that is, in its own shining image. . . . Once imbued with the idea of mission, a great nation easily assumes that it has the means as well as the duty to do God's work. The Lord, after all, would surely not choose you as His agent and then deny you the sword with which to work His will.[1]

According to Fulbright, this described the delusions to which Washington had succumbed since World War II. Among the chief fruits of those delusions was the disastrous and utterly unnecessary war then under way in Southeast Asia. The folly of those who insisted on fighting that war suggested that the United States was rapidly losing any "perspective on what exactly is within the realm of its power and what is beyond it." Fulbright stressed his unwillingness to question the motives of the war's architects: No doubt President Johnson and his advisers meant well. "What I do question," he wrote, "is the ability of the United States . . . to go into a small, alien, undeveloped Asian nation and create stability where there is chaos, the will to fight where there is defeatism, democracy where there is no tradition of it, and honest government where corruption is almost a way of life."[2]

Those wielding authority in Washington, he believed, had lost their ability to see the world as it actually existed. Foreign policy had become "a kind of voodoo," with incantations supplanting reasoned analysis. "Certain drums have to be beaten regularly to ward off evil spirits." Chief among the incantatory words meant to deflect all serious criticism were *appeasement, isolationism,* and the ever-present danger of *insufficient vigilance.* Impatient with complexity or nuance, policy makers found it easier to indulge "the crusading spirit" in places like Vietnam. "Who are the self-appointed emissaries of God who have wrought so much violence in the world?" Fulbright asked.

> They are men with doctrines . . . who believe in some cause without doubt and practice their beliefs without scruple, men who cease to be human beings . . . and become instead living, breathing, embodiments of some faith or ideology.[3]

For Fulbright, ideology and statecraft made for a combustible mix. "I think the world has endured about all it can of the crusades of high-minded men bent on the regeneration of the human race." Any people setting out "upon self-appointed missions to police the world, to defeat all tyrannies, to make their fellow men rich and happy and free" were less likely to advance the cause of world peace than to wreak "havoc, bringing misery to their intended beneficiaries and destruction upon themselves."[4]

Americans needed to rethink what it meant to lead. "Maybe we are not really cut out for the job of spreading the gospel of democracy," Fulbright suggested. "Maybe it would profit us to concentrate on our own democracy instead of trying to inflict our own particular version of it" on others. "If America has a service to perform in the world," he continued, "it is in large part the service of her own example. In our excessive involvement in the affairs of other countries we are not only living off our assets . . . we are also denying the world the example of a free society enjoying freedom to the fullest."[5]

Fulbright denied that he was advocating global disengagement. Instead he was proposing "a redress in the heavy imbalance" that privileged foreign affairs above the nation's domestic well-being. "An excessive preoccupation with foreign relations over a long period of time," he warned, "diverts a nation from the sources of its strength, which are in its domestic life. A nation immersed in foreign affairs is expending its capital, human as well as material." To heedlessly draw down that capital was to invite disaster. Fulbright compared an ambitious foreign policy supported by a deteriorating domestic base to "the light cast by an extinct star," destined to fade and fail. He judged it "unnatural and unhealthy for a nation to be engaged in global crusades for some principle or ideal while neglecting the needs of its own people." In the long run, "an effective policy abroad depends upon a healthy society at home."[6]

Then there was the matter of force. As Fulbright saw it, crusaders were too quick to reach for the gun. Although military action had "a deceptive appeal," with advocates of force promising "quick and easy solutions to difficult problems," the promises inevitably proved false and exacted a painful toll in blood. In Vietnam, Fulbright noted, the crusading burden fell largely on young Americans, few allies showing much willingness to assist; "while their young men go to school, get jobs, and raise families, they are quite reconciled to having American boys fight and die in the jungles of Southeast Asia." Fulbright rejected the notion that "force is the ultimate proof of superiority—that when a nation shows it has a stronger army, it is also proving that it has better people, better institutions, better principles, and, in general, a better civilization." In nations as in individuals, he wrote, "bellicosity is a mark of weakness and self-doubt rather than of strength and self-assurance," adding that "the true mark of greatness is not stridency but magnanimity."[7]

Magnanimity combined with realism might cure Americans of their tendency to view adversaries as abstractions ("Communists" in the 1960s, "terrorists" today). After all, Fulbright wrote, the communist world had "ceased to be the monolith it seemed to be in Stalin's time." To formulate policy according to some sort of strict ideological litmus test had become self-defeating. An obsession with communism had caused the United States "to see principles where there are only interests and conspiracy where there is only misfortune." The time had come to treat nations in the Eastern bloc not as puppets of the Kremlin but as distinctive entities.

Fulbright saw nationalism as a solvent that was eroding whatever bonds held together the Soviet Empire. "Far from being unified in a design for world conquest, the communist countries are deeply divided among themselves, with

widely varying foreign policies and widely varying concepts of their own national interests." In this diversity lay
opportunities for creative diplomacy. Fulbright wanted
Americans to become "the friends of social revolution," to
"make our society an example of human happiness," and to
"go beyond simple reciprocity in the effort to reconcile hostile worlds."[8]

Above all, Fulbright counseled modesty. Notwithstanding
the grandiose claims routinely made by American statesmen,
putting the world right and eliminating the woes afflicting
humankind lay well beyond the capacity of the United States
or any other nation to achieve. The best one might hope to
accomplish was to cope with history's complexities while promoting incremental improvements "to make life a little more
civilized, a little more satisfying, and a little more serene."
That defined success. "I think man is qualified to contemplate
metaphysics but not to practice it," Fulbright concluded. "The
practice of metaphysics is God's work."[9]

Like Fulbright, David Shoup was a son of the Middle
Border, born and raised in Indiana and carrying to Washington a wariness of East Coast elites. There the comparison ends. Unlike the sophisticated Fulbright, who attended
Oxford as a Rhodes Scholar, Shoup worked his way through
DePauw University, joining the ROTC to help pay for his
schooling. Finding this first brush with military life appeal-
ing, upon graduation he applied for and received a commission as a marine corps second lieutenant.

The corps soon became Shoup's life. Unrefined, even
uncouth, given to action rather than reflection, he became an
excellent marine. In 1943, for heroism while commanding a
battalion at Tarawa, he received the Medal of Honor. Although
wounded and "under constant, withering enemy fire," Shoup
led a series of "smashing attacks against unbelievably strong

and fanatically defended Japanese positions despite innumerable obstacles and heavy casualties." The capstone of
his career came in 1959 when President Eisenhower selected
Shoup, then a two-star general, to become the marine corps
commandant, vaulting him over the heads of several more
senior officers. He served in that position until retiring in
late 1963.[10]

As commandant, Shoup had reacted warily to the Kennedy administration's quest for innovative ways to employ
force. His own instincts were to avoid war except when the
issue really mattered: For Shoup, the survival of South Vietnam didn't qualify. When it was necessary to fight, Shoup
favored going in big: The romance of counterinsurgency and
nation building eluded him. A closeted dove, Shoup failed
while a serving officer and member of the JCS to resist the
drift toward direct intervention in Vietnam.

Only after leaving active duty did he discover his inner
Smedley Butler. Another cantankerous marine general and
Medal of Honor recipient, Butler in retirement had famously
declared that "war is a racket" and blasted U.S. foreign policy between the world wars as a game rigged in favor of Wall
Street. Butler spoke from a populist perspective. Shoup's
visceral opposition to the Vietnam War prodded him to formulate an analogous critique.

In a speech to a gathering of students in Los Angeles on
May 14, 1966, the former marine revealed his own populist
inclinations, targeting what he saw as the bogus rendering
of U.S. history that Americans had been conditioned to
accept. In surveying the landscape of the past, Shoup saw
mostly lies. When he looked at the present, he saw more lies,
all of them intended to produce citizens "about as thoughtful
as the inhabitants of a second-hand wax museum." The following passage captures the overall tone of his presentation:

> You are taught that our people can get what the major-
> ity wants, by the ballot. Well, we got President Wilson
> that way because his campaign slogan was, "He kept
> us out of war." A few days after his inauguration we
> were in the First World War.
>   I don't have to tell you what we have now [allud-
> ing to Vietnam], how we got it; nor what's happened
> since. You've seen it happen.

The Johnson administration had sold the war under false
pretenses.

> You read, you're televised to, you're radioed to, you're
> preached to that it is necessary that we have our
> armed forces fight, get killed and maimed, and kill
> and maim other human beings including women and
> children because now is the time we must stop some
> kind of unwanted ideology from creeping up on this
> nation.

Shoup mocked the notion of events in Vietnam—"8,000
miles away with water in between"—posing a threat to U.S.
security. "I don't think the whole of Southeast Asia, as
related to the present and future safety and freedom of the
people of this country, is worth the life or limb of a single
American."

Perhaps the people inhabiting the region deserved some
consideration. If so, what they deserved above all was the
chance to determine their own fate. Given half a chance,
they were perfectly capable of doing just that, Shoup
believed. If the United States kept its "dirty, bloody, dollar-
crooked fingers out of the business of these nations so full
of depressed, exploited people, they might well arrive at a

solution of their own." Although the creation of a just and equitable social order might require revolutionary upheaval, the United States should allow the local population to figure out what that revolution entailed rather than having some Washington-concocted blueprint "crammed down their throats."

When it came to communism, Shoup was even more dismissive than Fulbright. In explaining the origins of the Cold War, Shoup offered a strikingly revisionist perspective. After 1945, "Russia had no nuclear weapons. We encircled her with nuclear bombs and missiles. . . . From here it was easy [for Kremlin autocrats] to get these people to forego butter for guns. To sacrifice and toil cheerfully so they could have some weapons to protect their homeland from the threat of destruction."

Shoup acknowledged that the existing Soviet nuclear threat was real and menacing. Yet this was a problem that did not invite a military solution. By comparison, he characterized the Soviet ideological threat as mostly hype. "Don't let yourself get too shook-up by the over-advertised encroachment of communism," Shoup told his student audience. "Help people to get things and the idea of communism will strangle by its own umbilical cord."[11]

The former marine was by no means the only senior military officer to speak out in opposition to the Vietnam War. Gen. Matthew Ridgway and Gen. James Gavin, prominent army officers who became prominent critics of U.S. policy, also voiced concerns. Yet Shoup was far more vocal and far less nuanced. For a reporter looking for an outspoken former general, he became the go-to guy, willing to blast away with both barrels. Skewering the proponents of the so-called domino theory, for example, he remarked in one 1967 interview, "They just keep trying to keep the people worried about the communists crawling up the banks of Pearl Harbor, crawling up the Palisades, or crawling up the beaches of Los Angeles, which of course is a bunch of pure unadulterated poppycock."[12] Unlike Fulbright, he refused even to concede that the war's architects might be well intentioned. He depicted them as malevolent scoundrels.

In 1967 and again in 1968, just after the Tet Offensive that marked a dramatic turning point in the war, Shoup testified before Fulbright's Senate Foreign Relations Committee. In the latter case, Senator Albert Gore, Democrat of Tennessee, posed what had emerged as the central question of the day: "What do we win if we win?" Fulbright had remarked earlier in the proceedings that "this war is supposed to prove that aggression doesn't pay, not only in Vietnam, but everywhere else." Success in Vietnam would, it was claimed, preclude similar challenges elsewhere. "If we win this war," Fulbright continued, "and if we stay the course and if our will does not weaken, from now on all Communists are going to be good boys and there will be no more aggression. Isn't that the theory?"

Shoup responded that even if the United States managed to prevail militarily—an unlikely prospect—it would achieve nothing of value. "I do not think that the gain, no matter how greatly embellished," he told Gore, "will ever equal one one-thousandth of the cost." Assume victory, Shoup said: "[W]hat is the reason, where is the proof, that the same situation wouldn't break out within months in Laos, Cambodia, Thailand, Burma, Korea, and you could keep on going." Vietnam was a limited war conducted against the backdrop of putatively unlimited obligations and informed by an assumption of inexhaustible resources. But the assumption was false: "[S]omeplace up the line," Shoup argued, the United States was going to say, " 'it is too much for us,' and at that spot, whether we like it or not, we are going to have to say, 'we can't help.' " Regardless of the Vietnam War's immediate outcome, "there is no finality; no finish to this thing." The logic ostensibly impelling the United States to make a stand in Vietnam held out the prospect of war without end.[13]

The longer the fighting in Vietnam dragged on, the more radicalized Shoup became. By April 1969, when the *Atlantic* published his essay "The New American Militarism," Shoup might have passed himself off as a hard-core leftist. Fidel Castro himself would have found little in the essay with which to disagree.

The United States, Shoup now charged, had become "a militaristic and aggressive nation." Here lay the ultimate explanation for why Americans found themselves in the "tragic military and political morass of Vietnam." In describing the origins of this new militarism, Shoup suggested that there was plenty of blame to go around. Sharing in that blame were "pugnacious and chauvinistic" veterans groups; greedy defense contractors always keen to fatten their profit margins; a public deluged with manufactured images fostering a distorted understanding of combat; handsomely funded think tanks that fed "militaristic new philosophies into the Defense Department"; and, worst of all, generals eager to try out new toys, test young officers, or advance their own careers. For these groups, the phrase *communist aggression* served as an all-purpose justification for demanding more resources and more vigorous action. "Militarism in America is in full bloom," Shoup concluded, "and promises a future of vigorous self-pollination—unless the blight of Vietnam reveals that militarism is more a poisonous weed than a glorious blossom."[14]

Like a good marine, Shoup swung from the heels, holding

nothing back. Whereas Fulbright sought to educate and influence, Shoup had a different purpose: to chastise and de-
nounce. Fulbright was cool, Shoup white hot. Still, the angry
general created a stir. Together with Fulbright, he drove
home the point that the credo and the trinity had not been
handed down from Mount Sinai. Alternatives to the Washington rules did indeed exist. Whether Washington would
seriously entertain those alternatives was another matter.

PEACE WITH HONOR

By the time General Shoup's tirade against American militarism hit the newsstands, Richard M. Nixon had succeeded
Lyndon Johnson as president. Guided by Nixon's promise to
achieve "peace with honor," the process of getting out of
Vietnam proved nearly as protracted, and at least as costly,
as getting in.

The new president had little use for the moral daintiness
to which the proponents of flexible response had been prone.
Nixon's preferred modus operandi emphasized toughness.
By the time he ended the war—or at least ended direct U.S.
involvement in it—Strategic Air Command B-52s had rained
bombs on North Vietnamese cities with an intensity reminiscent of the raids that B-29s had conducted against Japanese cities nearly three decades earlier.

Operation Linebacker II, which deposited over twenty
thousand tons of high explosives on Hanoi and Hai Phong
from December 18 to December 29 in 1972, signified a brief
reversion to the Curtis LeMay school of power projection.
Yet this "Christmas bombing" marked that school's permanent closure. Rather than a portent of things to come, it was
a final backhanded salute. Never again would the United
States employ violence on such a scale with such little regard

for exactly who was being killed and what was being destroyed.

By this time, LeMay himself had become an embarrassment, mocked and vilified rather than venerated. Between the moment Johnson became president and the day he surrendered the office to Nixon, a tsunami had swept across American culture. Among the many things affected was the national security consensus. For ordinary citizens, especially younger ones viewed by the state as prime timber for military service, Washington's insistence on calling the shots globally no longer commanded automatic assent. To those who had been radicalized by the events of the 1960s, both at home and abroad, the notion that American values were universal values and that the United States should be granted special privileges in advancing those values seemed laughable.

Large numbers of Americans had lost faith in the sacred trinity as well. In the wake of Vietnam, they no longer believed that policies based on global presence, power projection, and interventionism worked or were morally justifiable. In the eyes of such critics, LeMay's approach, which had once defined the American way of war, now became so repugnant as to be unimaginable.

Hollywood, typically a lagging indicator of changes in the zeitgeist, managed in this instance to anticipate the shift in attitudes. During the early Cold War, films such as *Strategic Air Command* (1955), directed by Anthony Mann and starring James Stewart, and *Gathering of Eagles* (1963), directed by Delbert Mann and starring Rock Hudson, treated SAC—and LeMay—with a respect approaching reverence. The men charged with standing ready to wage nuclear war (for the women who stayed home tending the kids) were dedicated professionals, maintaining a firm grip on their humanity despite bearing the weightiest responsibilities.

By the time *Dr. Strangelove, or: How I Learned to Stop Worrying and Love the Bomb* appeared in 1964, a cultural switch was ready to flip. Directed by Stanley Kubrick and starring Peter Sellers, George C. Scott, Sterling Hayden, and Slim Pickens, *Dr. Strangelove* depicted SAC's ethos as an amalgam of arrogant condescension (Gen. Buck Turgidson), quasi-religious fanaticism (Brig. Gen. Jack D. Ripper), and mindless obedience (Maj. T. J. "King" Kong), laced with a tincture of Nazism (Dr. Strangelove himself). None of Kubrick's warrior-protagonists demonstrated more than a tenuous hold on reality.

Several decades later, *Strategic Air Command* and *Gathering of Eagles*, serious movies made by serious filmmakers, qualify as camp. Meanwhile, *Dr. Strangelove*, an exceedingly funny movie, retains its standing as a serious commentary on the absurdity of nuclear war and the madness of those who insisted upon seeing nuclear weapons as holding the key to peace and security.

From the late 1940s through the 1950s, a smattering of peaceniks apart, most Americans had seen nuclear weapons as legitimate, useable, even essential weapons. Across mainstream America during the age of Truman and Eisenhower, nukes had on balance been coded "good." Yet the general sense that nuclear weapons entrusted to the hands of responsible U.S. officials made war less rather than more likely did not survive the 1960s. Bit by bit, more or less in tandem with racial prejudice and anti-Semitism, nukes were recoded as "bad." Their use became unthinkable, their very existence a bane to humanity. To depart from these views was to mark oneself a Neanderthal.

By 1968, this had become LeMay's fate. As that year's vice presidential nominee of the American Independent Party running alongside George Wallace, the segregationist governor of Alabama, the aging general insisted that a few well-placed nuclear bombs could still reverse the tide in Vietnam and thereby made himself a laughingstock.

The former SAC commander's rapid descent from the status of national hero to dangerous buffoon offered a vivid expression of the damage incurred by proponents of the sacred trinity during the Vietnam era. Yet SAC was by no means the only instrument of power to emerge from the 1960s the worse for wear.

By the end of the Vietnam War, journalistic charges that the CIA had spied illegally on American citizens, compounded by accumulating reports of Agency malfeasance and ineptitude, prompted outrage. This was especially true among congressional Democrats awakened to the dangers of an imperial presidency now that Republicans once again occupied the White House.[15] "In the Congress," the CIA's chief historian has written, "there was no longer a consensus to support intelligence activities blindly." House and Senate leaders suddenly evinced a curiosity to know what the CIA had been up to all these years and to have a greater say in whatever it might do in the future. The upshot was that "[f]or the first time in the Agency's history, CIA officials faced hostile Congressional committees bent on the exposure of abuses by intelligence agencies and on major reforms."[16] The CIA also experienced a cultural recoding. It now became, in the phrase of the day, a "rogue elephant."

Yet if, by the 1970s, the legacies of Curtis LeMay and Allen Dulles appeared tarnished, the army emerged from the Vietnam War in truly dire shape, rife with indiscipline, racked by an epidemic of drug abuse, and divided internally along racial lines. Proponents of flexible response had looked to the army to bridge the gap between the extremes of nuclear warfare on the one hand and covert dirty tricks on the other. Maxwell Taylor had, in fact, touted his old service as a reservoir of capabilities. Yet the various methods implemented by the army in Vietnam—counterinsurgency, pacification, and nation building, along with the "search and destroy" tactics devised by Gen. William Westmoreland, the senior U.S. field commander in South Vietnam— had singularly failed. The cultural coding appended to the U.S. military as a whole now read "incompetent."

Worse, the resource most essential for replenishing the army's reservoir of capabilities—soldiers—had become a scarce commodity. Previously, the army had seemed attractive as an instrument of power projection, in part because of the ease with which it could be expanded. In Washington you opened the tap, increasing the monthly draft call, and the army got bigger. Relying chiefly on conscription, it had gone from 190,000 in 1939 to 8 million in 1944, from less than 600,000 in 1950 to 1.6 million by 1952, from 963,000 in 1965 to 1.5 million in 1968.[17] Draftees were cheap to boot: In 1965, as the U.S. commenced its buildup in South Vietnam, new recruits were paid $87.90 per month.[18]

Under the weight of Vietnam, however, conscription collapsed. Americans withdrew from the federal government the authority to order citizens to serve in uniform. President Nixon accepted that verdict and ended the draft. He anticipated—as events soon showed, correctly—that doing so would undercut the antiwar movement and thereby enable him to continue the war under the guise of seeking "peace with honor."

So, beginning in 1973, the U.S. military became an "allvolunteer" force. Power projection now became dependent

in part at least upon the Pentagon's ability to induce sufficient numbers of qualified young Americans to volunteer.
Given the existing antimilitary climate, this alone seemed
likely to oblige policy makers in Washington to demonstrate greater self-restraint. That the transformation of a
people's army into a professional force had the potential to
produce just the opposite effect—decision makers gaining a
free hand to use a military over which the American people
had forfeited any ownership—was a prospect few anticipated.

Vietnam adversely affected the remaining two elements
of the national security triad as well. The humiliating withdrawal from Southeast Asia made the need for a continuing
U.S. troop presence elsewhere the subject of debate. Senator
Mansfield, for example, questioned the need to garrison U.S.
troops in Europe. "I believe it is time," he argued, "for us to
insist that the European nations themselves take on the
primary military and financial responsibilities for their
defense."[19] For years thereafter Mansfield persisted in this
effort, which struck at the very heart of the proposition
that defending the United States against the communist
threat required the quasi-permanent forward positioning of
U.S. forces around the globe.[20]

Most severely challenged of all was the triad's third
element: the penchant for global interventionism. Vietnam
seemed to have exhausted the nation's appetite for liberating
the oppressed, subverting unfriendly governments, or otherwise meddling in the affairs of far-off countries. Responding to this "Vietnam syndrome," Congress acted to curtail
the authority of the commander in chief. The War Powers
Resolution, passed in 1973 over a Nixon veto, stated that the
president could "introduce United States Armed Forces into
hostilities, or into situations where imminent involvement

in hostilities is clearly indicated" only in response to a direct attack, a declaration of war, or "specific statutory authorization."[21] No longer could the chief executive act first and then seek permission later or maneuver Congress into a situation in which it seemingly had no choice but to rubber-stamp war policies concocted in the White House. This, at least, was what the sponsors of the resolution hoped to accomplish.

Soon thereafter came the Hughes-Ryan Act of 1974, requiring the president to provide Congress with advance notification of planned covert activities. The following year two investigative committees—one in the House, chaired by Representative Otis Pike, Democrat of New York; a second in the Senate, chaired by Frank Church, Democrat of Idaho—launched highly publicized hearings that reviewed the whole record of covert actions since the 1940s. These investigations eventually resulted in the passage of the Foreign Intelligence Surveillance Act of 1978, curbing domestic intelligence collection and mandating more thoroughgoing congressional oversight of sensitive intelligence activities. In the wake of Vietnam, the barriers to intervention, whether overt or covert, had risen appreciably. For any president inclined to surmount those barriers, so too had the political risks involved.

FAHGETTABOUDIT

In sum, failure in Vietnam seemingly left the Washington rules in tatters. That within five years of Saigon's fall they were well on their way to reconstitution qualifies as remarkable. That within another decade the American credo and sacred trinity had been fully restored deserves to be seen as astonishing. In retrospect, what distinguishes the legacy of Vietnam is not how much things changed, but how little.

Seldom has a war been so fervently memorialized even as it was being so thoroughly drained of meaning.

American elites, civilian and military, reacted to defeat in Vietnam much as German elites, civilian and military, did after the Great War of 1914 to 1918. Priority number one was to identify scapegoats. In both countries, stab-in-the-back theories flourished, Jews and leftists being blamed in Germany, liberals, academics, and biased media being singled out for abuse in the United States. Priority number two was to begin the hard work of reversing the war's apparent verdict. In each country, this undertaking met with considerable success, at least in the short term.

In the case of both Germany and the United States, a bitter defeat thought to mark a historical turning point turned out to be nothing of the sort. Fifteen years after the armistice of 1918, Germany was back, its ambitions bigger than ever, its confidence in the German soldier restored. Fifteen years after the fall of Saigon, the same could be said of the United States. By 1990, Washington had reasserted its claims to global leadership. Indeed, as the Cold War wound down, those claims became all the more expansive. The United States now donned the mantle of "sole superpower," having seemingly vanquished all challengers. Furthermore, Americans rediscovered the allure of garrisoning the planet, once again reconfigured the armed forces for global power projection, and restored military intervention to its status as preferred foreign policy option.

How to explain this turnaround? A large measure of credit belongs to those who bent themselves to the task of discerning and reinterpreting the lessons of failure. In post-1918 Germany, that work fell primarily to the officer corps, which reached conclusions that meshed (for a time) with the ambitions of the Nazi Party. In the United States, the search for lessons also preoccupied the officer corps, which reached conclusions that proved compatible (for a time) with the preferences of the permanent foreign policy establishment.

In the end, though, the views of the officer corps—both German and American soldiers were primarily intent on restoring the prestige and autonomy of the military profession—mattered less than those of the civilian elites.[22]

Elite concern elevated one issue above all others: repealing the outcome already decided on the field of battle. True in Germany during the 1920s, this was true as well in the United States during the late 1970s and 1980s.

Consider just one classic expression of elite opinion: *The Vietnam Legacy: The War, American Society, and the Future of American Foreign Policy*, a volume published in 1976 under the auspices of the august Council on Foreign Relations. The book collected the perspectives of twenty-four observers, described by Anthony Lake, who presided over the project, as "authors of diverse backgrounds and points of view." Lake, who by resigning in protest from Nixon's National Security Council staff had demonstrated what in Washington passed for independence and integrity, added that the essays produced by this diverse group "differ in style, in substance, and in method of expression."[23]

In fact, a more accurate description of the group would be *clubby* and of its findings *homogenized*. The roster of contributors assembled by Lake was all-white, all-male, and with only two exceptions—a British academic and a French journalist—consisted entirely of Americans. The group included name-brand politicians (Senators Hubert Humphrey of Minnesota and John Tower of Texas), once-and-future high-ranking officials (Richard Holbrooke and Paul Warnke), well-known academics (Ernest May and Edward Shils), and prominent journalists (Leslie Gelb and Irving

Kristol), along with various representatives of the think-tank world. They were, to a man, eminently respectable and eminently reliable, known quantities who could be counted on to confine their disagreements to matters where disagreement was deemed permissible. If tempted to rock the boat, they would do so politely and gently.

In short, the outcome of Lake's project was predetermined by the roster of participants. As is so often the case in Washington—from Maxwell Taylor's inquiry into the Bay of Pigs down to the various investigations conducted in the wake of the Abu Ghraib torture and abuse scandal—what purported to be a searching examination was in reality a carefully staged exercise intended to foreclose unwanted conclusions.

None of Lake's contributors possessed the capacity to assess the war from a Vietnamese perspective, nor did any even think it worth bothering to try. None had served in Vietnam as combatants. The one soldier recruited for the project was, predictably enough, Maxwell Taylor. Although the war had fostered fundamental cleavages in American society, none of the contributors offered an antiestablishment or countercultural take on the war. There were no voices that might even remotely qualify as radical—no socialists, Marxists, pacifists, one-worlders, neo-agrarians, or libertarians. There was no room for Senator Fulbright or General Shoup. The 1960s had given rise to a "New Left," which was then all the rage in the hipper quarters of academe. No New Left figure made the cut. Nor did any exponent of the anti-interventionist tradition, commonly if inaccurately referred to as isolationism. Lake included a single token contrarian: Richard J. Barnet, of the left-leaning Institute for Policy Studies, who made the case for putting

social justice and human rights at the forefront of U.S. policy objectives.

During the course of the Vietnam War, none of Lake's
contributors had gone to jail, gone underground, or gone
into exile. They had, instead, gone to the White House, the
Pentagon, and the Capitol. A single participant had actively
engaged in antiwar protest at something approximating the
grassroots level. Yet Sam Brown, a founder of the Vietnam
Moratorium Committee in 1969, titled his essay "The Defeat
of the Antiwar Movement." Brown launched his assessment
by bluntly declaring that opposition to the war had "had
little lasting influence on the nature of either American society or its approach to the world," thereby obviating any need
for further discussion. By implication, popular grassroots
opposition to U.S. policy had been an epiphenomenon, lacking in real significance.[24]

For the participants in Lake's study, significance lay
in identifying what precisely had gone wrong—mistakes
made that, once identified, could put Vietnam definitively to
rest. In his introduction, Lake approvingly quoted Henry
Kissinger, no longer an obscure professor, who insisted that
unearthing such lessons was essential "if we are not going
to have another disaster that may have a quite different look
but will have the same essential flaws."[25]

When it came to specifying those flaws, the participants
in Lake's study did not reach a uniform set of conclusions.
They did, however, adhere to a common analytical framework, one that treated Vietnam as an anomaly. The big
problem was the loss of consensus, control, and legitimacy
that failure in Vietnam had prompted. For Professor Shils of
the University of Chicago, all the controversy over the war
had stirred up "ideas of participatory democracy" along

with populism, "bohemianism, animosity against business-men and politicians, and muckraking."[26] Plain folk had got-ten uppity, which undermined the authority of institutions long in the habit of exercising authority.

Irving Kristol, remembered today as a founding father of neoconservatism, assessed the foreign policy consensus as "under powerful attack" by both "the educated, idealistic 'cosmopolitans'" who had created it back in the 1940s and by "the bulk of 'provincial' America," which had never espe-cially cared for that consensus in the first place.[27] According to Kristol, the cosmopolitans needed to recover their nerve; the provincials needed to relearn their place.

This erosion of consensus, control, and legitimacy threat-ened to open the door to irresponsible behavior, usually described as some variant of "isolationism." Only by stem-ming that erosion would it be possible to get national secu-rity policy back on track. Humphrey, the former vice president who had returned to the Senate, bemoaned the fact that after Vietnam so many Americans "seem afflicted with syndromes of self-condemnation over our past mis-takes and self-pity over what we perceive as a lack of appreciation."[28] The United States may have overreached in Vietnam, but people needed to pull up their socks and move on. David Abshire of the Center for Strategic and Interna-tional Studies urged "a true dialogue on foreign policy out of which can emerge a new and sound consensus."[29] To reassure confused and angry Americans, elites in Washing-ton needed to reconstitute a bipartisan image of confidence and self-assurance.

For his part, Lake warned against the possibility that the United States might succumb to a "mean-spirited foreign policy," reminiscent of the period between the world wars. He worried that "a Vietnam analogy" could "amend or replace the Munich analogy," with Americans concluding "that the United States should avoid foreign wars not by nipping them in the bud, but simply by staying out of them."[30]

Until Vietnam intruded, had U.S. national security policy since World War II consisted of nipping foreign wars in the bud? Only a true believer in the Washington rules, devoted to the proposition that American global preeminence had been and remained benign, essential, and irreplaceable, could think so. Yet there exists no reason to question Lake's sincerity.

After Vietnam, the noisiest and most noxious of the 1960s revolutionaries gravitated to academe, eventually becoming "tenured radicals." These devout leftists seized control of American colleges and universities and severely compromised the quality of American higher education—this at least is the perception that persists, even today, among devout right wingers.

Yet even if we stipulate for the sake of argument that this is true, a mirror image of that process occurred in the realm of national security policy. With real, if by no means radical, change in the wind—amending or replacing the Munich analogy does not exactly qualify as storming the Bastille— defenders of the Washington rules rallied, intent on restoring consensus, control, and legitimacy. They quietly but firmly excluded from serious consideration views that smacked, however remotely, of being heretical. They dismissed the charge coming from the Vietnam War's most vehement critics that the war itself testified to something essential (and essentially defective) about U.S. policy and American society—that Vietnam, in the words of Martin Luther King, had been "but a symptom of a far deeper malady within the American spirit."[31]

Members of the foreign policy establishment offered a

carefully crafted interpretation of the war's significance that
served ultimately to demonstrate its insignificance. The
conclusion was obvious: Revisiting or reassessing the core
assumptions informing U.S. policy was simply unnecessary. Things went awry in Vietnam as a result of specific
misjudgments and miscalculations, not deep-seated sys-
temic flaws in the American way of life, in the American
tradition of statecraft, or in the triad of principles guiding
U.S. military policy: This defined their position.

The rebuttal, of which *The Vietnam Legacy* is an artifact,
succeeded brilliantly. The defenders of the Washington
rules achieved—and retain today—a level of mastery that
"tenured radicals" on university campuses can only dream
of.[32] Indeed, the range of acceptable opinion in a typical fac-
ulty lounge is orders of magnitude greater than that which
prevails in precincts where U.S. national security policy
gets discussed and formulated.

So, in remarkably short order, Vietnam became enshrined
as a one-off event. Briefly challenged during the 1960s, the
conventions to which Washington remained devoted
emerged unscathed. The precepts of American global leadership remained fixed. Even the Democratic Party—acutely
burned by its association with Vietnam and presumably
more sensitive to the dangers of any recurrence—wasted
little time in abandoning its flirtation with the idea of America "coming home."

By 1980, Vietnam's relevance to policy had all but vanished, with both political parties tacitly agreeing to airbrush
the episode out of existence. The Republican Party platform
of that year, a forty-three-page document compiled to support former governor Ronald Reagan's challenge to incumbent president Jimmy Carter, contained not a single reference
to the Vietnam War. The platform did, however, signal

the party's adherence to the preexisting national security consensus. To "hearten and fortify the love of freedom everywhere in the world; and to achieve a secure environment in the world in which freedom, democracy, and justice may flourish"—this was America's calling, one that required the United States to "reach the position of military superiority that the American people demand." Amid much bashing of President Carter's performance, the GOP made clear its commitment to a definition of American global assertiveness unaffected by the events of Vietnam.[33]

Not surprisingly, the Democratic Party platform of that same year offered a different take on Carter's record. Yet when it came to national security policy, Democrats and Republicans occupied the same page. The Democratic platform contained but a single cryptic reference to "a tragic war in Asia." Apart from promising to study the effects of Agent Orange and to support "the construction of a memorial in the nation's capital to those who died in service to their country in Southeast Asia," the Democrats did not trouble themselves to reflect on the causes, consequences, or implications of that tragedy. When it came to national security policy, Democrats—intent on refuting the charge that theirs had become the cut-and-run party—wanted it known that their views did not differ appreciably from their rivals'. America's purpose was "to be a beacon of liberty," employing American power and American ideals "as a means of shaping not only a more secure, but also a more decent world."

The drafters of the Democratic platform made it clear that *power* meant military power. "America's military strength is and must be unsurpassed," they asserted. Yet unsurpassed was not good enough and Democrats vowed to "strengthen the military security of the United States" even further by increasing the level of Pentagon spending—a promise on which Carter and members of his party had, in fact, already begun to make good.

The point of citing these two documents is not to suggest that they represent serious statements of policy. The drafting of platforms is an exercise in political posturing. Yet this quadrennial compendium of grand aspirations and ponderous clichés does testify to the prevailing national mood, as interpreted by the political class. By 1980, both major parties had concluded that Vietnam was best forgotten while the energetic reassertion of American global leadership, backed by plentiful supplies of firepower, had once more become the order of the day.

Running to depose Carter, candidate Reagan described the American misadventure in Southeast Asia as a "noble cause," adding, "For too long we have lived with the Vietnam syndrome."[34] Reagan's election in November sealed the triumph of Vietnam revisionism. A mere five years after the fall of Saigon, antiwar or anti-interventionist views had once again been consigned to the fringes of American politics.

As events soon demonstrated, Anthony Lake need not have fretted about the United States seeking to avoid wars by staying out of them. During the 1980s, opportunities to "nip wars in the bud" by committing U.S. forces to Beirut, Grenada, Libya, and Central America and in the waters of the Persian Gulf proved legion. If Vietnam had induced a reluctance to act, that reluctance faded remarkably quickly.

In search of historical analogies to justify this renewed activism, Reagan and his successors ignored Vietnam in favor of Munich. "Neville Chamberlain thought of peace as a vague policy in the 1930s," Reagan remarked in a 1983 speech, "and the result brought us closer to World War II. History teaches us that by being strong and resolute we can keep the peace." George H. W. Bush concurred. "Half a century ago, the world had the chance to stop a ruthless aggressor and missed it," he declared in explaining his intended response to Saddam Hussein's 1990 invasion of Kuwait. "I pledge to you: We will not make the same mistake again."[35] Within months, Bush, having—so it seemed—handily disposed of Saddam in Gulf War I, announced with satisfaction that "we've kicked the Vietnam syndrome." Demonstrating an even greater penchant for military activism, Bush's successor Bill Clinton affirmed that judgment.[36] To justify the use of force, Clinton too deployed the lessons of Munich.[37] Appeasement rather than overreaction had once again become the sin to be avoided at all costs.

For Reagan, Bush, Clinton, and the entire foreign policy establishment, the most important conclusion to be derived from Vietnam was that the American experience there was sui generis. This meant, of course, that the war had no truly important lessons to teach, none at least that should call into question the larger record of U.S. policy or alter its future course. Reflecting on the past took a backseat to looking ahead.

Henry Kissinger himself both anticipated and helped to ensure this outcome. For public consumption, Kissinger made a show of wanting to plumb the Vietnam experience for whatever it had to teach. Behind closed doors, he took the position that combing through the debris left by the U.S. failure would yield little of value. Already in 1975, in a memo drafted for President Gerald Ford, Kissinger, then secretary of state, called it "remarkable, considering how long the war lasted and how intensely it was reported and commented [upon], that there are really not very many lessons from our experience in Vietnam that can be usefully applied elsewhere despite the obvious temptation to try." Kissinger continued:

> Vietnam represented a unique situation, geographi-
> cally, ethnically, politically, militarily, and diplomati-
> cally. We should probably be grateful for that and
> should recognize it for what it is, instead of trying to
> apply the "lessons of Vietnam" as universally as we
> once tried to apply the "lessons of Munich." . . . [T]he
> war had almost universal effects but it did not pro-
> vide a universal catechism.[38]

Regarding Vietnam's policy significance, Kissinger proved
remarkably prescient. Within a decade, Washington had all
but forgotten Vietnam. The catechism to which policy makers
adhered during the 1980s and beyond did not differ percep-
tibly from the one that landed the United States in Vietnam
in the first place.

SEAMLESS TRANSITION

If the disaster of Vietnam posed only a momentary challenge, the passing of the Cold War and the disintegration of
the Soviet Empire posed none at all. It was after all the threat
of totalitarianism originating during the middle third of the
twentieth century that had ostensibly summoned the United
States to shoulder unprecedented burdens. As it turned out,
however, the disappearance of the totalitarian threat in no
way eased those burdens. The emergency that had begun in
the 1930s finally ended; the imperative for exercising global
leadership persisted.

Beginning with Franklin Roosevelt, every U.S. president
had insisted that at the far side of America's resistance to
totalitarianism world peace awaited. The reward for exertions today was to be a reduced need for exertions on the
morrow.

Yet the fall of the Berlin Wall in 1989 and the disappearance of Ronald Reagan's "Evil Empire" in 1991 elicited a
chorus of warnings against any hint of backsliding. According to people in the know, peace was not in the offing, not
yet anyway. Indeed, according to proponents of the Washington rules, the end of the Cold War confronted the United
States with new, even more daunting challenges. In a world
of ever-growing complexity, with the tempo of change accel-
erating, dangers loomed. The Red Menace had disappeared,
but humankind more than ever needed the United States to
show the way.

It was a great paradox. On the one hand, triumphalists
celebrated the end of the Cold War as an achievement of
profound significance. On the other hand, those who celebrated this victory were quick to caution against entertaining the notion that Americans could afford to rest on their
laurels. The Promised Land still beckoned just yonder. Now
more than ever it became essential to protect Americans
from thinking that the best way to avoid wars was to stay
out of them.

To illustrate this point, consider the testimony of Madeleine Albright. During the brief interval between the Cold
War and the global war on terror, Albright cut a wide swath.
Serving successively as UN ambassador and then as secretary of state, the first woman ever to hold the latter post, she
did much to advance the cause of gender equality in public
life. That said, her substantive contributions to diplomacy
were exceedingly thin. Unlike, say, George C. Marshall, she
launched no major policy initiatives that outlived her tenure. Unlike Kissinger, she did not engineer the reordering
of great-power relationships. There is today no distinctive
Albright Doctrine or Albright Plan or Albright Principle that
animates or even influences U.S. policy.

Yet historians of American statecraft will surely grant Albright a prominent place, less for anything she did than for things she said. During her years in the spotlight, Albright held forth as the preeminent booster and exponent of a recalibrated Washington consensus. Although never especially eloquent and possessing little personal charisma, she had a gift for rhetorical repackaging. More effectively than any of the men who dominated the world in which she worked, she described, justified, and celebrated a version of American global assertiveness said to account for the new conditions created by the passing of the Cold War.

In making these points, Albright was expressing conclusions widely shared by her male colleagues and competitors. Yet she spoke with a clarity, directness, and transparent sincerity that few of them could muster. She really believed what she was saying.

Four of Albright's utterances serve to illustrate the post–Cold War modifications made to the Washington rules that preserved their essence.

In the first, Albright offered her synopsis of contemporary history: "My mind-set is Munich. Most of my generation's is Vietnam."[39] Albright flattered herself in fancying that her views differed from those of others in her circle. In truth, at a moment when Washington had drunk deeply from the waters of triumphalism, Albright's comment neatly summarized views common to that circle: Remembering 1938 qualified as a categorical imperative; brooding over 1965 was counterproductive and would get you nowhere.

By reducing history to an either/or proposition—take your choice: Munich or Vietnam—Albright foreclosed the possibility of including other events as reference points for policy. This, too, fit nicely with the preferences of the foreign policy establishment. To grant the overthrow of Mossa-

degh or the Bay of Pigs, not to mention cataclysms like World
War I or Hiroshima, equal standing with Munich as a source
of policy relevance would have meant raising murky questions about the efficacy and moral legitimacy of American
preeminence that Albright and other advocates of the Washington consensus refused even to consider. Better to keep
things simple: good vs. evil; courage vs. cowardice; resistance vs. appeasement; freedom vs. slavery; survival vs.
holocaust.

In her second remark, Albright described the status to
which the United States had risen as a consequence of its
participation in the immense historical drama centered on
Munich. In this case, the immediate context was one of the
recurring dustups with Saddam Hussein that punctuated
the decade after Operation Desert Storm. "If we have to use
force," Albright declared with regard to the possibility of
renewed air attacks against Iraq, "it is because we are America. We are the indispensable nation. We stand tall. We see
further . . . into the future."[40]

The pretentiousness of the language—especially, perhaps, the grating use of the imperial "we"—all but cries out
for a deflating rebuttal. Yet to sneer is to miss the importance of Albright's claims. That she herself was speaking in
deadly earnest is certain. Equally certain is that she was
expressing sentiments widely shared across the foreign policy elite.

That American leadership is indispensable, that Americans possess a unique grasp of history's purpose, that these
factors should empower the United States to act: As far as
Washington is concerned, these remain unimpeachable
truths. Conservatives and liberals, Republicans and Democrats, President George H. W. Bush and President Bill Clinton, the editors of the right-leaning *National Review* and

those of the left-leaning *New Republic*, not to mention the Joint Chiefs of Staff and the titans of Wall Street, all fervently subscribed to Albright's belief that the United States is unique, irreplaceable, and able to see things that other more ordinary (or evil) nations are unable to discern.

There might be disagreement on just when to pull the trigger or just how big a gun to use, but on the fundamentals, broad agreement existed. Albright's contribution was to describe and affirm that agreement in no uncertain terms.

Albright's third remark went further still in explaining the proper role of military power. On this occasion, her subject was a proposed intervention in the Balkans. The ultranationalist Serb dictator Slobodan Milošević was threatening to overrun the region. Seeing Milošević as the reincarnation of Adolf Hitler, Albright wanted him stopped. In this instance, however, the Joint Chiefs of Staff, led by Gen. Colin Powell, counseled caution. Undeterred, Albright pressed for action. In his memoirs, Powell quoted her memorable challenge: "What's the point of having this superb military that you're always talking about if we can't use it?"[41]

Again, however intemperate her language, Albright was expressing a view that was then gaining considerable traction. An inverted Vietnam syndrome was taking Washington by storm: The idea was to be bold, take some risks, and employ American arms as a force for good, confident that victory was a foregone conclusion. This implied easing restraints on the use of violence, at least when wielded by the United States. Who, after all, could possibly prevent the United States military from achieving its noble purposes? In 1993, when Albright's confrontation with Powell occurred, the answer seemed self-evident: no one.

Finally, there is this: During a 1996 television interview, a journalist invited Albright to respond to a report that sanctions imposed on the regime of Saddam Hussein in 1990, and kept in place at U.S. insistence ever since, had resulted in the deaths of half a million Iraqi children. Rather than disputing the charge, she implicitly affirmed it. "It's a hard choice," she responded, "but I think, we, think, it's worth it."[42]

Albright's response once again expressed a perspective that enjoyed wide currency and that still remains central to the Washington consensus. American purposes are by definition enlightened. ("I've never seen America as an imperialist or colonialist or meddling country," Albright remarked on another occasion.)[43] The pursuit of exalted ends empowers the United States to employ whatever means it deems necessary. If U.S.-enforced sanctions had indeed caused the deaths of 500,000 Iraqi children, at least those children had died in a worthy cause. This was not cynicism or hypocrisy on Albright's part. It was conviction encased in an implacable sense of righteousness.

It was also an instance of life imitating art. Albright's judgment recalls the attitude of the fictional CIA operative Alden Pyle in Graham Greene's famous 1955 novel *The Quiet American*, set in Indochina during the early days of U.S. involvement there. A plot organized by Pyle in Saigon has gone awry, killing or maiming innocent Vietnamese bystanders. Contemplating the results of his handiwork, Pyle reassures himself that the victims "died for democracy." Their deaths were a "pity," he remarks, "but you can't always hit your target. Anyway they died in the right cause." Pyle's conscience was clear. So, too, was Madeleine Albright's.

In her farewell to the State Department on January 19, 2001, Secretary Albright likened the events of her tenure to those recounted in *Present at the Creation*, the famous memoir of postwar diplomacy written by Dean Acheson, who had headed the State Department under President Truman.

"Together, you and I have been present at the transition from one era to the next," she asserted. With her colleagues she had shouldered the "responsibility to build or adapt institutions that would enhance security, prosperity and freedom for generations to come." This work was certain to continue under her successor. In the American system, she said, "the parties and the personalities may change, but the principles that guide our republic do not."[44]

Her comments contained a kernel of truth. In the midst of an ostensibly momentous global transformation, Albright had ensured the preservation of the principles guiding American statecraft, successfully insulating them from serious scrutiny. That accomplished, she now handed off to a new administration the responsibility for applying those principles.

As events soon demonstrated, leading members of this new administration shared Albright's perspective, to a far greater extent than she or they would readily admit. George W. Bush and his chief lieutenants believed with her that the lessons of Munich took precedence over any putative lessons of Vietnam: Evildoers were not to be tolerated. They concurred in her conviction that the United States is uniquely equipped to peer into the future and discern history's purpose (which, it transpired, centered on the elimination of tyranny and even evil itself). When it came to using force, they too bridled at constraints and were even more eager than she had been to put American military power to work. Not least of all, like her, President Bush and those around him subscribed to a moral calculus in which the ends justified the means. Whatever mayhem might occur as a result of U.S. actions, good intentions ensured that American innocence remained unstained and uncompromised.

Unlike Dean Acheson, who not only witnessed but contributed directly to a period of considerable creativity, Albright had created nothing. Her contributions were those of a midwife. Yet viewed from that perspective, her achievement qualifies as noteworthy: She had delivered the Washington rules, fully refurbished, into a new millennium.

4

RECONSTITUTING THE TRINITY

BY THE 1980S, THE AMERICAN PENCHANT FOR INTERVEN-
tion was already showing signs of robust recovery, with
defenders of the Washington consensus enjoying similar
success in reshaping the instruments of global power projection and fending off calls to scale back the U.S. global
presence. By the end of the century, the whole sacred trinity
was back, bigger and better than ever.

The Soviet Union had done its best to help, as had adherents of radical Islam. The Soviet invasion of Afghanistan in
1979, along with Soviet military and economic assistance to
leftist revolutionaries in Central America during the 1980s,
fostered the impression, fueled by hawks in the United
States, that the Red Menace was reaching new heights. The
overthrow of the Shah of Iran, also in 1979, leading to the
creation of the Islamic Republic of Iran and the humiliating
capture of American diplomats by radical Iranian students,
supposedly demonstrated the consequences of giving the

impression that the United States was becoming weak and pusillanimous. Iranians saw the ensuing 444-day hostage crisis as just retribution—payback for Washington's incessant meddling in Iranian affairs. Americans chose to see it as an unwarranted assault on innocent representatives of a well-meaning nation.

To the extent that Vietnam had inspired any inclination to shrink the Pentagon's global "footprint," that inclination quickly ebbed and, by the end of the 1970s, had all but disappeared. Over the course of the next two decades, what occurred was not retrenchment but reconfiguration. U.S. troops did withdraw from Southeast Asia (though retaining a foothold in Thailand) and Taiwan (part of the price paid for Richard Nixon's opening to China). A nearly century-long U.S. military presence in the Philippines also ended, felled by Filipino anticolonialism and the 1991 eruption of Mount Pinatubo, which wrecked Clark Air Force Base and the American naval station at Subic Bay. Yet U.S. forces remained in Japan, operating a network of bases in both the home islands and Okinawa.

Running for president in 1976, Jimmy Carter vowed to remove American troops from the Korean peninsula, an effort that failed in the face of concerted military and congressional opposition. In the meantime, the Pentagon gained access to Singapore, improved its facilities on the Pacific island of Guam, and began developing a major new base in the Indian Ocean on the British-owned island of Diego Garcia—a project that entailed expelling the island's inhabitants.[1]

As the Soviet threat subsided and then disappeared, so too did the traditional rationale for this continuing presence. So the Pentagon devised a new rationale. Rather than defending key allies from external attack, U.S. forces abroad were now needed to facilitate the emergence of a new world order. In any case, they had to stay.

The Pentagon's post–Cold War mission, explained Secretary of Defense William S. Cohen in 1998, was "to shape the environment," creating conditions conducive to international stability and economic growth. "How do we do that? We have to be forward deployed." Although other elements of national policy might change, Cohen insisted, the presence of U.S. troops on bases worldwide remained absolutely essential.

> [W]e're going to keep 100,000 people in the Asia Pacific region, so that's off the table; and we're going to keep 100,000 people in Europe [so] that's off the table.
>
> We have to be forward deployed in Europe and in Asia in order to shape people's opinions about us in ways that are favorable to us. To shape events that will affect our livelihood and our security. And we can do that when people see us, they see our power, they see our professionalism, they see our patriotism, and they say that's a country that we want to be with. So we are shaping events on a daily basis in ways that are favorable to our interests. You can only do that if you're forward deployed.

Presence not only reassured your friends, it also impressed anyone tempted to be unfriendly. Forward-deployed forces, Cohen continued, influenced the views of would-be adversaries, persuading them "that they really don't want to challenge us in any given situation."[2] That such a presence might actually provoke rather than allay challenge, or that prolonged exposure to U.S. forces might evoke antagonism rather than respect, were propositions the defense secretary and others in the Pentagon were not prepared to contemplate.

Cohen was reciting what now became the textbook explanation for maintaining the Pentagon's global footprint. Even if the demise of the Soviet empire had rendered Europe whole and free, that did not mean American troops were coming home anytime soon. Over the course of nearly two centuries, a series of warlords—Napoleon, the kaisers of Imperial Germany, Adolf Hitler, Josef Stalin—had endangered European peace and stability. After 1989 the warlords had finished their run: Europeans faced negligible security threats. Yet American soldiers, sailors, and airmen remained at their stations in Belgium, Germany, Greece, Italy, Portugal, Spain, Turkey, and the United Kingdom anyway.

Beyond Europe and Asia, the Pentagon assigned top priority to reinforcing the U.S. military presence in areas where it had previously been insignificant. In this regard, attention focused especially on the Persian Gulf. President Carter had declared in 1980 that the United States would henceforth view an attempt by any outside power to gain control of this region "as an assault on the vital interests of the United States of America," to "be repelled by any means necessary, including military force." Putting teeth into this new Carter Doctrine meant the Pentagon needed to secure the use of nearby airfields, seaports, and other facilities, while improving local infrastructure and pre-positioning military stocks—doing, that is, all things necessary to make military intervention in the energy heartlands of the planet feasible and sustainable.

The significance of the shift in military posture that Carter set in motion can hardly be overstated. Inured to reports of U.S. forces operating out of or moving through places like Bahrain, Egypt, Kuwait, Oman, Qatar, Saudi Arabia, and the United Arab Emirates, not to mention Iraq and Afghanistan, Americans have forgotten how recently all of this activity began. Until 1980, the U.S. military footprint in what is today commonly called the Greater Middle East was so light as to be almost invisible. Thirty years later it is massive, seemingly permanent, and overshadows in importance the American military presence anywhere else in the world.

Indeed, after 9/11, the Pentagon dropped the pretense that the United States kept forces forward deployed simply so that others could bear witness to the power, professionalism, and patriotism of the American military. *Activism* now became the watchword. Forces were positioned abroad not to be "seen" but to expedite their future commitment to potential hot spots. A new term of art emerged: Overseas garrisons now became *forward operating bases*—springboards from which air, ground, and naval units could launch into zones of conflict.

Vice Adm. Arthur Cebrowski, an influential military thinker, described these facilities as "nodes or hubs in a worldwide system of moving U.S. military forces anywhere we need them to go." The "main purpose" of that system, explained one analyst, was "to facilitate the rapid deployment of U.S. forces throughout the world." Rather than "deterring undesired operations by another nation's traditional military forces," global presence provided "a means to move preemptively against non-national groups for whom traditional deterrence has little meaning."[3]

The activities of the navy to which Cebrowski devoted his life exemplified this shift in purpose. The modern U.S. Navy, created in the closing decades of the nineteenth century, was designed to take on opposing battlefleets. By 1945 it had fought its way to a position of dominance, securing what the naval theorist Alfred Thayer Mahan had once called "command of the seas." During the Cold War, maintaining command of the seas in the face of Soviet submarines had at least nominally been the navy's primary mission. In practice, however, its purpose was evolving: Beginning with the Korean War, its ships—above all its aircraft carriers—were employed as floating fire support platforms used to strike targets far inland.

As the Soviet threat faded, the fleet no longer held itself in readiness to do battle at sea. Instead, it went into the business of raining bombs and missiles on places like Tripoli, Beirut, Baghdad, Belgrade, and Kandahar. Taking command of the seas for granted—perhaps too quickly, as the emergence of twenty-first-century piracy might suggest— the navy employed its eleven massive aircraft carriers as mobile components within the system of nodes and hubs that Cebrowski described. Terminology lagged behind actual practice. Eventually, however, the traditional term *carrier battle group* disappeared—after all, no U.S. carrier has engaged in battle since World War II—to be replaced by the more aptly descriptive *carrier strike group*. This defines the navy's core function today. It has become a strike force, delivering ordnance against land targets wherever Washington wants to send a signal, reduce a potential threat, or retaliate against some real or fancied insult.

Overall, America's far-flung empire of bases prospered during the decades following Vietnam, adapting itself to a notable reshuffling of U.S. strategic priorities. As the empire changed, the foot soldiers manning its ramparts learned to accommodate themselves to new environments. U.S. forces used to worry about operating in subfreezing temperatures or in the midst of monsoons; today they cope with sand-storms while trying to avoid heatstroke. American military vernacular had formerly incorporated bits of German, Korean, and Vietnamese, often off-color. In our own day GI scatology has taken on Arabic overtones. Rather than beer steins, souvenir-collecting soldiers bring home hookah pipes and prayer rugs. The upshot is that the U.S. military since Vietnam has sustained and even expanded its global presence.

REINVENTING WAR

More striking still was the post-Vietnam rehabilitation of the Pentagon's power-projection capabilities. Superficially, this was simply a matter of loosening constraints, persuading Americans (and American soldiers) that the risks entailed in sending U.S. forces into action in some far-off land were tolerable and the likelihood of a new "quagmire" remote. More fundamentally, the goal was to make war once again purposeful, refuting the lingering Vietnam-era impression that committing forces abroad almost inevitably yielded only meaningless slaughter.

Between 1981 and 2000, three presidents—Ronald Reagan, George H. W. Bush, and Bill Clinton—collaborated to lift the constraints that Vietnam had seemingly imposed. Each of the three vowed as commander in chief to take a vigorous, assertive approach to military intervention—no shilly-shallying. Each made good on that promise.

Over these two decades, the use of force by the United States became both notably more frequent and less controversial. Bit by bit, the concept of deterrence as a cornerstone of national security strategy lost its salience. In its place emerged a clear preference for putting U.S. forces to work rather than holding them in reserve.

At one end of this narrative stands the U.S. involvement in the El Salvadoran civil war, Ronald Reagan's 1981 decision to send a grand total of fifty-five U.S. military "trainers" to assist the Salvadoran army, evoking from panicky observers predictions that the United States was plunging headlong into another Vietnam. At the other end stand Bill Clinton's efforts to "contain" Saddam Hussein during the 1990s, which saw U.S. combat aircraft penetrating Iraqi airspace on a daily basis for years on end—tens of thousands of sorties flown, thousands of weapons expended in attacking Iraqi targets—with few Americans even bothering to take notice.[4]

In between were a slew of combat and quasi-combat missions that saw American troops going into action everywhere from Latin America to the Caribbean, the Balkans to the Persian Gulf, East Africa to Asia Minor. By the dawn of the twenty-first century, the War Powers Act of 1973, and therefore any congressional brake on decisions related to war, had become a dead letter. To a greater extent than any earlier period in U.S. history, Americans had come to accept the use of force as routine.

In the wake of 9/11, this trend found its ultimate expression in the Bush Doctrine of preventive war, which swept aside any lingering reticence about employing force. When acting in the role of commander in chief, the president now claimed—and exercised—essentially unlimited entitlements. Anything he and his advisers judged necessary to "keep America safe" became legitimate. In the midst of the Watergate scandal that ultimately proved his undoing, President Richard Nixon had advanced the argument that "if the president does it, that means it's not illegal." Nixon's removal from office had seemingly discredited this claim; after 9/11, this perverse Nixon Doctrine returned to favor.

All of this happened in plain sight. If the American people did not actively endorse the ever greater militarization of foreign policy and the concentration of ever more power in the Oval Office, they passively assented. White House advisers increasingly operated on the assumption that the benefits of using force outweighed the risks. At a minimum, dropping a few bombs all but guaranteed an uptick in a president's approval rating. Even when an operation went awry, as in the case of Bill Clinton's bungled war in Somalia, the negative fallout quickly passed. Everyone knew this; hence the joke—or was it a joke?— that the best way for a president to get out of hot water at home was to conjure up a war abroad, an insight brilliantly captured in director Barry Levinson's cynical 1997 movie, *Wag the Dog*.

A president could now—it seemed—take the nation to war without Americans being noticeably discomfited. War, after all, had become a spectacle, not a phenomenon that inflicted pain and suffering on citizens of the United States.

Behind the scenes, the reformulation of the American way of war involved sustained conflict, pitting an officer corps still bearing the scars of Vietnam against a new generation of civilian semiwarriors keen to prove Vietnam's irrelevance. Both camps were committed to restoring the utility of force. Each camp entertained its own specific vision of what that should entail. Yet note carefully: Although soldiers and semiwarriors disagreed on matters of technique, they were united in their commitment to restoring the credibility of America's armed forces as an instrument of global power projection. That the Department of Defense might define its purpose as defending the United States never received serious consideration.

This process of reinventing war occurred in two stages. For a time, the officer corps had the upper hand. After 9/11, the semiwarriors gained the advantage. The defining events in this saga were Operation Desert Storm in 1991 and Operation Iraqi Freedom in 2003. The first was Gen. Colin Powell's war, its conduct reflecting precepts to which Powell and the officer corps as a whole had become deeply devoted. The second was Secretary of Defense Donald Rumsfeld's war, its conduct—in its early stages at least—reflecting the way that he and his fellow semiwarriors believed the United States ought to fight.

Operation Desert Storm represented the culmination of a reform project that had absorbed the energies of the officer corps ever since the Vietnam War ended. Its principal theme was the reconstitution of conventional warfare—the clash of regular forces on non-nuclear battlefields uncluttered with civilians, directed by generals insulated from meddling politicians and intrusive media, and culminating in an operationally decisive outcome. From Vietnam, officers like Powell had drawn this lesson: Long wars spelled institutional disaster and were to be avoided at all costs. The military's version of a new American way of war aimed to preclude protracted fighting and therefore all of the political and moral complications that had made Vietnam such a frustrating and agonizing experience.

Largely conceived by the officer corps itself at installations such as Fort Leavenworth, Kansas, and Fort Monroe, Virginia, the reforms instituted during the period leading up to Desert Storm looked to the past as much as the future. For inspiration, they drew upon World War II (emphasizing Europe over the Pacific) and to a lesser extent on the Israeli military experience (focusing on the ostensibly decisive Six-Day War of 1967). Military reformers consciously disregarded the U.S. experience of Vietnam altogether. Indeed, a central purpose of the reform project was to purge the armed forces of the effects of Vietnam and avert the recurrence of anything even remotely similar. Counterinsurgency, nation building, winning hearts and minds: Officers who had served in Vietnam invariably viewed these as anathema.

Although styled as bold and innovative, the spirit of this enterprise was deeply conservative. This becomes especially evident when considering how the military chose to spend its money during the bountiful years of the Reagan defense buildup. The signature weapons that had defined the services prior to Vietnam continued to define them afterward: For the army, this meant, above all, the tank; for the navy, the aircraft carrier; for the air force, the long-range bomber and manned supersonic fighter.

In virtually every case, weapons design reflected a commitment to incremental refinements. So, although the M1 Abrams tank fielded in the 1980s was a wonder to behold, it expressed a vision of land combat that dated back to World War I and had reached maturity in the 1940s. Much the same could be said of the navy's post-Vietnam Nimitz-class carriers and of the air force's new B-1 bomber and F-15 and F-16 fighters. An officer from any of the services transported from the 1940s to the 1980s would have been impressed with the hardware available—everything was faster, bigger, and sleeker—but would have found the organization, operations, and institutional culture that went with these weapons comfortably familiar.

The new generation of weapons did differ from their predecessors in one respect: They were exceedingly expensive. Even the generous budgets of the 1980s funded their purchase in only limited numbers. A similar limitation applied to the procurement of volunteers for the all-volunteer force: They cost a lot and were not easily replaced. So the post-Vietnam reforms also saw the services shift from a traditional reliance on sheer mass to destroy any adversary, as epitomized by the LeMay approach to strategic bombing, to a greater stress on quality. Among other things, this meant placing greater emphasis on training and retention. Those volunteering to serve became an increasingly valued commodity.

This increased attention to quality fostered one exception to the Pentagon's otherwise consistent preoccupation with conventional warfare. In the wake of Vietnam, so-called special operations forces proliferated. Elite units—among them navy SEALs and the army's Rangers, Green Berets, Delta Force, and 160th Aviation Regiment—assumed responsibility for an array of unconventional tasks ranging from clandestine reconnaissance and counterterror missions to hostage rescue, psychological operations (PSYOPS), and support for friendly indigenous forces. In 1987, Congress acknowledged the growing importance of these activities by creating a new four-star Special Operations Command, signifying that the members of this "community" had achieved a status separate from but at least equal to the bulk of U.S. forces.

Americans quickly learned that most of what happens in the world of special operations lies beyond their purview. Capabilities, activities, and even budgets are all classified. Public accountability is minimal. In effect, after Vietnam the Pentagon increased its presence in the "black world," encroaching upon and then moving well beyond the territory originally staked out by Allen Dulles and his colleagues.

When it came to covert action, the CIA no longer enjoyed even the approximation of a monopoly.

From the perspective of the officer corps, the post-Vietnam reform project reached its apotheosis in the Persian Gulf War of 1990–1991. For the armed services, and especially for Powell, then serving as chairman of the Joint Chiefs, Operation Desert Storm came as validation and vindication. Victory over Iraq, generously credited by the Department of Defense with possessing "the fourth largest army in the world, an army hardened in long years of combat against Iran," vanquished the memory of defeat in Southeast Asia.[5]

By assembling a combat force of several hundred thousand soldiers in a harsh, unforgiving environment, Powell and his fellow Vietnam veterans had reaffirmed the unequaled ability of the United States to reposition massive amounts of combat power just about anywhere on the planet. Powell had promised to destroy the Iraqi army— "First, we're going to cut it off, and then we're going to kill it"—and U.S. troops had seemingly made good on that promise.[6] At first blush, Operation Desert Storm appeared a stupendous achievement, a victory without parallel in the annals of warfare.

It promptly vaulted Powell to the status of national hero. The general wasted no time in advertising the just-completed campaign as the approved template for all future American wars. This was the way it was supposed to be done: When (and only when) truly vital interests were at stake, the United States should employ what Powell called "overwhelming force" to make short work of any adversary. Now that U.S. forces had proven their ability to do just that, however, Powell was not eager to place the military's gains at risk by repeating the feat elsewhere. With the Iraqis kicked out of Kuwait, his priority, widely shared through-out the officer corps, was to consolidate the gains that the armed services had worked so hard to achieve since Vietnam.

Within the military, the inevitable search for relevant lessons focused on identifying "what is important to protect and preserve in our military capability." According to the Pentagon, five key elements had contributed to victory in the Gulf: a decisive president who "not only gave the military the tools to do the job but . . . provided it with clear objectives and the support to carry out its assigned tasks" (that is, a president who avoided the errors charged to Lyndon Johnson); technological superiority, especially a new generation of precision weapons that "gave our forces the edge"; the professionalism and competence of U.S. troops and their commanders; the availability of forward-deployed units along with the bases that made their commitment to combat possible; and finally the accumulated benefit of intense preparation over the course of many years. "It takes a long time to build the high quality forces and systems that gave us success." Implicit in that concluding point was a warning: Abuse this force and you'll break it; once broken, recovery won't come easily.[7]

Looking ahead, the Pentagon identified two key priorities: first, "to retain our technological edge out into the future," and second, to "be ready for the next Desert Storm–like contingency that comes along."[8] In sum, by 1991 the military establishment felt that it had achieved something approximating the summit of perfection. The last thing soldiers needed or wanted was for someone to start tinkering with a machine so painstakingly assembled. Powell's priority and the priority of the officer corps was to preserve what had been regained.

There was an alternative view, however, according to which the results achieved against Iraq fell well short of being decisive. After all, Saddam had survived. So, too, had the most capable parts of his large, if not especially competent, army. To deal with this continuing "threat," U.S. forces remained in Saudi Arabia and elsewhere in the region, a decision consistent with the principle that the presence of American forces abroad contributed to security and stability yet one provoking deep resentment throughout much of the Islamic world. In the end, a brief campaign touted as a great victory had settled little, while creating new complications; the historic feat of arms over which Colin Powell had presided turned out to be something of a bust politically and strategically.

Proponents of this view—for the most part civilians ensconced in universities like Harvard and Chicago, in security-oriented think tanks, and in an obscure but influential Pentagon directorate called the Office of Net Assessment—saw Operation Desert Storm not as a great victory but as a missed opportunity, not as the culmination of a process of reform but as a harbinger of better things to come. In the campaign to expel the Iraqi army from Kuwait, they glimpsed stupendous possibilities. America's armed services stood on the cusp of what they called a Revolution in Military Affairs or RMA. Properly exploited, they believed, this revolution promised to invest force with unprecedented effectiveness and utility.

Considered from this perspective, Operation Desert Storm signaled not the perfection of industrial-age warfare but its death knell. According to RMA enthusiasts a new era of Information Age warfare was dawning. Primacy in the cyberworld held the promise of primacy in the real world: This was their conviction.

During most of the twentieth century, machines had dominated the battlefield. As the twenty-first century beckoned, information networks were emerging as key determinants of victory. A nation's capacity to manufacture armor plate had once figured as a measure of its military potential; what mattered now was the ability of a nation's military forces to access and manage bandwidth. Machines remained, of course, but ensuring their effectiveness now centered on making them "smart." As the fate of the Iraqi army in Kuwait suggested, the machine that was not smart became simply a target.

This RMA implied a new aesthetic of war. Past conflicts had tended to be confusing brawls; in the digital age, military operations were to become carefully choreographed performances. Information would lift the millennia-old fog of war; things that had been hidden would become visible; tasks that had seemed dauntingly difficult would become routine. No matter the conditions on the ground, the advent of the Information Age promised to unshackle armies, transforming war much as it was said to be transforming business, journalism, and mass culture. Agility, precision, synchronization, and speed: In the realm of military affairs, these were now emerging as the attributes defining operational excellence.[9]

The RMA's semiwarriors believed that the United States was uniquely placed to exploit the opportunities offered by this revolution. If the Pentagon acted promptly, they felt certain that something approaching permanent military dominion would all but fall into the country's lap. The mere contemplation of this prospect generated a sense of excitement verging on the erotic.

The implications of supremacy extended far beyond matters of tactics, of course. The appeal of the RMA lay not in the promise of winning battles but of changing the world, while making the global Pax Americana all but permanent. What the new semiwarriors glimpsed was the possibility of removing war from the realm of chance and uncertainty.

For the United States, armed conflict henceforth promised to become a low-risk enterprise. All but assured that future wars would be limited affairs ending in success, Americans would no longer hesitate before pulling the trigger. Policy makers could contemplate the prospect of intervention abroad, confident that any ensuing conflict would be brief and economical, that they would be able to anticipate and control its course, and that (in contrast to Desert Storm) the result would be politically decisive. As never before, force would provide the essential instrument for cutting through the vagaries of history, paving the way for peace, security, and the further spread of American values.

And that was not all: Once fully demonstrated to a shocked-and-awed world, these capabilities, uniquely possessed by U.S. forces, promised to reduce the necessity of actually pulling that trigger. In most cases, the mere prospect of the United States flexing its military muscles was likely to dissuade anyone from challenging the existing order or violating American norms. If, as Dean Acheson once remarked, "influence is the shadow of power," the RMA promised to endow the United States with a level of influence surpassing anything the world had ever seen. Possession of unrivaled military capabilities would make the Washington rules unassailable. Washington's rule would be complete. Washington itself, the seat of American power, would affirm its standing as the New Rome.

As an added bonus, the project would likely pay for itself. In 1991, the governments of Kuwait, Saudi Arabia,

Germany, and Japan had reimbursed the Pentagon for costs incurred in conducting Operation Desert Storm. If U.S. forces demonstrated the ability to maintain international peace and security to the general benefit of all, was it unreasonable to expect other nations—rich but debellicized—to underwrite the expenses involved? With military service voluntary and with other nations footing the bill, the yoke borne by the American people promised to be so light as to be unnoticeable.

So now was not the time for the Pentagon to rest on its laurels as Powell and his military contemporaries preferred. To wait passively for the next Desert Storm to come along—years might pass!—could mean forfeiting the initiative. Standing pat might allow would-be competitors (China seemed the most likely candidate) to catch up. Rather than consolidation, aggressive exploitation of the new revolutionary age of warfare defined the order of the day.

The expectations generated by RMA theorists—forces optimized for "network centric" warfare providing the foundation for lasting American primacy—grew out of a specific context in which post–Cold War triumphalism blended with a rising faith in the transformative power of technology married to the forces of globalization. In a fast, flat, and wide-open world, this new way of war offered an enticing blueprint for extracting the maximum benefit from the arena in which the United States enjoyed unquestioned superiority. Unlike LeMay's SAC, instruments of violence designed to fit RMA precepts wouldn't risk blowing up the world. Unlike Dulles's CIA with its limited repertoire of dirty tricks, those forces would possess broad utility. Best of all, for the moment at least, the United States owned the RMA franchise.

Yet strip away the cyberjargon and the RMA bore more

than a passing resemblance to flexible response. The new generation of semiwarriors—Democrats like Madeleine Albright eager to succor the afflicted; Republicans like Donald Rumsfeld, pursuing more overtly imperial ambitions—were, in fact, the heirs of Taylor, McNamara, and Bundy. In the RMA they saw the possibility of fulfilling the promise of flexible response, dashed by Vietnam: Here once again was the prospect of devising a broader array of power projection options; here once again was the seductive vision of force employed in a controlled and limited manner, with costs contained and risks minimized.

The debate over the new American way of war, pitting those who saw Desert Storm as perfection against those who saw it as portent, extended throughout the 1990s and did not come to a head until after 9/11. By that time, Rumsfeld, a self-described conservative who, on matters related to the future of war, entertained genuinely radical views, had become secretary of defense. His agenda upon taking command of the Pentagon reduced to a single word: transformation.

Rumsfeld was intent on breaking military resistance to the RMA and then remolding the services according to its dictates. During the first eight months of his tenure he made frustratingly little progress. The attacks of September 11, 2001, changed all that. The global war on terror promptly declared by the Bush administration presented a made-to-order opportunity to shatter that resistance once and for all. Rumsfeld grasped the opportunity with alacrity.

SPEED KILLS

America's crusade to extirpate terrorism—in size, scope, and significance comparable to the world wars of the last century, according to some observers—opened on a seem-ingly promising note.[10] In the fall of 2001, U.S. forces launched Operation Enduring Freedom, toppling the Taliban regime that had provided Osama bin Laden sanctuary and putting Al Qaeda to flight. Dazzled by this apparent success, the Bush administration almost immediately began shifting its attention to Iraq, identifying the overthrow of Saddam Hussein as its main objective. Although top U.S. officials did not expect the global war on terror to end with Sad-dam's removal, they felt certain that removing the Iraqi dic-tator would yield large strategic gains. Once Washington had removed Saddam, further successes would come easily.

As with the campaign in Afghanistan, Operation Iraqi Freedom began on a promising note. Within a matter of weeks, U.S. forces had shattered the Iraqi army and cap-tured Baghdad. Speaking on the deck of the USS *Abraham Lincoln* against the backdrop of a banner reading MISSION ACCOMPLISHED, a giddy President Bush announced on May 1, 2003, that major combat operations in Iraq had ended.

The president spoke prematurely, however. Saddam's ouster had decided nothing. Things became not easier, but more difficult.

Intended to solve problems, Saddam's elimination instead confronted Washington with fresh complications. In Bagh-dad, regime change unleashed forces—a civil war com-bined with an anti-Western insurgency and rampant criminality—to which U.S. occupation authorities in Iraq responded clumsily and ineffectually. As the Bush adminis-tration preoccupied itself with trying to prevent Iraq from imploding, the larger global war on terror stalled. Expecta-tions that a concerted exercise of American power would eliminate the conditions giving rise to violent jihadism and affirm Washington's claim to global dominion lost all coherence and credibility.

No sooner had U.S. forces managed to impose some faint semblance of order on Iraq in 2008, than deteriorating conditions in Afghanistan revealed that earlier claims of victory there had likewise been overstated. The Taliban were once again on the march and the United States found itself back at square one. By the time Barack Obama succeeded George W. Bush as president in January 2009, the phrase *global war on terror* had become an epithet, redolent with deception, stupidity, and monumental waste. Soon thereafter it faded from the lexicon of American politics.

Donald Rumsfeld's transformation initiative followed a similar trajectory and suffered a similar fate. What seemed ever so briefly to be evidence of creative genius—Rumsfeld prodding, cajoling, and lashing hidebound generals into doing things his way with spectacular results—turned out to be illusory, and the RMA's much-hyped formula for military supremacy ersatz.

Campaigns in Afghanistan and Iraq intended to showcase an unprecedented mastery of war demonstrated the folly of imagining that war could be mastered. When he finally left the Pentagon in late 2006, Rumsfeld found himself running neck and neck with Robert McNamara for the title of worst defense secretary in U.S. history. The concept of transformation had become a symbol of the overweening arrogance and hucksterism that had characterized his entire tenure in office. Yet Rumsfeld's failure—the bungled wars that discredited his military reform project—deserves careful examination for one specific reason: Out of that failure came yet another misguided effort to refashion the sacred trinity, namely the new era of counterinsurgency in which the United States finds itself today.

President Bush and his chief advisers intended the global war on terror to serve several purposes, not least among them to shore up the basic approach to national security that had prevailed since World War II. For Rumsfeld and others in the administration, transformation and the conflict initiated in response to 9/11 were component parts of a even larger enterprise. Their overarching goal was to affirm and even deepen the Washington consensus, while removing any remaining constraints on the use of American military power.

Forged during the early Cold War, the Washington rules once underpinned a strategy of containment: Washington's declared aim had been to avert a domino effect, the loss of any one country to communism presumably leading to the loss of many others. As reconfigured in the wake of 9/11, the Washington rules provided the basis for the United States to promote its own domino effect, the forceful "liberation" of one or two countries in the Islamic world expected to unleash a wave of change eventually rippling across the entire Greater Middle East.

Yet implementing this new domino theory required the United States to shed any lingering reticence when it came to the actual use of force. Here lay the inspiration for the Bush Doctrine of preventive war: It offered the means to advance Bush's Freedom Agenda. Rather than merely containing threats to national security, the United States would anticipate, confront, and eliminate threats before they actually posed a danger. By embracing preventive war, the Bush administration added a codicil to the Washington consensus, with massive (although largely unexamined) moral, political, and strategic implications. What made this doctrine of preventive war appear plausible—even alluring, in the eyes of some—was the Revolution in Military Affairs. Selling the

American people on the global war on terror meant selling them on the new American way of war it implied.

In congressional testimony presented barely three weeks after September 11, Paul Wolfowitz, Rumsfeld's influential deputy, explained the connection between the war just begun and the national security practices to which the United States had adhered for decades. Although "terrorist movements and totalitarian regimes of the world have a variety of motives and goals," Wolfowitz explained, in a broader sense they shared a single unifying purpose: "a desire to see America driven into retreat and isolation."

> Usama bin Laden, Saddam Hussein, Kim Jong Il and other such tyrants all want to see America out of critical regions of the world, constrained from coming to the aid of friends and allies, and unable to project power in the defense of our interests and ideals.
>
> By holding our people hostage to terror and fear, their intention is for America to be intimidated into withdrawal and inaction—leaving them free to impose their will on their peoples and neighbors unmolested by America's military might.
>
> All of these capabilities serve their common objective of keeping America out of their regions and unable to project force in the defense of freedom. To meet the challenges over the horizon, we must transform our Armed Forces more rapidly, more creatively, and even more radically than we had previously planned. . . .
>
> It is a fact of life that countries frequently prepare to fight the last war. We spent much of the 1990s planning to re-fight the Gulf War. . . . [To wage the wars of the future,] we will need forces and capabili-

> ties that give the President an even wider range of
> military options.
>
> The goal of [military] transformation is to main-
> tain a substantial advantage over any potential
> adversaries. . . . If we can do this, we can reduce our
> own chances of being surprised, and increase our
> ability to create our own surprises, if we choose.[11]

Wolfowitz's glib allusion to the historical dyad was standard fare: assertive leadership as prescribed by the American credo versus retreat and isolationism. As always for
defenders of the Washington consensus, these defined the
sole alternatives. More imaginative was Wolfowitz's depic-
tion of how a motley collection of B-list foes had banded
together to lay siege to the national security triad. Rolling
back the U.S. military presence abroad, neutralizing the Pentagon's capacity for power projection, intimidating Americans into passivity: This defined the common agenda to
which such disparate figures as Al Qaeda's radical jihadist
leader, Iraq's secular authoritarian, and North Korea's erratic
dictator all ostensibly subscribed.

According to Wolfowitz, "transformation" offered the
essential means of thwarting this nefarious partnership.
Radically reforming the Pentagon consistent with the principles of the RMA promised to provide Washington—that
is, people like Rumsfeld and Wolfowitz—with inviting new
opportunities to act. Rather than being surprised as on
9/11, the United States would spring surprises on bin Laden,
Saddam Hussein, Kim Jong Il, and anyone else said to pose
a threat.

Within days after Wolfowitz spoke, the invasion of
Afghanistan provided a preliminary demonstration of what
he and Rumsfeld had in mind. Small numbers of special

operations troops (assisted by CIA paramilitaries) linked to an impressive array of firepower—mostly sophisticated aircraft delivering precision munitions—and local allies on the ground made short work of the Taliban. Operation Enduring Freedom began on October 7, 2001. By November 14, the Afghan capital, Kabul, had fallen.

President Bush wasted no time in explaining what it all meant. Afghanistan had provided "a proving ground" for a new American approach to war, he announced to the assembled cadets at the Citadel in Charleston, South Carolina. Yet this was a work in progress: More remained to be done. "This revolution in our military is only beginning," Bush continued, "and it promises to change the face of battle."

> These past two months have shown that an innovative doctrine and high-tech weaponry can shape and then dominate an unconventional conflict. The brave men and women of our military are rewriting the rules of war. . . . Our commanders are gaining a real-time picture of the entire battlefield and are able to get targeting information from sensor to shooter almost instantly. . . . We're striking with greater effectiveness, at greater range, with fewer civilian casualties. More and more, our weapons can hit moving targets. When all of our military can continuously locate and track moving targets with surveillance from air and space, warfare will be truly revolutionized.[12]

The march on Baghdad served to highlight these capabilities on an even larger scale. Operation Iraqi Freedom began on March 20, 2003. By April 9, U.S. forces had taken the Iraqi capital, Saddam Hussein was in hiding, and his army had all but ceased to exist.

Administration officials immediately set out to interpret the military significance of what had occurred. The deed was done. The Pentagon had, in fact, consummated a revolution. History had rounded a corner and was entering the home stretch.

During his presentation on the deck of the *Abraham Lincoln* that May 1, a cocky President Bush, already referring to Operation Iraqi Freedom in the past tense, elaborated on the significance of the campaign now (apparently) concluding. The invasion of Iraq, he rhapsodized, "was carried out with a combination of precision and speed and boldness the enemy did not expect and the world had not seen before. In the images of falling statues," the president continued,

> we have witnessed the arrival of a new era. For a hundred years of war, culminating in the nuclear age, military technology was designed and deployed to inflict casualties on an ever-growing scale. . . . Military power was used to end a regime by breaking a nation. Today, we have the greater power to free a nation by breaking a dangerous and aggressive regime. With new tactics and precision weapons, we can achieve military objectives without directing violence against civilians. No device of man can remove the tragedy from war; yet it is a great moral advance when the guilty have far more to fear from war than the innocent.[13]

In an appearance at a conservative Washington think tank that same day, Vice President Dick Cheney seconded his boss, declaring that "Iraqi Freedom has been one of the most extraordinary military campaigns ever conducted." Victory in Iraq offered "proof positive of the success of our efforts to transform our military to meet the challenges of the twenty-first century." Transformation had "allowed us to integrate joint operations much more effectively than ever before, thereby enabling commanders to make decisions more rapidly, to target strikes more precisely, to minimize human casualties, civilian casualties, and to accomplish the missions more successfully."[14]

In testimony before the House Government Reform Committee on May 6, Wolfowitz went even further:

> Our unparalleled ability to conduct night operations has allowed us to virtually own the night, and the close integration of our forces has resulted in an order of magnitude change in how precise we are in finding and hitting targets from just a decade ago. . . .
>
> As we have seen so vividly in recent days, lives depend, not just on technology, but on a culture that fosters leadership, flexibility, agility and adaptability. The American people need and deserve a transformed Defense Department.[15]

Out of this cascade of self-congratulation, one word pulled away from the pack to emerge as the signature for the new American way of war: *speed*. U.S. forces possessed the ability to dictate the tempo of events. They acted; the enemy reacted, belatedly and ineffectively. The United States "owned the clock," a priceless asset.[16]

In a hastily prepared history of the Iraq invasion, retired Maj. Gen. Robert Scales cut to the essence:

In war, speed kills, especially if military forces move fast enough to disrupt the enemy's ability to make decisions. [U.S. commanders in Iraq] maintained the speed of movement by making the tip of the spear as supple, mobile, and flexible as possible. They had clearly learned the lesson of the Gulf War [of 1991] that a fundamental law of Newtonian physics applies also to military maneuver: one can achieve over-whelming force by substituting velocity for mass.[17]

Rumsfeld himself returned repeatedly to this point. In the invasion of Iraq, "speed was more important than mass," he emphasized during a television interview on April 13.[18] Speed facilitated the good and precluded the unwanted. At a meeting with Pentagon employees soon after Baghdad fell, Rumsfeld expanded on this theme: "What's happened is amazing for the speed with which it was executed, but also for all the things that did not happen, all the bad things that could have happened [but didn't] because of that speed." Speed cleansed war of undesired collateral effects that tra-ditionally compromised its utility. Thanks to the speed and precision of U.S. operations, he continued,

There are no large masses of refugees fleeing across borders into the neighboring countries. And human-itarian relief is flowing in through ports and rail and roads to assist the Iraqi people. There has not been large-scale collateral damage. The infrastructure of the country is largely intact. Bridges were not blown, for the most part, and rail lines were protected. The dams were not broken and floods did not occur. And there have not been massive civilian casualties because the coalition forces took such enormous care to protect the lives of innocent civilians.[19]

Rumsfeld had shaped the design of Operation Iraqi Freedom to validate his concept of transformation. He now
declared his test a success. Together, Operations Enduring
Freedom and Iraqi Freedom had seemingly buried the putative lessons that Colin Powell had drawn from Desert Storm.
Numerically large armies with their "big footprint" were
now problematic. Small contingents of highly trained, high-
tech ground forces moving like quicksilver: Here was the
template for all future U.S. military operations. Deliberate
planning, massed formations, top-down control, operations unfolding according to a ponderous, predetermined
sequence: All of these had become as obsolete as close-
order drill. Swift, precise, flexible, agile, adaptable: These
qualities had now become the hallmarks of U.S. military
operations.

As Afghanistan and Iraq seemed to indicate, to commit
U.S. forces to battle was to achieve assured victory. Washington need no longer view force as a last resort. Among the
instruments available to policy makers, force now ranked
as the preferred option.

Bush, Cheney, Rumsfeld, and Wolfowitz may not have
hankered for war, something with which they had no direct
personal experience. What they and other semiwarriors
craved was not slaughter but submission—unquestioned
political dominance as an expected by-product of unquestioned military dominion. Writing not long after the fall of
Baghdad, one enthusiast put it this way:

> [T]he strategic imperative of patrolling the perime-
> ter of the Pax Americana is transforming the U.S.
> military . . . into the cavalry of a global, liberal inter-
> national order. Like the cavalry of the Old West, their
> job is one part warrior and one part policeman—

both of which are entirely within the tradition of the American military.

Even as the military remains ready to wage a full-scale war focused against a specific aggressor nation, the realignment of our network of overseas bases into a system of frontier stockades is necessary to win a long-term struggle against an amorphous enemy across the arc of instability. . . . Although countless questions about transformation remain unanswered, one lesson is already clear: American power is on the move.[20]

This defined the brand of militarism to which Washington now fell prey.

WAIST DEEP IN THE EUPHRATES

During the run-up to, and execution of, Operations Enduring Freedom and Iraqi Freedom, Rumsfeld had broached no opposition from within the officer corps. Confronted with contrary views, he moved quickly to crush them, Gen. Eric Shinseki, the army chief of staff who told Congress that occupying Iraq might pose considerable challenges, being his most famous victim. (A paradox of Rumsfeld's tenure in office: Intolerant of generals within the Pentagon who disagreed with him, the defense secretary evinced remarkable patience for senior commanders in Afghanistan and Iraq who performed ineptly.)

With the fall of Baghdad, Rumsfeld succeeded in silencing RMA skeptics. Senior officers—at least those wishing to remain in the defense secretary's good graces—now dutifully parroted the language of transformation. Here, for example, is army Lt. Gen. Robert Wagner riffing on the

future of warfare, less than a year into Operation Iraqi
Freedom:

> We envision the future from an information age
> perspective where operations are conducted in a
> battlespace, not a battlefield. . . . We are now able to
> create decision superiority that is enabled by net-
> worked systems, new sensors and command and
> control capabilities that are producing near real-
> time situational awareness. . . . [O]ur operations in
> Afghanistan and Iraq [have demonstrated the] oper-
> ational attributes that an adaptive joint force must
> possess in the modern Battlespace. To dominate this
> battlespace, the joint force must be "knowledge
> centric," "coherently joint," "fully networked and
> collaborative" interdependent in organization and
> employment and uniquely designed for "Effects-
> Based Operations." Certainly any future joint force
> must be capable of conducting rapid, decisive combat
> operations. But we have found that a future joint
> force must also apply these operational attributes
> synergistically across the entire range of military
> operations. We must be decisive in every operation,
> not just the high-end portion of war but across the
> full range of military operations. . . . The advent of
> reliable and secure digital communications, a new
> level of battlespace awareness borne from joint and
> combined interoperability, and precision weapons
> have created the potential for a new type of force.[21]

Some readers may flinch from wading through this gas-
eous passage. Yet it deserves careful consideration. Take a
moment to read it a second time. Savor the vocabulary:
seamless, digital, networked, effects-based, coherently joint,

along with the reference to precision and, of course, speed, all of it redolent of a pitch marketing an info-tech start-up rather than an activity involving death and destruction, risk and uncertainty (all of which go unmentioned). Note the references to synergism, interoperability, and situational awareness, which suggest the absence of fog and friction. Ponder Wagner's jaw-dropping assurance that forces organized consistent with such principles will "be decisive in every operation," apparently without exception.

General Wagner's testimony recalls H. L. Mencken's famous assessment of President Warren G. Harding's oratory:

> It is so bad that a sort of grandeur creeps into it. It drags itself out of a dark abysm of pish, and crawls insanely up the topmost pinnacle of posh. It is rumble and bumble, it is flap and doodle. It is balder and dash.

The bloviating of hack politicians offers a suitable subject for comedy and satire. Balderdash that presumes to express the truth about war does not: The stakes are too high. The views expressed by General Wagner, a Vietnam veteran to boot, illustrate the extent to which, midway through the Age of Rumsfeld, the officer corps, its ranks normally filled with sober empiricists, had become unhinged. A soldier transported from the 1940s—or even the 1990s—would have found General Wagner's incantations all but incomprehensible.

Not only were such views divorced from the historical experience of warfare, they were also radically at odds with ongoing events. Wagner spoke in late February 2004. That month, 19 American soldiers lost their lives in Iraq with another 150 wounded. The following month the totals would rise to 52 killed and 323 wounded, and in April to 136 killed and 1,214 wounded.[22]

In the "battlespace" where this was occurring, the Revolution in Military Affairs provided U.S. forces with no discernible advantage. The Americans certainly did not "own the clock." Despite all the technological paraphernalia in their possession, U.S. forces were effectively fighting blind. Lacking adequate intelligence, they conducted massive nighttime "sweeps" in which they knocked down doors, terrorized Iraqi women and children, and detained large numbers of military-age men. They threw innocent and guilty alike into overcrowded detention camps that then served as incubators of anti-American resistance.

The result was not to suppress but further inflame an insurgency that was destabilizing Iraq. As U.S. troops moved about Baghdad and other cities, they found themselves continually ambushed. Relying increasingly on roadside bombs and other explosive devices, insurgents called the tune; the Americans danced. Meanwhile, the Abu Ghraib scandal was in full flower, with photographs of GIs sadistically abusing Iraqi detainees demolishing Washington's pretensions to moral superiority.

As things went from bad to worse, Rumsfeld's knowledge-centric, coherently joint, fully networked concept of military transformation offered little of value. The RMA ostensibly provided a surefire formula for making wars short and decisive. In Iraq, the formula failed, abysmally. The Bush administration's official narrative of a brief encounter ending neatly in "mission accomplished" disintegrated. The war became incoherent. Fighting simply went on and on, with U.S. forces groping ineffectually to regain control. Caught in the middle were Iraqi civilians who suffered and died or simply fled their homes or the country in alarming numbers, giving the lie to claims that the United States had discovered a more discriminating and humane approach to waging war.

During the opening stages of the Iraq War, Western observers had had great fun at the expense of Muhammad Saeed al-Sahhaf, the Iraqi information minister. Mockingly known as Baghdad Bob, al-Sahhaf had periodically provided Western reporters in Baghdad with the Iraqi government's version of events. As late as April 8, 2003, with U.S. armored columns already cruising through the Iraqi capital, he was still predicting that coalition forces were "going to surrender or be burned in their tanks." Victory over the invaders, he insisted, was just around the corner. Baghdad Bob's assessments evoked gales of laughter: Only a knave or a fool could express views so obviously at odds with reality.

By the spring and summer of 2004, those presenting the official U.S. interpretation of events in Iraq were sounding more than a little like Baghdad Bob. President Bush, for example, clung to the delusion that the restoration of Iraqi sovereignty, scheduled for June 30, held the key to restoring peace and harmony across that nation. Speaking at a press conference on April 13, the president was once again ready to declare the mission accomplished.

> The nation of Iraq is moving toward self-rule, and Iraqis and Americans will see evidence in the months to come. On June 30th, when the flag of free Iraq is raised, Iraqi officials will assume full responsibility for the ministries of Government. On that day, the transitional administrative law, including a bill of rights that is unprecedented in the Arab world, will take full effect.[23]

Donald Rumsfeld shared this upbeat assessment of Iraq's prospects. "They've got the schools open," he told a television interviewer on April 29. "They've got the hospitals open. They've got the clinics open. There was not a humanitarian crisis. Food is there and available to the people. The people are able to form a part of an Olympic team. They've got a symphony that's started."[24] Undersecretary of Defense Douglas Feith corroborated these findings. In a speech at a conservative think tank on May 4, he reported that over the course of the previous twelve months, "Iraq has been transformed." The economy was booming. Everywhere there were signs of progress. The restoration of sovereignty on June 30 would seal the deal.[25]

On May 10, 2004, Bush was still justifying the ongoing war as central to American efforts to encourage "the spread of freedom throughout the world." U.S. forces were "steadily defeating" the enemy, he reported. American troops were "on the offensive, conducting hundreds of patrols and raids every day . . . . responding with precision and discipline and restraint, [while] taking every precaution to avoid hurting the innocent as we deliver justice to the guilty." The president expressed confidence that things were well in hand. "We're fielding the most technologically advanced military forces ever assembled, forces that are agile and flexible, able to strike in darkness and in light."[26]

All of this was fantasy. June 30 came and went, with the restoration of Iraqi sovereignty largely a fiction. Little of substance changed. The violence worsened. Tens of thousands of foreign troops continued to occupy Iraq and operate as their commanders saw fit. The war continued.

Rather than liberating Iraq en route to liberating the remainder of the Greater Middle East, the Bush administration had blundered into an immense cul-de-sac, from which it could not extricate itself. The campaign intended to high-light American military capabilities without precedent became instead an open sore—the very war that Colin Powell, while a serving officer, had vowed to avoid.

In November 2001, with U.S. intervention in Afghanistan just under way, Paul Wolfowitz had touted the Pentagon's plans for reforming the military even as it waged the global war on terror. "We are getting it right," he declared. "I guarantee you."[27]

Wolfowitz's promise reflected the confidence then pervading the ranks of the semiwarriors. Like so much else undertaken by the Bush administration, the guarantee proved worthless. Rumsfeld's attempt to use the global war on terror as a device to validate his transformation agenda proved to be a massive miscalculation. Marrying the two together resulted in the undoing of both.

5

COUNTERFEIT COIN

PRESIDENT BUSH HAD EMBARKED UPON SUCCESSIVE WARS in Afghanistan and Iraq expecting each to end quickly and decisively. Yet in each theater—with Iraq attracting the lion's share of attention—fighting dragged on, increased in intensity, turned ugly, and consumed prodigious amounts of blood and treasure. The global war on terror morphed into what the Pentagon began styling the Long War, a conflict defined not by purpose, adversary, or location but by duration, which was indeterminate. For members of the U.S. military, war—not a cold war, but engagement in actual hostilities—was establishing itself as the new normalcy.

This new normalcy imparted a radical twist to the Washington rules. Not even the most hawkish proponent of American global leadership—not Allen Dulles or Curtis LeMay, not Maxwell Taylor or McGeorge Bundy—had ever proposed committing the United States to a policy of war without foreseeable end. Yet over the course of George W. Bush's presidency, open-ended war became accepted policy, hardly more controversial than the practice of stationing U.S. troops abroad. Speaking in 2006, Brig. Gen. Mark O. Schissler, a senior Pentagon planner, bluntly put into words what had already emerged as a prevailing assumption: "We're in a generational war." He himself expected that conflict to last another fifty or one hundred years.[1]

More extraordinary still was the extent to which the country's military leaders, and the American people more generally, accommodated themselves to this prospect. Even as the course of events (especially in Iraq) evoked widespread consternation, questions about the origins of the predicament in which the United States found itself remained unasked. It was a classic example of a symptom masking the disease. Even as a growing chorus of critics raged against President Bush's "mismanagement" of the Long War, the national security consensus that provided the real, if unacknowledged, foundation for the enterprise attracted little or no critical attention.

Yet as the bills piled up and the toll in casualties mounted (and as memories of 9/11 faded), the American people grew restive. Both Bush and the wars he had begun became increasingly unpopular. Someone had obviously screwed up. An angry season of finger-pointing ensued with the president and Secretary of Defense Rumsfeld, along with a few hapless generals, the favored targets.

The administration acknowledged the challenges it was facing, but remained determined. Rumsfeld famously described the road to victory in Iraq and Afghanistan as "a long, hard slog." Yet the defense secretary did not waver in his conviction that "the coalition can win . . . in one way or another."[2]

Loyalists committed to the Long War did not conceal their disappointment, but insisted on the need to stay the

course. They combed reports from the battlefield in search
of good news. They hailed the arrival of successive "turning
points" that, in practice, never quite panned out. Max Boot,
a senior fellow at the Council on Foreign Relations, was
typical of those counseling patience. Writing five years after
9/11 when the situation in Iraq appeared particularly grim,
Boot rejected the charge that "the Bush doctrine is a bust,"
insisting that "it is far too soon to judge the results of the
President's grand strategy of transforming the Middle East."
Persistence was sure to pay off. "The Muslim masses just
need to be shown that it's possible to set themselves free."
Although there might be some bumps along the way, "vigorous American leadership can lower the body count and
hasten freedom's triumph," which Boot characterized as
"virtually foreordained."[3]

For the Democratic Party, the Iraq War served as a rally-
ing point, notwithstanding the fact that party leaders like
Senators John Kerry of Massachusetts and Hillary Clinton
of New York had voted in favor of the resolution giving a
congressional stamp of approval to the 2003 invasion. Cal-
culation rather than conviction shaped the party's behavior:
Iraq offered a perfect opportunity to make hay at Republican expense. Democrats denounced Bush's war policies not
because they were reevaluating the fundamentals of national
security strategy, but because they found fault with the
implementation of that strategy in Iraq. Having tendered
their ritual denunciations, they then routinely voted the
money needed to ensure the war's continuation, tacitly signaling their continuing fealty to the Washington consensus.

Unwilling to take a principled stand against a conflict
key members denounced as an unmitigated disaster, the
Democratic Party made itself complicit in the war's perpetuation. Claiming to oppose the war while supporting the

troops, most Democrats staked out a position designed to maximize partisan advantage while minimizing political risk.

These maneuvers paid off handsomely in the 2006 midterm elections, which Democrats cast as a referendum on Iraq, promising that, if given control of Congress, they would act promptly to shut down the war. Invited to render a verdict, voters handed Bush and his party a crushing setback. In the House of Representatives, the Republicans lost thirty-one seats. In the Senate, six Republican incumbents went down to defeat. Now in the driver's seat, incoming House Speaker Nancy Pelosi confirmed that "my highest priority, immediately, is to stop the war in Iraq."[4] Democrats wasted little time reneging on that commitment. What ensued was not a concerted effort to end the Iraq War, but a hastily contrived Republican effort to salvage it. Neither for the first time nor the last, an election touted as being about change produced results that served primarily to affirm the status quo.

For anyone with a taste for irony, the three years that followed offered a veritable banquet. President Bush opened the period by dramatically announcing a new course for Iraq. His successor, Barack Obama, closed it by deepening the U.S. military commitment in Afghanistan. In the interval between these two announcements came three singular developments, for which the two presidents could rightly claim joint credit.

First, even as the enterprise once known as the global war on terror continued, it lost all coherence and began to metastasize. As the end of that war's first decade approached, the United States found itself strategically adrift. Even as Afghanistan replaced Iraq as the primary focus of attention, a surreptitious collaboration between the Pentagon and the

CIA was opening up two additional fronts, in Pakistan and Yemen. Meanwhile, hawks clamored for direct military action against Iran. There could be no doubt that the Long War stretched well into the future. Yet where it led was anyone's guess.

Second, yet another American way of war made a dramatic appearance or, perhaps more accurately, reappearance: Counterinsurgency (COIN) displaced the discredited concept of "shock and awe" in which Rumsfeld and others had invested such lofty expectations. In fact, COIN offered no plausible remedy to violent anti-Western jihadism, the threat from which the Long War derived its ostensible rationale. By restoring an *appearance* of purposefulness to military activity, however, it helped distract attention from the strategic crisis confronting Washington. Here, in fact, lay COIN's chief political appeal along with the true measure of its perniciousness: It enabled senior civilian and military officials to sustain the pretense of having reasserted a measure of control over a situation in which they exercised next to none.

Finally, helped in part by the illusions propagated by counterinsurgency advocates, the Washington rules survived. Notwithstanding the aimlessness of the Long War, their proponents, both in and out of government and in and out of uniform, were able to quash rising popular doubts about the credo and the trinity. In this regard, as the Age of Bush gave way to the Era of Obama, little of substance changed. That was the greatest irony of all.

COURSE CORRECTION

Had Nancy Pelosi and her fellow Democrats made good on their promises to shut down the Iraq War, the implications

might well have been profound. President Bush had repeatedly declared Iraq to be the global war on terror's primary
front, the must-win theater. Replace that must-win designation with not-worth-fighting and the idea that global war
offered an antidote to violent jihadism would have collapsed.
Americans might then just possibly have entertained second
thoughts about the reigning conception of global leadership.

President Bush and his lieutenants were dead set against
allowing that to happen. To forestall such a prospect—which
Democratic leaders such as Pelosi never seriously contemplated anyway—Bush responded to electoral defeat by ordering a course change. He sacked the widely reviled Rumsfeld
and jettisoned the approach to fighting the Iraq War his
administration had steadfastly defended over the three previous years. In January 2007, he unveiled a new approach to
be implemented by a new command team in Baghdad.

At its heart, as the president explained in a nationally
televised address, was a freshly discovered determination
"to protect the local population." Rather than defeating the
Iraqi insurgency, the United States would persuade the Iraqi
people to deny the insurgents their support. Rather than
periodically venturing out from large fortified base camps
in hot pursuit of bad guys, U.S. forces would saturate and
safeguard Iraqi cities, living among the people in small (and
necessarily vulnerable) contingents.

To implement this new policy, the president announced
his intention to increase the total number of U.S. troops in
Iraq. Reinforcements told only part of the story, however. "A
successful strategy for Iraq goes beyond military operations,"
Bush emphasized. "Ordinary Iraqi citizens must see that military operations are accompanied by visible improvements in
their neighborhoods and communities."

In a country riven with ethnic, sectarian, and tribal divisions, reduced violence combined with good governance promised to make life better for the average Iraqi and thereby "help make [national] reconciliation possible." Hard days and heavy sacrifices still lay ahead, the president acknowledged. Yet he vowed to prevail. "Victory will not look like the ones our fathers and grandfathers achieved," he conceded. "There will be no surrender ceremony on the deck of a battleship." Yet the struggle was a necessary one; its outcome was certain to "set the course for a new century."[5]

In reality, Bush no more understood the implications of committing U.S. forces "to protect the local population" than he had the "innovative doctrine and high-tech weaponry" he once proudly proclaimed were revolutionizing warfare. Yet in unveiling this new approach—subsequently enshrined as "the surge"—he officially buried the previous new American way of war. Events had already rendered shock and awe defunct. As a slogan for waging modern war, "speed kills" had long since fallen from favor. Now it disappeared altogether.

The old script having lost its power to persuade, the president recited a new text that others had thrust into his hands. Staring defeat in the face and seeing no alternative, he decided to give counterinsurgency a whirl. Thus did a self-described conservative Republican endorse national security techniques last employed with disastrous results by liberal Democrats during the Kennedy-Johnson era.

The shift marked another sea change in American military thought and practice. To shore up the Washington consensus, Washington was once again reinventing war. Winning hearts and minds now displaced fire and maneuver atop the pyramid of soldierly priorities.

Among the unwritten duties that every modern president must shoulder is to explain to the American people "why we fight." Up to this point, in justifying the Long War, Bush had expressed himself using the ideologically charged language typically employed by his predecessors. The global conflict begun on 9/11, he had regularly insisted, represented a continuation of a long-standing commitment to spreading liberal democratic values.

Throughout U.S. history, such imagery has resonated with many (perhaps most) Americans, even those who, in the ever shorter interval between wars, evidenced little concern for the inalienable rights of unfortunates beyond America's own borders. Yet when presidents use phrases like *fighting for freedom, eliminating tyranny,* and *liberating the oppressed,* they speak in code. Their real meaning, easily deciphered by their listeners, is this: Safeguarding the American way of life requires that others conform to American values. Military victory offers the medium through which American warriors impose that conformity. Given the stakes, forcing adversaries to submit becomes a political and moral imperative. Gen. Douglas MacArthur captured the essence of this imperative in the aphorism for which he is best remembered: "There is no substitute for victory."

With the advent of the surge, President Bush quietly detached the Long War's political rationale from any expectations of victory. By the end of 2006, the purpose of Operation Iraqi Freedom was no longer Iraqi freedom. American warriors were now fighting not to advance the cause of liberty but to create conditions that might enable them to leave Iraq without acknowledging explicit defeat. The principles defining the sacred trinity were being pressed into service in support of an amorphous conception of warfare in which victory had essentially become indefinable and the benefits accruing to Americans were at best obscure.

Designating the surge the basis of a new "strategy" had a further effect: It devalued, even trivialized, the very concept of strategy. The Bush administration had, after all, originally conceived of the Iraq War as but part of a global war, one campaign among several intended to transform the Islamic world.

By 2007, even the president had abandoned any expectations of presiding over such a regional (or civilizational) transformation. The Bush administration's post-9/11 domino theory—its reliance on American power to remove regimes hostile to American values—had misfired. Instead of toppling forward, the dominoes were now threatening to fall backward, fostering the further spread of violent jihadism rather than its elimination. U.S. forces in Iraq and Afghanistan wished for nothing more than to prop the dominoes up again and depart.

So the bold talk of eliminating tyranny disappeared. The president's minions ceased to lecture foreign leaders in places like Egypt and Saudi Arabia on their duty to implement American-style liberal reforms. Apart from bitter-enders bunkered in the editorial offices of the *Weekly Standard* or the *National Review*, even devout right wingers were increasingly hard-pressed to take the Freedom Agenda seriously. "Everyone wants to go to Baghdad," they had once chanted. "Real men want to go to Tehran."[6] By 2007, simply keeping Tehran out of Baghdad seemed a sufficiently ambitious goal.

In reality, the operative rationale for continuing the struggle in Iraq no longer extended beyond that country's borders. In a global war that had become devoid of discernible purpose, the surge now served as the administration's substitute for strategy. Nowhere was the absence of overarching strategic purpose more apparent than with respect to Afghanistan, the "forgotten war," orphaned as a direct result of an ever-intensifying preoccupation with Iraq. Unlike Saddam Hussein, the Afghan Taliban had actually provided support and sanctuary to Al Qaeda in the run-up to 9/11; yet in a war that ostensibly aimed to destroy Al Qaeda, members of Bush's inner circle continued to obsess about Iraq, while allowing Afghanistan to languish.

Among die-hard boosters of the global war on terror, the appeal of Bush's course change in Iraq derived in considerable part from the opportunity it offered to change the topic. To describe the surge as a strategy was to distract attention from the extent to which strategy as such had ceased to exist.

So it was déjà vu all over again. As in the early 1960s, counterinsurgency—armed nation building to preserve a weak state beset with internal violence—took Washington by storm as the latest embodiment of military fashion. The administration quietly shelved expectations for an Information Age version of blitzkrieg enabling it to liberate—or impose its will on—the Islamic world. The surge did not constitute a new blueprint for eliminating global jihadism: President Bush did not contemplate U.S. forces employing COIN to pacify the Greater Middle East neighborhood by neighborhood and village by village. He was merely attempting to prevent the Iraq War from ending in the sort of outright defeat that might call attention to the defects of the Washington rules.

KING DAVID

Given the Republican Party's professed aversion to anything that even remotely smacks of social engineering, the Bush administration's revival of counterinsurgency qualifies as astonishing. That the original impetus for that revival came from within the officer corps makes it more astonishing still.

At the outset of the Long War, members of the officer corps had harbored about as much interest in counterinsurgency as in trench warfare. Although U.S. troops had repeatedly clashed with insurgents over the course of American history, little of that experience, ranging from the ethnic cleansing of Native Americans who impeded westward expansion to suppressing Asian or Latin American opposition to the rising American empire, had been positive. By their very nature, counterinsurgencies tended to be drawn-out, dirty affairs. They taxed the patience of the American people and rarely did much to improve the standing or well-being of military institutions. Seldom did they yield anything approximating clear-cut victory. The biggest of all American counterinsurgencies—the agonizing Vietnam War—had ended in abject humiliation.

Despite this unpromising record, an officer corps that found itself mired in Iraq and Afghanistan decided that counterinsurgency deserved a fresh look. The mounting frustrations of the Long War persuaded influential figures in the army and marine corps—most navy and air force officers tended to a different view—that the post-Vietnam military had grotesquely misconstrued the true nature of contemporary warfare. In the struggle against violent jihadism, the methods employed in Iraq and Afghanistan not only didn't work, but were making things worse. Only a wholesale revision of military methodology could correct the problem.

This insight triggered a campaign within the officer corps to displace military practices devised for wars between armies in favor of techniques suitable for what some had begun to call "war amongst the people"—a phrase coined by Gen. Sir Rupert Smith, a British officer who had commanded NATO forces in the Balkans. "Our conflicts tend to be timeless," Smith wrote in his book *The Utility of Force*, "even endless."[7] Sir Rupert thereby put his finger on one key element of the gradually emerging conventional wisdom in the U.S. military: An officer corps that had once resolved to avoid protracted war at all costs now contemplated an era of conflict without end.

The commitment of the post-Vietnam officer corps to the sacred trinity had been contingent on expectations that political leaders, having assimilated the "lessons" of Vietnam, would employ armed force prudently, even sparingly. As those expectations went by the board and as peace became the exception and war the rule, from within the officer corps itself came an urge to counterinsurge.

Chief among the proponents of this intraservice insurgency was Gen. David Petraeus, an ambitious soldier who first came to public attention as a media-savvy, politically adroit, and very successful division commander during the 2003 invasion of Iraq. (En route to Baghdad, confiding in a receptive *Washington Post* reporter, Petraeus posed what proved to be the most elusive yet emblematic question of the decade: "Tell me how this ends.")[8]

Petraeus was a gifted officer, identified early in his career as someone meant for big things. Among his most prominent gifts were those of a courtier: The young Petraeus displayed a considerable talent for cultivating influential figures, both in and out of uniform, who might prove useful in advancing his own prospects. And he was nothing if not smart. On his way to the top, he had acquired a Princeton Ph.D., choosing as the subject of his dissertation "The American Military and the Lessons of Vietnam." Writing in the mid-1980s, Major Petraeus hewed to the then-existing military consensus, and so questioned the wisdom of any U.S. "involvement in counterinsurgencies unless specific, perhaps unlikely, circumstances obtain—i.e., domestic public support, the promise of a brief campaign, and freedom to employ whatever force is necessary to achieve rapid victory."

"In light of such criteria," Petraeus wrote, "committing U.S. units to counterinsurgencies appears to be a very problematic proposition, difficult to conclude before domestic support erodes and costly enough to threaten the well-being of all America's military forces (and hence the country's national security), not just those involved in the actual counterinsurgency."[9]

For Petraeus, then, the key lesson of Vietnam reduced to this: When the United States went to war, time—the overriding necessity of securing a decisive outcome in short order—was of the essence. The American people demanded prompt results and American political leaders were hard-pressed to resist such demands. Petraeus put it this way: "Recognizing the perishability of public support for military action abroad, the post-Vietnam military have come to regard time as the principal limit in limited wars."[10]

Domestic support for Vietnam had eroded because the public sensed that things were going badly, a perception that hardened as violence escalated from one year to the next. When, in the wake of the 1968 Tet Offensive, President Johnson himself bought into that perception, all was lost. Whether or not the United States had succeeded militarily in thwarting the communist offensive was beside the point. "Perceptions of reality," wrote Petraeus, "more so than objective reality, are crucial to the decisions of statesmen. What policy makers believe to have taken place in any particular case is what matters more than what actually occurred."[11] In

Washington, Tet was widely seen as a disastrous setback. Once established, this impression proved difficult to dislodge.

Yet perceptions were not necessarily immutable, the young Petraeus surmised. Changing the way that a war was perceived—whether within the inner circle of power or in the eyes of the public—could be tantamount to changing reality itself. In a time of crisis, the soldier who demonstrated a capacity to alter perceptions might well parlay military authority into influence extending well beyond the narrow realm of military affairs. This describes the central achievement of General Petraeus in Iraq some twenty years after Major Petraeus claimed his Princeton degree.

In 2005, as a three-star general commanding the U.S. Army Combined Arms Center (CAC) at Fort Leavenworth, Kansas, Petraeus found himself in a position to act on the insights derived from his study of Vietnam. The CAC commander is to the army what the Prefect of the Congregation for the Doctrine of the Faith is to the Roman Catholic Church: the chief guardian of orthodoxy, charged with ensuring conformity to Truth. Yet Petraeus consciously set out to overturn orthodoxy and promulgate an alternative version of truth, consisting of ideas long regarded as rank heresy. More specifically, in collaboration with Lt. Gen. James Mattis, a like-minded marine, he launched a crash program to revise and republish the army's counterinsurgency manual, offering it as the corrective to all the frustrations that soldiers and marines were encountering in Iraq and Afghanistan.

In Washington, Rumsfeld was still counseling patience. Out on the plains of Kansas, Petraeus had concluded that *patience* was just another word for incremental, inexorable failure.

FM 3-24, to employ the army's designation for the new manual, appeared in December 2006. Rarely has a military publication garnered such instantaneous and widespread public attention. Within weeks of publication it had been downloaded 1.5 million times.[12] In a matter of months, a prestigious university press rushed into print a paperback edition, adding for the benefit of civilian readers an interpretive commentary elucidating on the significance of this doctrinal rediscovery. Petraeus himself provided a glowing blurb for what was, in effect, his own book: "Surely a manual that's on the bedside table of the president, vice president, secretary of defense, 21 of 25 members of the Senate Armed Services Committee and many others deserves a place at your bedside too."[13]

What was all the fuss about?

"This publication's purpose," FM 3-24 began, "is to help prepare Army and Marine Corps leaders to conduct COIN operations anywhere in the world." Although acknowledging that insurgencies have been around for centuries, Petraeus's manual argued that an especially malignant variant, "one that seeks to impose revolutionary change worldwide," afflicted the present age. Al Qaeda, which "seeks to transform the Islamic world," offered but one example of an insurgent movement fired by vast global aspirations. Countering this threat demanded a comparably expansive riposte, "a global strategic response, one that addresses the array of linked resources and conflicts that sustain these movements while tactically addressing the local grievances that feed them." In short, when the manual referred to the "conduct of COIN operations anywhere in the world," the word *anywhere* was synonymous with *everywhere*.[14]

No doubt the manual's authors intended this statement

to be taken at face value, even though FM 3-24 offered no estimates on the cost or duration of the proposed global response. Yet Petraeus's purpose in revising U.S. counterinsurgency doctrine was not to evaluate COIN but to sell it.

As such, the text was conducive to multiple interpretations. At one level, FM 3-24 could serve as a handbook. At a deeper level, it was an exercise in deconstruction, dismantling hallowed conceptions of warfare while contriving a substitute suited to the exercise of great power politics in the twilight of modernity. In the postmodern age, after all, what matters most is not originality but novelty, not intrinsic value but marketing, not product but packaging. FM 3-24 was suffused with the spirit of the age in which it was written.

Trafficking in the standard array of postmodernist tropes—irony, paradox, bricolage, and sly self-referential jokes—Petraeus's manual was all about subverting conventions. Yet where it pretended to speak most authoritatively, it managed to say next to nothing. There was lots of foam, but not much beer.

Consider the "Paradoxes of Counterinsurgency" that formed the centerpiece of FM 3-24's first chapter.[15]

"Sometimes," the manual counseled, "the more you protect your force, the less secure you may be." At other times, by implication, the reverse could well be true. Similarly, "Sometimes, the more force is used, the less effective it is," a precept suggesting that on occasion, more force might do the trick. Further, "[s]ometimes doing nothing is the best reaction." So less could be more, more could be less, and nothing could be most of all—sometimes.

"Tactical success," the manual opines, "guarantees nothing"—as if discovering a genuine pearl of wisdom. Yet it never has: Consider what German tactical prowess achieved in two world wars. Or consider the performance of Israeli forces in any number of conflicts with the Arabs.

"If a tactic works this week, it might not work next week; if it works in this province, it might not work in the next"— a truism applicable to any war, small or large, conventional or unconventional.

"Some of the best weapons for counterinsurgents do not shoot"—a contention that applies equally to weapons generally. It was, after all, precisely this argument that Curtis LeMay employed in the 1950s: Give me more bombs and more bombers for SAC and I'll keep the peace.

Finally, there was this: "Many important decisions are not made by generals." When was this ever not obviously the case, except perhaps in the eyes of generals and their groupies?

Yet implicit in the "Paradoxes of Counterinsurgency" and in FM 3-24 generally was this subversive proposition: As an autonomous instrument of statecraft, armed force had lost its viability. Bluntly, war as such—war as traditionally defined by the officer corps itself—no longer worked.

Since time immemorial, the purpose of armies has been to fight battles, thereby enabling nations to win wars. Through battle an army imposes its will on the enemy, thereby restoring peace. Inherent in this assertion are two further claims: that war (if undertaken to restore peace) can be morally justifiable, and that warriors (uniquely charged with responsibility for waging war) occupy a special niche in society. These two claims also provide the essential rationale for creating a distinctive military profession. Society accords physicians an exalted status in deference to their presumably unique ability to diagnose and heal. Political leaders and society in general accord members of the officer corps respect and singular responsibilities based on the assumption that only

within its ranks is found the expertise needed to win battles.

Petraeus's manual tacitly rendered each of these propositions null and void. FM 3-24 expanded and blurred the definition of warfare, describing it not as a contest between
opposing armed forces, but as a "violent clash of interests
between organized groups." In modern war, the army's
primary purpose was no longer to fight. The manual's
detailed and lengthy index contained not a single entry for
"battle" or "battlefield" and made only passing reference to
"combat."

In 1997, Petraeus had written an article subtitled "Never
Send a Man When You Can Send a Bullet."[16] He now took
precisely the opposite view. Indeed, his manual warned
pointedly against the mistake of "overemphasizing killing
and capturing the enemy." Rather than vainly attempting
to destroy an adversary, counterinsurgent forces should
concentrate instead on "securing and engaging the popu-
lace," at first compensating for the absence of safety and basic
services and then resurrecting (or creating from scratch)
"host nation" institutions capable of providing them.
"Counterinsurgents," FM 3-24 boldly declared, "take upon
themselves responsibility for the people's well-being in all
its manifestations."[17]

The ultimate aim was not primarily to dismantle or
defeat an insurgency, but to "foster effective governance"
in an environment where governance was notably absent.
"Legitimacy is the main objective," the manual declared.[18]
Yet legitimacy is a notoriously slippery concept, difficult to
define, much less measure. To designate the creation of
legitimacy as a primary wartime goal is equivalent to designating the pursuit of wealth as a primary goal in life. In
effect, you have embarked upon an infinitely expansible

enterprise. When is a government sufficiently legitimate? When is a tycoon sufficiently rich? Who decides? According to what criteria? The endpoint of such a venture is necessarily arbitrary, subject to redefinition, and revocable.

Furthermore, the promotion of legitimacy is not a sphere in which the officer corps can claim unique or even notable competency. In a counterinsurgency, military expertise becomes one skill set among many that have to be mobilized, deployed, and integrated. FM 3-24 concedes as much, emphasizing that COIN is a collaborative undertaking involving not simply military forces but a wide range of other government agencies, along with private contractors, international entities like the United Nations, and nongovernmental organizations that may or may not even share U.S. policy objectives.

Why senior military officers should preside over such enterprise is by no means clear. When it comes to enhancing "host nation" capacity, functionaries drawn from entirely different professional backgrounds might have as much or more to offer than four-star generals unschooled in law enforcement, economic development, or institution building.[19] When it comes to providing for "the people's well-being," a successful big-city mayor, police chief, or director of social services is likely to possess experience more relevant than that accrued over the course of a career devoted to soldiering.

In sum, an officer corps that accepts FM 3-24 as its guide has abandoned war as its principal raison d'être. In doing so, it forfeits any claim to singularity. Rather than exercising exclusive control over a specific, clearly distinguishable realm of human activity, the army becomes but one institution among many attempting to temper the world's most grievous political and economic failures. Having dispensed with the pursuit of victory, such an army devotes itself to social work with guns. As with such work undertaken in places like Los Angeles or Chicago, the social work inherent in FM 3-24's call for a "global strategic response" to the problem of global insurgency promises to be a project literally without end.

For the U.S. military, war among peoples—not really war but something more akin to imperial policing combined with the systematic distribution of alms—now became de rigueur. Here is Lt. Gen. William B. Caldwell, Petraeus's successor at Fort Leavenworth, holding forth on the military future with all the confidence and certainty of the senior officers who, just years earlier, had touted the wonders of shock and awe.

> The future is not one of major battles and engagements fought by armies on battlefields devoid of population; instead, the course of conflict will be decided by forces operating among the people of the world. Here, the margin of victory will be measured in far different terms from the wars of our past. The allegiance, trust, and confidence of populations will be the final arbiters of success.[20]

The entire military reform project of the post-Vietnam era—indeed of the entire era since Hiroshima—had sought to restore the concept of war as an instrument of decision and the exclusive purview of soldiers. The proponents of counterinsurgency effectively declared that effort a failure. Winning hearts and minds had now become the essence of the soldier's calling. This describes the revolution in military thought engineered by David Petraeus, a revolution to which George W. Bush signed on when he gave up on victory in Iraq without giving up on war.

THE SURGE

In his Princeton Ph.D. dissertation, Petraeus quoted Col. Harry Summers, a noted military commentator, reflecting on the counterinsurgency doctrine devised during the Vietnam era: "Reading it today sounds more like a description of a new liturgy than a discussion of strategic doctrine." For the U.S. Army and Marine Corps, the manual reviving that liturgy, with the mud from rice paddies wiped clean, now became holy writ.

Tapped by Bush to turn around the failing effort in Iraq, Petraeus took his bible to Baghdad and used it to implement "the surge." In pulling Iraq back from the abyss, the general vaulted to rock star status, acquiring in Washington a reputation for infallibility not unlike that claimed by the Bishop of Rome.

The cult of personality that soon enveloped Petraeus served to obscure this reality: Despite innumerable claims to the contrary, the campaign he directed in Iraq in 2007–2008 fell well short of success. The surge did avert Iraq's outright collapse, a not inconsiderable achievement. It also provided a modicum of breathing space for a deeply divided Iraqi political establishment. Yet it did not deliver the promised reconciliation of the various factions vying for power. If it substantially reduced the incidence of terrorist attacks in Baghdad and other cities, violence, targeting both symbols of authority and the civilian population, persisted at levels that would elsewhere have been deemed evidence of impending state failure.

In Baghdad, the *New York Times* reported, mayhem

remained a constant companion, "with attackers able to plant and detonate bombs across the city seemingly with impunity."[21] The surge did weaken the insurgency threatening the Iraqi government. Yet it failed to destroy that insurgency, as Gen. Raymond Odierno, Petraeus's successor in Baghdad, bluntly acknowledged. Two and a half years after the surge began, a reporter pressed Odierno to say when he expected armed resistance to the Iraqi government finally to subside. "It's not going to end, OK?" Odierno snapped. "There'll always be some sort of low-level insurgency in Iraq for the next 5, 10, 15 years."[22]

Exactly who or what deserved credit for the gains achieved during Petraeus's tenure in Baghdad was less clear than the general's legions of fans let on. In reality, improvements in Iraqi security during the period derived from a complex array of factors. Among them were the increased U.S. troop commitment ordered by President Bush, the abandonment of heavy-handed coalition tactics that alienated Iraqis during the occupation's first three years, and Iraq's violent effective partition along ethnic and sectarian lines, largely accomplished prior to Petraeus's arrival.

Most important of all were the effects of the so-called Sunni Awakening, which Petraeus did not instigate but upon which he shrewdly capitalized. In the wake of the 2003 invasion, Sunni tribal chiefs in the crucially important Anbar Province of western Iraq had forged an anti-American alliance with Al Qaeda in Iraq (AQI), an especially brutal jihadist movement that the invasion itself had ushered into existence. By September 2006, having concluded that AQI posed a threat to their own authority, the Sunni chieftains called off that alliance, turned on their erstwhile partners, and offered a marriage of convenience to the Americans. In essence, Sunnis who had been in the forefront of the insurgency resisting the American occupation signaled a willingness to be bought. The U.S. military accommodated that request. In another context, this might have been called appeasement. Petraeus's supporters preferred to call it brilliant.

Meanwhile, Petraeus's contributions notwithstanding, the larger purposes that had ostensibly impelled the United States to invade Iraq remained unfulfilled. U.S. forces never did find the weapons of mass destruction that had imbued the invasion with such purported urgency. The promised documentation linking Saddam Hussein to the jihadists who had plotted the 9/11 attacks never materialized. Expectations that the liberation of Iraq would trigger a wave of democratic change across the Islamic world remained a pipe dream. No road to peace in Jerusalem was ever discovered in downtown Baghdad. The presence of U.S. forces in Iraq failed to cow the mullahs ruling neighboring Iran. If anything, Operation Iraqi Freedom boosted Iranian influence. Members of the Shiite-dominated government installed in Baghdad, some of whom had fled Saddam Hussein's Iraq to find sanctuary in Iran, proved remarkably sympathetic to the Islamic government in Tehran.

Based on the justifications advanced for the war by its architects and supporters, in other words, Operation Iraqi Freedom remained as unsuccessful (not to mention unnecessary) after Petraeus's tenure in command as it had been before he arrived.

These were facts, stubborn and incontrovertible. Yet in a dazzling demonstration of how perceptions skillfully manipulated can trump reality, an audaciously revised Iraq story line rendered facts irrelevant.

FM 3-24 contains this nugget, almost a parody of postmodernism:

> The central mechanism through which [insurgent]
> ideologies are expressed and absorbed is the narrative.
> A narrative is an organizational scheme expressed in
> story form. . . . Stories are often the basis for strategies
> and actions, as well as for interpreting others' inten-
> tions.[23]

In the wake of the surge, insurgents in Washington intent
on installing counterinsurgency as the *new* new American
way of war wasted no time in constructing their own narrative. Lionizing "King David," as they had lionized Stormin'
Norman Schwarzkopf in 1991 and Tommy Franks in 2003, a
claque of semiwarriors replotted the entire Iraq War. They
enshrined the surge as the war's defining moment, with full
credit assigned to Petraeus himself.

To celebrate his genius was to bask in his reflected glory.
Military analysts Frederick W. Kagan and Kimberly Kagan
could scarcely contain themselves. "Great commanders
often come in pairs," they announced: "Eisenhower and
Patton, Grant and Sherman, Napoleon and Davout, Marl-
borough and Eugene, Caesar and Labienus. Generals David
Petraeus and Raymond Odierno can now be added to the
list."[24] Or as another member of the Petraeus fan club put it:
"God has apparently seen fit to give the U.S. Army a great
general in this time of need."[25]

This was myth making of a high order. Just as Americans had once pointed to Andrew Jackson's victory at the
Battle of New Orleans as proof that the United States had
defeated Great Britain in the (already concluded) War of
1812, so now many came to see the surge as proof that U.S.
forces, led by the redoubtable Petraeus with his gift for
counterinsurgency, had emerged victorious in Iraq.

Myth making in relation to war is never innocent. Those

keen to install Petraeus in the pantheon of great captains alongside Ulysses S. Grant and Napoleon Bonaparte did so to advance a specific agenda. For both military practice and basic national security policy, the implications of proclaiming the surge a historic victory on a par with, say, Gettysburg or Stalingrad loomed large indeed. Energetically hawked by various national security analysts, retired generals, and jingoistic pundits, the legacy of the revised Iraq narrative consisted of four elements.

First, with Petraeus lionized for all but single-handedly redeeming a lost cause, the surge tilted the balance of civil-military authority back in favor of the top brass. Listening to General Petraeus and giving him a free hand had, so the story went, enabled George W. Bush to bring the Iraq War to a successful conclusion. With the professional malpractice perpetrated by the several commanders who had preceded Petraeus in Baghdad erased from memory, the reputation of American generalship rebounded.

Yet not all senior officers accrued additional clout. The institutional influence of the Joint Chiefs of Staff remained at an all-time low: Through the Long War's first decade, there was no major issue on which the Chiefs collectively can be said to have had a major impact. True before the surge, this remained no less so afterward. The JCS chairman, nominally occupying the uppermost rung of the military profession, wielded about as much influence as a moderately prominent assistant secretary of defense. As for the service chiefs, charged with building and maintaining the various uniformed services, they had long since been banished from the inner circle of power.

The principal beneficiaries of the postsurge shift in civil-military relations were senior field commanders. Self-styled warfighters now became figures to reckon with, their influence extending well beyond mere operational matters. In Washington, their views carried great weight. For the foreseeable future, therefore, politicians presuming to trust their own judgment over that of whoever happened to be commanding U.S. forces in Baghdad or Kabul did so at considerable risk.

Second, the surge became the occasion when the officer corps kicked its own Vietnam syndrome. A determination to avoid protracted conflict had been a core conviction for the generation of officers who had served in Vietnam. According to Gen. Colin Powell, the best-known member of that generation, wars should occur infrequently. For Powell the supreme value was not warfighting but preparedness: A force holding itself ready to fight would deter others, thereby reducing the actual prevalence of war. When conflict did occur, Powell favored the employment of overwhelming force to end the fighting quickly and achieve decisive results.

The generation of officers represented by Petraeus now reached different conclusions. They came to view war as commonplace, a quasi-permanent aspect of everyday reality. Moreover, their experiences in Iraq and Afghanistan persuaded them to see armed conflict as an open-ended enterprise. To be a soldier was either to be serving in a war zone or to be recently returned—in which case preparations for the next combat deployment were already under way or soon would be. Wars no longer ended. At best, they subsided, a semblance of order replacing disorder and a semblance of stability displacing instability—with even this limited achievement requiring many years of struggle.

Generals Schwarzkopf and Franks had enjoyed their brief star turns because each had seemingly demonstrated an ability to deliver definitive (and relatively cheap) battlefield victory. When events exposed those victories as specious, each general's reputation suffered a sharp reverse. En route to achieving even greater celebrity, General Petraeus had abandoned the very pretense that combat might yield quick and decisive outcomes. The use of violence to impose one's will on the enemy no longer described the central activity for which soldiers prepared themselves. Instead of winning battles, they now sought to pacify populations.

Third, the surge reduced the significance of time as a constraint in the planning and conduct of war. Counterinsurgency demands enormous patience. "COIN campaigns are often long and difficult," as FM 3-24 put it. "Progress can be hard to measure."[26]

From his study of Vietnam, Petraeus had concluded that the American public and their elected representatives do not possess great stores of patience. In implementing the surge, he set out to change that. "The Washington clock is moving more rapidly than the Baghdad clock," he remarked during the course of a television interview several weeks after taking over as commander in Iraq. "So we're obviously trying to speed up the Baghdad clock a bit and to produce some progress on the ground that can, perhaps . . . put a little more time on the Washington clock."[27]

The surge achieved that and more. Remarkably, the Washington clock stopped altogether. In Iraq, even after Petraeus had reaped his own "mission accomplished" rewards, war continued, but the American people and their elected representatives—among them Democrats who had denounced the war only so long as doing so yielded a partisan advantage—ceased to pay it much attention.

The agreed-upon post-surge narrative offered little explanation for the bombs that continued to detonate in Baghdad and other Iraqi cities. So even when reported, these developments remained essentially inexplicable. Hearing of some bloody incident in a mosque, marketplace, or government ministry, Americans shrugged their shoulders or averted their eyes, while carefully avoiding the question of what it all might mean: Even to permit such a question was to expose the flimsiness of the claim that Petraeus had engineered a triumph in the manner of the Emperor Napoleon. The general's most noteworthy achievement was actually this: that in the Age of Petraeus, American soldiers and the American people tacitly endorsed Rupert Smith's proposition—modern wars had indeed become "endless."

Ironically, the surge thereby served to vindicate Robert McNamara. Back in 1965 McNamara had believed that Vietnam's "greatest contribution" was that it was teaching the United States "to go to war without arousing the public ire." Persuading the public to tune out, he believed, was "almost a necessity in our history, because this is the kind of war we'll likely be facing for the next fifty years."[28] McNamara had misread the temperament of his countrymen during the 1960s; yet his error proved to be merely one of timing. By the time he died in 2009, Americans had learned to tune out their wars.

Finally, and most important, Petraeus's putative success made it seemingly unnecessary to inquire further into exactly how the United States had bollixed things up so badly in the first place. If the collapse of Bush's Freedom Agenda had cracked open a window for debating policy fundamentals, the surge slammed that window shut. In salvaging something from the wreckage of the Iraq War, Petraeus also managed to salvage the Washington consensus itself.

"Korea came along and saved us," former secretary of state Dean Acheson once cynically observed, alluding to the way the outbreak of the Korean War in 1950 ended political resistance to a controversial U.S. military buildup Acheson had been advocating.[29] Advocates of the Long War and of the militarized approach to policy from which it derived could say much the same thing: In their darkest hour, the surge had come along and saved them.

The campaign to choose a successor to President Bush in 2008 told the tale. As is usually the case in U.S. elections, the contestants portrayed their differences as fundamental, notably so with regard to national security. Yet what actually ensued was a contest between different species of hawks. In one camp were those like Republicans John McCain and Sarah Palin who insisted that the Iraq War, having always been necessary and justified, was now—thanks to the surge—successful as well. In the other camp were those like Barack Obama and Joseph Biden who derided the Iraq War as disastrous, but pointed to Afghanistan as a war that needed to be won. No prominent figure in either party came within ten feet of questioning the logic of configuring U.S. forces for global power projection or the wisdom of maintaining a global military presence. When it came to the use of force, the various candidates vied with one another to demonstrate their bellicosity. Inevitably in such a contest, the hawks won.

By early 2009, when Bush handed the reins of power to Barack Obama, the Washington rules had once more been restored. In expressing his determination to shift the weight of U.S. military efforts from Iraq to Afghanistan—"This is not a war of choice. This is a war of necessity."—President Obama put his own seal of approval on that restoration.[30] The promise of change that had formed the centerpiece of Obama's run for the presidency left the American credo and the sacred trinity untouched. In Iraq, the outcome remained uncertain. In Washington, the verdict was in: Here is where General Petraeus had left his mark.

GCOIN: SON OF SURGE

The onset of the Obama era found members of the Petraeus lobby eager to press on. They had big ideas.

Prominent among those interpreting the significance of the surge was John Nagl, former soldier, counterinsurgency expert, and sometime Petraeus adviser. According to Nagl, although *population security* might well constitute "the first requirement of success in counterinsurgency," it was by no means the only requirement. Indeed, it was only the beginning.

> Economic development, good governance, and the provision of essential services, all occurring within a matrix of effective information operations, must all improve simultaneously and steadily over a long period of time if America's determined insurgent enemies are to be defeated.

The key, according to COIN advocates like Nagl, was for the United States to mount a "global counterinsurgency campaign."[31] With the world besieged by ideologically driven insurgents, and with events in Iraq having supposedly demonstrated the efficacy of FM 3-24, Nagl was among those promoting counterinsurgency as perhaps the only plausible response to the threat posed by violent anti-Western jihadism.

As Obama entered the White House in January 2009, global counterinsurgency—GCOIN some were already calling it—showed every sign of emerging as an Idea Whose Time Had Come. Senator John Kerry of Massachusetts went on record calling for the conversion of the global war on terror into "the global counterinsurgency campaign it always should have been—namely, a battle for hearts and minds."[32] In the month of Obama's inauguration, Bruce Hoffman, a well-known terrorism expert, was promoting GCOIN as the basis for "the development and execution of long-term 'hearts and minds' programs."[33]

Army Brig. Gen. Bennet Sacolick concurred. A career special operations officer, Sacolick opined that "eradicating terrorists alone will not win the war on terror; frankly, it won't even put a dent in" the problem. The United States needed to send troops into countries that served as "the breeding ground for terrorism" in order to address head-on the conditions giving rise to anti-American violence. The key task was now "nation-building."[34] Meanwhile, the journal of the U.S. Army War College published an article with the imposing title "Global Counterinsurgency: Strategic Clarity for the Long War." GCOIN, wrote its author, Col. Daniel S. Roper, provided the correct "intellectual framework" to repair the strategic confusion that had prevailed during much of the Bush era.[35]

Proponents of GCOIN, in other words, did not view Iraq as a one-off event. Facing the prospect of defeat, President Bush launched the surge in an act of desperation. In the eyes of Nagl and other members of the Petraeus lobby, Iraq in 2007–2008 had served as a feasibility study. In the broken quarters of the world, many more Iraqs waited.

Across the Greater Middle East hundreds of millions of people were in dire need of "economic development, good governance, and the provision of essential services." GCOIN

offered the way to meet those needs and thereby nip terrorism in the bud.

Yet any GCOIN campaign worthy of the name would
necessarily require the pacification of Afghanistan (population 28.4 million, in an area approximately the size of Texas)
and of Pakistan (176.2 million, roughly twice the size of
California), both facing imminent insurgent threats. Then
there was Somalia (9.8 million, slightly smaller than Texas)
and Yemen (23.8 million, more than twice as large as Wyo-
ming), both known as countries in which the recruitment
and training of violent jihadists were commonplace. Lurk-
ing in the wings were Iran (66.4 million, slightly smaller
than Alaska), widely condemned for underwriting terrorist activity, and perhaps even Egypt (83.1 million, three
times larger than New Mexico), a simmering caldron of
radical Islamist sentiment.[36] Only counterinsurgency on
an epic scale could possibly satisfy the needs of all these
people.

The road ahead promised to be long and arduous. Yet for
American soldiers, relieved to put Iraq in their rearview
mirror, the immediate requirement was not to move ahead
but to reverse course. Making a sharp about-face, they headed
back to Afghanistan.

RESET

At his inauguration on January 20, 2009, President Barack
Obama immediately became a wartime commander in chief,
responsible for not one, but two ongoing conflicts. Obama's
opposition to the Iraq War had provided much of the initial
impetus for his candidacy. Once in office, the new president
happily, if not quite explicitly, endorsed the verdict that the

surge had achieved a notable success: Doing so offered a readily available rationale for winding down direct U.S. military involvement in Iraq, something that as a candidate he had vowed to do.

In Afghanistan, Obama faced a more difficult problem. To protect himself from the charge of being a national security wimp, candidate Obama had vowed, if elected, to reenergize the military effort there. Within weeks of taking office, he signaled his intention to make good on that promise. Just shy of a month after becoming president, Obama ordered an additional twenty-one thousand troops into the war zone. "This increase is necessary to stabilize a deteriorating situation in Afghanistan, which has not received the strategic attention, direction and resources it urgently requires," the president announced.[37]

Getting things back on track was going to require more than just troops, however. Taliban fighters were on the march. Both literally and figuratively, the United States and its allies were losing ground. The new administration wanted "fresh thinking" and "fresh eyes." So in May, Obama unceremoniously fired the commander immediately responsible for operations in Afghanistan. Deemed too stodgy and too conventional, Gen. David McKiernan was out. Gen. Stanley McChrystal, a career special operations officer close to Petraeus and specializing in counterterrorism—that is, targeted assassination—now reinvented himself as an expert in COIN.[38]

Commentators had wasted little time in dubbing Afghanistan "Obama's War." McChrystal's job was to figure out how to bring that war to a successful conclusion. Under the tutelage of Petraeus—appointed by the outgoing President Bush to command U.S. Central Command and therefore McChrystal's immediate boss—the new commander set out to do just that, undertaking a crash reevaluation of U.S. and allied efforts.

The revived cult of generalship endowed McChrystal with instant celebrity. Journalists wasted no time in designating Prince Stanley heir to King David. A gushing profile in the *New York Times Magazine* made the case succinctly: "And so if it was Petraeus who saved Iraq from cataclysm, it now falls to McChrystal to save Afghanistan."[39] *Newsweek* likewise depicted McChrystal in quasi-messianic terms, describing him as a "Zen warrior," who "eats one meal a day, works out obsessively every morning at 5, and is so free of body fat that he looks gaunt."[40] Tall, lanky, earnest, and "fit as a tuning fork" was *Time*'s description, noting with approval that McChrystal's Kindle included "serious tomes on Pakistan, Lincoln and Vietnam."[41] Here, according to a raft of press accounts, was no mere mortal, but something close to a superman.

After "consulting" with various civilian experts who had helped market the Petraeus surge in Iraq,[42] McChrystal completed his assessment on August 30, 2009. Within three weeks, his report had leaked, landing in the lap of the *Washington Post*'s Bob Woodward. The entire sixty-six-page document, intended for the president and his most senior advisers, promptly became available to anyone with Internet access. The impact was instantaneous: General McChrystal's views now framed the ensuing Afghanistan debate. Would the president support his field commander? Or would he deny McChrystal the tools needed to get the job done?

The COIN experts to whom McChrystal had looked for advice promptly took to the op-ed pages and airways to demand that Obama accede to his general's request. Max Boot called on Obama "to back General McChrystal who is a terrific general who has a great team with him, and has done a very careful study of the situation."[43] In the *Weekly Standard*, Frederick Kagan contemplated "the cost of dithering," castigating Obama for not promptly giving McChrystal the green light. The White House had "deliberately refused even to review" McChrystal's recommendations, instead wasting time conducting "a series of seminars on Afghanistan and the region."[44] Kagan was tired of talk. He wanted action.

To save Afghanistan, General McChrystal proposed to save its people, consistent with the methods detailed in FM 3-24. "Success," he wrote, "demands a comprehensive counterinsurgency (COIN) campaign," one that "earns the support of the Afghan people and provides them with a secure environment." Gaining the support of Afghans meant that Western armies in their country had to acquire "a better understanding of the people's choices and needs." A major impediment was the existing mind-set of U.S. and allied occupiers: "Our conventional warfare culture is part of the problem." Western forces were "inexperienced in local languages and culture" and "poorly configured for COIN."[45]

To grasp the true nature of Afghan culture, the prevailing Western military culture itself needed to undergo a wholesale transformation. "We must do things dramatically differently—even uncomfortably differently—to change how we operate, and also how we think." Implicit in the McChrystal plan was an assumption that cultural sensitivity is like marksmanship: a skill in which soldiers can be trained. (Despite innumerable references to culture, the plan was oddly silent on the issue of religion, addressing neither Islam's significance as a factor shaping Afghan identity nor the post-Christian milieu in which most American and other allied soldiers had been formed.)

According to McChrystal, the task of securing the Afghan people broke down into two requirements, each to be pursued simultaneously. One was to defeat a "resilient and growing insurgency"; the other, to remedy a widespread "crisis of confidence." The roots of this crisis were complex and included "the weakness of [Afghan political] institutions, the unpunished abuse of power by corrupt officials and powerbrokers, a widespread sense of political disenfranchisement, and a longstanding lack of economic opportunity."

The comprehensive counterinsurgency program devised by McChrystal would provide an antidote to each of these afflictions. Because properly resourcing that campaign would entail more money and more boots on the ground, McChrystal requested an additional forty thousand troops beyond the reinforcements that President Obama had already approved.

McChrystal ventured no estimates on how much his proposed counterinsurgency campaign was likely to cost. The commander's reticence was perhaps understandable: The numbers, whether measured in dollars expended or lives lost, were almost certain to be daunting. One optimistic retired four-star general put the bill at approximately $600 billion: "In 10 years of $5 billion a month and with a significant front-end security component, we can leave an Afghan national army and police force and a viable government and roads and universities."[46]

Nor did General McChrystal say how long saving Afghanistan was likely to take, choosing instead to emphasize that the months just ahead were sure to prove pivotal. "Failure to gain the initiative and reverse insurgent momentum in the near-term," he wrote, "risks an outcome where defeating the insurgency is no longer possible." The United

States could not afford to tarry. The imperative was to act, the sooner the better.

On one point McChrystal was adamant: To reject his advice was to ensure failure. Asked during a presentation at London's International Institute of Strategic Studies whether a more modest approach with more modest goals (reportedly suggested by Vice President Joe Biden) could possibly work, McChrystal minced no words. "The short answer is: no. A strategy that does not leave Afghanistan in a stable position is probably a short-sighted strategy."[47] Or as he put it during an interview for a PBS documentary: "There is no alternative."[48]

MISSING THE OFF-RAMP

How to save Afghanistan now displaced all other issues atop the U.S. national security agenda. Whether or not Afghans wished to be saved and how exactly they viewed salvation were matters that attracted scant attention. Virtually all of Washington agreed on two points: With Iraq now largely forgotten, Afghanistan posed an urgent problem, and it was incumbent upon the United States to fix that problem forthwith.

In at least a nominal sense, the final decision on how to proceed was left to the commander in chief. Yet even though the president's national security team went through the motions of presenting him with a range of choices, the options actually on offer amounted to variations on a single theme. All involved extending and deepening U.S. military involvement in an eight-year-old conflict that the previous administration had treated as a stepchild. One option, of course, remained conspicuously "off the table": getting out.

The weeks between the McChrystal report leak and a presidential speech at West Point in which he announced his decision provided an extraordinary demonstration of how Washington both rules and enforces its rules. Through the fall of 2009, the world waited for the "most powerful man in the world" to reveal how he intended to proceed in Afghanistan. Obama's critics chided him for "dithering." His supporters commended his careful deliberation. Parties on all sides agreed that whichever way the president came down, the implications were sure to be momentous.

In fact, however, even as Obama pondered the question of whether to send ten thousand or twenty thousand or thirty thousand or forty thousand additional reinforcements to Afghanistan, the actual ability to exercise choice had already passed from his hands. In essence, the president found himself in the position of a man shopping for a new suit who is told that he can pick any color so long as it's some shade of khaki.

The issues that should properly have claimed presidential attention in light of the failure of President Bush's Freedom Agenda—evaluating the Long War's purpose and prospects while identifying the principles that could form the basis for a realistic response to violent jihadism (and then applying those principles to Afghanistan)— never seemingly made it to his desk. The issue actually allotted to the president, selecting the right approach to pacifying Afghanistan, was the one he was least qualified to make. It was as if Franklin Roosevelt had spent World War II planning amphibious invasions, while assuming that the formulation of overall strategy would take care of itself.

On December 1, just days before traveling to Oslo to accept the Nobel Peace Prize, Obama announced that he was ordering an additional thirty thousand troops to Afghanistan. (By the next day, that number had risen to thirty-three thousand; with seven thousand in additional NATO reinforcements promised, McChrystal got his forty thousand exactly.) By escalating the U.S. military commitment there the president in effect ratified the Long War. In doing so, he made it all but certain that Obama's War would become a central theme of his presidency. Whatever the talk of "off-ramps" and "exit strategies," the president had effectively forfeited his opportunity to undertake a serious reassessment of the basic approach to national security formulated over the course of the preceding six decades.

Obama would not challenge the tradition that Curtis LeMay and Allen Dulles had done so much to erect. In the counsels of government, the views and voices of the semi-warriors would continue to command respect—indeed, the heirs of McGeorge Bundy and Robert McNamara applauded Obama's determination to see things through in Afghanistan. Meanwhile, the warriors themselves—Generals Petraeus and McChrystal taking the place of generals like Maxwell Taylor—provided the rationale for why fixing Helmand Province should take precedence over fixing Cleveland and Detroit. As it had with the lessons of Vietnam, Washington now successfully absorbed (and trivialized) the lessons of Iraq so as to ensure that nothing of importance would be learned and little would change. The essential elements of the Washington consensus were thereby preserved.

Given the record of Washington's devotion to that consensus, Obama's decision to affirm the status quo hardly qualifies as a surprise. Yet given the hopes of real change to which his election had given rise, many of the president's most devoted supporters found his decision disheartening. Real change would apparently have to wait for another day.

6

CULTIVATING OUR OWN GARDEN

As a boy growing up in the Midwest during the early years of the Cold War, I developed a clear understanding of what differentiated Americans from their communist adversaries. Simply put, we were pragmatists and they were ideologues. On our side flexibility and common sense prevailed; whatever worked, we were for it. In contrast, the people on the other side were rigid and dogmatic; bombast and posturing mattered more than results. The newsreels of the time told the tale: Communist leaders barked ridiculous demands; the docile masses chanted prescribed slogans. It was impossible to imagine Americans tolerating such nonsense.

However belatedly, learning has overturned these youthful impressions. "Whatever works" no longer seems to guide everyday American behavior, if it ever did. Americans view it as their birthright that reality should satisfy desire. Forget *e pluribus unum*. "Whatever I want" has become the operative national motto. In the meantime, when it comes to politics, Americans do put up with nonsense. Week in and week out, members of a jaded governing class, purporting to speak for "the American people," mouth tired clichés that would have caused members of the Soviet Politburo to blush with embarrassment.

The Washington rules provide a sterling example of this tendency to disregard what actually works and stubbornly cling instead to familiar practices that manifestly fail to deliver what they promise: in this case, ensuring the safety and well-being of the United States at a reasonable cost while keeping faith with professed American values.

The world—we are incessantly told—is becoming ever smaller, more complex, and more dangerous. Therefore, it becomes necessary for the nation to intensify the efforts undertaken to "keep America safe," while also, of course, advancing the cause of world peace. Achieving these aims—it is said—requires the United States to funnel ever greater sums of money to the Pentagon to develop new means of projecting power, and to hold itself in readiness for new expeditions deemed essential to pacify (or liberate) some dark and troubled quarter of the globe.

At one level, we can with little difficulty calculate the cost of these efforts: The untold billions of dollars added annually to the national debt and the mounting toll of dead and wounded U.S. troops provide one gauge.

At a deeper level, the costs of adhering to the Washington consensus defy measurement: families shattered by loss; veterans bearing the physical or psychological scars of combat; the perpetuation of ponderous bureaucracies subsisting in a climate of secrecy, dissembling, and outright deception; the distortion of national priorities as the military-industrial complex siphons off scarce resources; environmental devastation produced as a by-product of war and the preparation for war; the evisceration of civic culture that results when a small praetorian guard shoulders the burden of waging perpetual war, while the great majority of citizens purport to revere its members, even as they ignore or profit from their service.

Furthermore, there is no end in sight, even though the conditions that first gave rise to the Washington rules have ceased to exist. U.S. allies in Western Europe and East Asia, weak and vulnerable in the immediate wake of World War II, are today stable, prosperous, and perfectly capable of defending themselves. The totalitarian ideologies that challenged liberalism in the twentieth century have definitively and irrevocably failed. Josef Stalin is long gone, as is the Soviet Empire. Red China has become simply China, valued by Americans as a bountiful source of credit and consumer goods. Although Communists still call the shots in Beijing, promoting exports ranks well above promoting Mao's teachings in the party's list of priorities. In the Islamic Republic of Iran, once thought to be the incubator of powerful revolutionary forces, the mullahs find themselves hard-pressed just to maintain order in the streets. Washington's quasi-official enemies list now consists mostly of pygmies: North Korea, a nation unable to feed its own population; Syria, an Israeli punching bag; Venezuela, governed by a clown; and, for old times' sake, Cuba.

The world has by no means entered an era of peace and harmony. Far from it. Yet the threats demanding attention today—terrorism, climate change, drug cartels, Third World underdevelopment and instability, perhaps above all the proliferation of genocidal weapons invented and first employed by the West—bear scant resemblance to the threats that inspired Washington to devise its sacred trinity in the first place.

The problem set has changed, while the solutions proffered by Washington remain largely the same. The conviction that the obligations of leadership require the United States to maintain a global military presence, configure its armed forces for power projection, and employ them to impose change abroad persists, forms the enduring leitmotif of U.S. national security policy. Washington clings to its credo and trinity not out of necessity, but out of parochial self-interest laced with inertia.

Dwight D. Eisenhower for one would have been appalled. Early in his first term as president, Ike contemplated the awful predicament wrought by the Cold War during its first decade. "What can the world, or any nation in it, hope for," he asked, "if no turning is found on this dread road?" The president proceeded to answer his own question. The worst to be feared would be a ruinous nuclear war.

> The best would be this: a life of perpetual fear and tension; a burden of arms draining the wealth and the labor of all peoples; a wasting of strength that defies the American system or the Soviet system or any system to achieve true abundance and happiness for the peoples of this earth.
>
> Every gun that is made, every warship launched, every rocket fired signifies, in the final sense, a theft from those who hunger and are not fed, those who are cold and are not clothed.

The president illustrated his point with specifics:

The cost of one modern heavy bomber is this: a modern brick school in more than 30 cities. It is two electric power plants, each serving a town of 60,000 population. It is two fine, fully equipped hospitals. It is some fifty miles of concrete pavement.

We pay for a single fighter plane with a half million bushels of wheat. We pay for a single destroyer with new homes that could have housed more than 8,000 people.

This is, I repeat, the best way of life to be found on the road the world has been taking.

This is not a way of life at all, in any true sense. Under the cloud of threatening war, it is humanity hanging from a cross of iron.[1]

Eisenhower urged Soviet leaders to join him in lifting humankind from its iron gibbet. His speech had little practical effect. Perhaps inevitably, the Cold War and its associated arms race continued. Worth recalling, however, is this soldier-statesman's acute discomfort with the progressive militarization of U.S. policy.

Today, for most Americans, the Cold War has become a distant memory. Yet the "life of perpetual fear and tension" that Eisenhower described in 1953, the "burden of arms" that he decried, and "the wasting of strength" that undercuts the prospect of Americans achieving "true abundance and happiness" all persist. In Washington, the pattern of behavior that Eisenhower lamented has become deeply entrenched. Practices that Eisenhower viewed as temporary expedients are now etched in stone.

Contemplate these three examples: the size of the Pentagon budget, the dimensions of the nuclear arsenal, and the extent of its overseas military presence. If, rather than exceeding the military spending of the rest of the planet, Pentagon outlays merely equaled the combined defense budgets of, say, Russia, China, Iran, North Korea, Syria, Venezuela, and Cuba, would the United States face great peril? If the U.S. nuclear stockpile consisted of several hundred weapons rather than several thousand, would the United States find itself appreciably more vulnerable to nuclear blackmail or attack? Were the United States, sixty-plus years after the end of World War II, finally to withdraw its forces from Germany, Italy, and the rest of Europe, would Americans sleep less easily in their beds at night?

Consider these questions pragmatically and the answer to each is self-evidently *no*. Consider them from a vantage point within the Washington consensus and you'll reach a different conclusion.

Adherents of that consensus categorically reject the notion that the defense spending of would-be adversaries could provide a gauge for our own military budget. They argue instead that America's unique responsibilities require extraordinary capabilities, rendering external constraints unacceptable. Even as U.S. officials condemn others for merely contemplating the acquisition of nuclear weapons, they reject unilateral action to reduce America's own arsenal—the fancied risks of doing so being too great to contemplate. As for withdrawing U.S. troops from Europe, doing so might—so the argument goes—call into question America's commitment to its allies and could therefore send the wrong "signal" to unnamed potential enemies. Thus do the Washington rules enforce discipline, precluding the intrusion of aberrant thinking that might engender an actual policy debate in our nation's capital.

Cui bono? Who benefits from the perpetuation of the Washington rules? The answer to that question helps explain why the national security consensus persists.

The answer, needless to say, is that Washington itself benefits. The Washington rules deliver profit, power, and privilege to a long list of beneficiaries: elected and appointed officials, corporate executives and corporate lobbyists, admirals and generals, functionaries staffing the national security apparatus, media personalities, and policy intellectuals from universities and research organizations. Each year the Pentagon expends hundreds of billions of dollars to raise and support U.S. military forces. This money lubricates American politics, filling campaign coffers and providing a source of largesse—jobs and contracts—for distribution to constituents. It provides lucrative "second careers" for retired U.S. military officers hired by weapons manufacturers or by consulting firms appropriately known as "Beltway Bandits." It funds the activities of think tanks that relentlessly advocate for policies guaranteed to fend off challenges to established conventions. "Military-industrial complex" no longer suffices to describe the congeries of interests profiting from and committed to preserving the national security status quo.

Nor are the benefits simply measurable in cold cash or political influence. The appeal of the Washington rules is psychic as well as substantive. For many, the payoff includes the added, if largely illusory, attraction of occupying a seat within or near what is imagined to be the very cockpit of contemporary history. Before power corrupts it attracts and then seduces. The claims implicit in the American credo and the opportunities inherent in the sacred trinity combine to make the imperial city on the Potomac one of the

most captivating, corrupt, and corrupting places on the face
of the earth.

COMING HOME

For these very reasons, the Washington rules are likely to
remain securely in place for the foreseeable future. Or they
will until the strain laid on a military that is perpetually at
war and on an economy propped up by perpetual borrow-
ing causes one or both to collapse.

Yet even that eventuality, should it occur, is less likely to
nudge Americans onto a path of sobriety and good sense
than to produce a panicky rush to assign blame—a steady
supply of McNamaras and Rumsfelds guarantees the availability of suitable scapegoats—and announce "reforms"
while further sweetening the Pentagon's budget. President
Obama's response to the economic crisis that began in 2008
illustrates this tendency: His administration's vow to reduce
federal deficits in "the long term" served to justify increased
spending in the near term, with anything even remotely
related to national security explicitly exempted from even
the slightest belt tightening.

So proposing to replace the American credo and the
sacred trinity might seem a fanciful exercise, unlikely to
yield anything of immediate practical value. Still, the effort is worth attempting, if only to lay down a marker.
Before the movement comes the conviction—an awareness
of things amiss combined with a broad vision of how to
make them right. Challenging the Washington consensus
requires first establishing the proposition that viable alternatives to permanent war *do* exist—that a different
credo and trinity might offer a better way of ensuring the

safety and well-being of the American people and even perhaps of fulfilling the mission that Americans persist in believing God or Providence has bestowed upon the United States.

The existing American credo assumes that the world is plastic, that American leaders are uniquely capable of divining whatever God or Providence intends, and that with its unequaled reserves of power the United States is uniquely positioned to fulfill those intentions. Experience since the dawn of the American Century in 1941, and especially over the course of the last decade, offers little support for these propositions.

The record of American statecraft during the era that began with U.S. entry into World War II and that culminates today with the Long War does not easily reduce to a simple report card. Overall that record is mixed, combining wisdom with folly, generosity with shortsightedness, moments of insight with periods of profound blindness, admirable achievements with reckless misjudgments. The president who devised the Marshall Plan also ordered the bombing of Hiroshima. The president who created the Peace Corps also dabbled in assassination plots. The president who vowed to eliminate evil secretly authorized torture and then either could not bring himself to acknowledge the fact or simply lied about it.

Critics fasten on these contradictions as evidence of Washington's hypocrisy. What they actually reveal is the intractability of the human condition. Even the self-assigned agent of salvation persistently strays from the path of righteousness. No wonder the world at large remains stubbornly resistant to redemption. Notwithstanding prophetic pronouncements issued by American leaders, when it comes to discerning the future they, like other statesmen, fly blind.

The leader of the Free World, surrounded by his impressively credentialed advisers, is hardly more capable of divining the global future than is a roomful of reasonably well-informed high school students.

As with American clairvoyance, so too with American power: Events have exposed its limits. Especially in economic terms, it is today a wasting asset.

Any new credo must surely take into account these lessons of the era now drawing to a close, acknowledging the recalcitrance of humankind, the difficulty of deciphering history's purposes, and the importance of husbanding American power.

Note, however, that these very insights formed the basis of an earlier credo, nurtured across many generations until swept aside by the conceits of the American Century. Proponents of this earlier credo did not question the existence of an American mission. Embracing John Winthrop's charge, issued to his followers on the eve of founding Massachusetts Bay Colony in 1630, they too sought to create a "city upon a hill." This defined America's obligation.[2] Yet in discharging that obligation, in their view, the city's inhabitants should seek not to compel or enforce, but to exemplify and illuminate.

For the Founders, and for the generations that followed them, here was the basis of a distinctively American approach to leadership, informed by a conviction that self-mastery should take precedence over mastering others. This Founders' credo was neither liberal nor conservative. It transcended partisanship, blending both idealism and realism, emphasizing patience rather than immediacy, preferring influence to coercion. Until the end of the nineteenth century, this conception of America as exemplar, endorsed by figures as varied in outlook and disposition as George

Washington and John Quincy Adams, commanded wide-spread assent.

In his farewell address to the nation, a document that for decades enjoyed a standing akin to divine scripture, President Washington urged his countrymen to chart an independent course, enabling the United States "to give to mankind the magnanimous and too novel example of a people always guided by an exalted justice and benevolence." Washington had an acute appreciation of the extraordinarily fortunate circumstances in which the young republic found itself. "Why forego the advantages of so peculiar a situation?" he asked.

> Why quit our own to stand upon foreign ground?
> Why, by interweaving our destiny with that of any
> part of Europe, entangle our peace and prosperity in
> the toils of European ambition, rivalship, interest,
> humor or caprice?[3]

In a presentation to the House of Representatives on July 4, 1821, Secretary of State Adams elaborated on Washington's theme. The United States, he insisted, "goes not abroad, in search of monsters to destroy."

> She is the well-wisher to the freedom and indepen-
> dence of all. She is the champion and vindicator only
> of her own. She will commend the general cause by
> the countenance of her voice, and the benignant sym-
> pathy of her example.
>   She well knows that by once enlisting under
> other banners than her own, were they even the ban-
> ners of foreign independence, she would involve her-
> self beyond the power of extrication, in all the wars
> of interest and intrigue, of individual avarice, envy,

and ambition, which assume the colors and usurp
the standard of freedom.

The fundamental maxims of her policy would
insensibly change from liberty to force. . . . She might
become the dictatress of the world. She would be no
longer the ruler of her own spirit.[4]

For most Americans, most of the time, the policies prescribed by Washington and Adams defined the nation's
proper orientation toward the outside world, a view that
prevailed throughout the nineteenth century.

America's impulsive if abbreviated fling with European-
style imperialism in 1898 signaled the impending demise
of this tradition. "We used to believe . . . that we were of a
different clay from other nations," Harvard's William James
reflected when contemplating the resulting American
empire. But this had turned out to be "pure Fourth of July
fancy, scattered in five minutes by the first temptation."[5]

U.S. entry into World War I at the urging of President
Woodrow Wilson in 1917 dealt a mortal blow to the belief that
Americans were made of different clay than the warring
peoples of Europe. Dissenters remained, but now they seemed
to lag behind in their understanding of history's summons.
Prominent among those dissenters was the radical journalist
Randolph Bourne, who offered this impassioned defense of
America's true mission in a world consumed by violence:

If America has lost its political isolation, it is all the
more obligated to retain its spiritual integrity. This
does not mean any smug retreat from the world, with
a belief that the truth is in us and can only be con-
taminated by contact. It means that the promise of
American life is not yet achieved . . . and that, until it

is, there is nothing for us but stern and intensive cultivation of our garden.[6]

With the advent of World War II, the tradition of America as exemplar—now widely and erroneously characterized as isolationism—stood almost completely discredited, finding favor with only a handful of cranks, malcontents, and anti-Semites. In Washington after 1945, it carried no weight at all. If not entirely forgotten, the cultivation of our own garden now figured at best as an afterthought. In official circles, fixing the world now took precedence over remedying whatever ailments afflicted the United States.

Outside of such circles, an awareness of America's own imperfections—social, political, cultural, and moral—survived. The advent of the postwar American credo, with all of the costly undertakings that trailed in its wake, fostered for a minority a renewed appreciation of the all but forgotten Founders' credo. Among critics of U.S. foreign policy, the old tradition of America as exemplar enjoyed a quiet renaissance.

Those critics questioned the wisdom and feasibility of forcibly attempting to remake the world in America's image. They believed that even to make the attempt was to court corruption in the form of imperialism and militarism, thereby compromising republican institutions at home. Representing no one party but instead a great diversity of perspectives, they insisted that, if America has a mission, that mission is to *model* freedom rather than to impose it.

The famed diplomat-turned-historian George Kennan, a cultural conservative, was one such critic. Senator J. William Fulbright, a died-in-wool liberal internationalist, was another. The influential social critic Christopher Lasch, a self-professed radical, was a third. Martin Luther King, arguably the dominant moral figure of the American Century, was a fourth.

Writing to an acquaintance in the midst of the Korean War, Kennan argued that Americans had for too long subjected their garden to abuse. "It seems to me," he wrote, "that our country bristles with imperfections—and some of them very serious ones—of which we are almost universally aware, but lack the resolution and civic vigor to correct." Here lay the real danger. "What is at stake here is our duty to ourselves and our own national ideals."[7] In a contemporaneous lecture, Kennan returned to this theme. To observers abroad, he suggested,

> the sight of an America in which there is visible no higher social goal than the self-enrichment of the individual, and where that self-enrichment takes place primarily in material goods and gadgets that are of doubtful utility in the achievement of the deeper satisfactions of life—this sight fails to inspire either confidence or enthusiasm.

Rather than obsessing about the threat posed by the Soviet Union, the nation needed to set its own house in order. By demonstrating a capacity to nurture "a genuinely healthy relationship both of man to nature and of man to himself," Kennan believed, Americans might "then, for the first time, have something to say to people elsewhere," perhaps even becoming "a source of inspiration" to others.[8]

A decade after Kennan, in the midst of another dubious war, Senator Fulbright assessed the implications of believing that America's own well-being required constant meddling abroad. It was, he wrote, "neither the duty nor the right of the United States to sort out" all of the world's problems. "[M]any things happen in many places," wrote the chairman of the Senate Foreign Relations Committee, "that are either none of our business or in any case are beyond the range of our power, resources, and wisdom." It was long past time for the United States to "confine herself to doing only that good in the world which she *can* do, both by direct effort and by the force of her example," abandoning her "missionary idea full of pretensions about being the world's policeman."[9]

Lasch, who spent decades ruthlessly dissecting American culture, concurred. "The real promise of American life," he insisted, was to be found in "the hope that a self-governing republic can serve as a source of moral and political inspiration to the rest of the world, not as the center of a new world empire."[10]

Martin Luther King went even further. In the spring of 1967, preaching on the raging Vietnam War, he insisted that the time had come "for all people of conscience to call upon America to come back home." Before attempting to save others, the nation needed to acknowledge and correct its own sins and failings.

To none of these men did coming home imply passivity or so-called isolationism. It did, however, mean revising the hierarchy of national priorities. In that regard, the militarization of U.S. policy, exemplified above all by the Vietnam War, had diverted the nation's attention from pursuing its true calling. The arduous work of creating a free society remained far from finished. Only by turning away from war would the United States be able to tackle what King referred to as the "giant triplets of racism, extreme materialism, and militarism."[11]

The essential credo to which each of these figures subscribed, a variant of the convictions first articulated by the

Founders, deserves renewed consideration today. Its essence is simply this: *America's purpose is to be America, striving to fulfill the aspirations expressed in the Declaration of Independence and the Constitution as reinterpreted with the passage of time and in light of hard-earned experience.*

The proper aim of American statecraft, therefore, is not to redeem humankind or to prescribe some specific world order, nor to police the planet by force of arms. Its purpose is to permit Americans to avail themselves of the right of self-determination as they seek to create at home a "more perfect union." Any policy impeding that enterprise—as open-ended war surely does—is misguided and pernicious.

By demonstrating the feasibility of creating a way of life based on humane, liberal values, the United States might help illuminate the path ahead for others who seek free-dom. Or as Randolph Bourne once put it, "a turning within" is essential "in order that we may have something to give without." Yet this "giving without" qualifies as an extra benefit—a bonus or dividend—not as the central purpose of American life.

In short, if the United States has a saving mission, it is, first and foremost, to save itself. In that regard, Dr. King's list of evils may need a bit of tweaking. In our own day, the sins requiring expiation number more than three. Yet in his insis-tence that we first heal ourselves—"Come home, America!"—King remains today the prophet Americans would do well to heed.[12]

Come home and resurrecting the nation's true vocation becomes a possibility. Cling to the existing American credo and the betrayal of that vocation is assured. For anyone genuinely interested in education—a category that neces-sarily excludes partisans and ideologues—surely this stands out as a conclusion that the events of the post-9/11 era, and indeed of the entire American Century, have made manifest.

No doubt the case can, and probably will, be made that the obligations of global leadership demand that the United States take on the problems besetting Pakistan, Yemen, and Somalia, much as it has addressed those besetting Afghanistan and Iraq.

Little evidence exists to suggest that such efforts are likely to have a positive effect, however. No evidence exists—none—to suggest that U.S. efforts will advance the cause of global peace. If, as many suspect, Washington's actual aim is something more akin to dominance or hegemony, then evidence exists in abundance demonstrating that the project is a self-defeating one.

A NEW TRINITY

Even if self-determination qualifies as a right, it is certainly not a gift. As with any right, it requires safeguards. To ensure that others will refrain from interfering with its efforts to create a more perfect union, the United States requires power. Yet in light of the credo described above, how precisely should the United States formulate and wield that power?

Here, too, there exists an alternative tradition to which Americans today could repair, should they choose to do so. This tradition harks back to the nearly forgotten anti-imperial origins of the Republic. Succinctly captured in the motto "Don't Tread on Me," this tradition is one that does not seek trouble but insists that others will accord the United States respect. Updated for our own time, it might translate into the following substitute for the existing sacred trinity.

First, the purpose of the U.S. military is not to combat evil or remake the world, but to defend the United States and its most vital interests. However necessary, military power itself is neither good nor inherently desirable. Any nation defining itself in terms of military might is well down the road to perdition, as earlier generations of Americans instinctively understood. As for military supremacy, the lessons of the past are quite clear. It is an illusion and its pursuit an invitation to mischief, if not disaster. Therefore, the United States should maintain only those forces required to accomplish the defense establishment's core mission.

Second, the primary duty station of the American soldier is in America. Just as the U.S. military should not be a global police force, so too it should not be a global occupation force. Specific circumstances may from time to time require the United States on a temporary basis to establish a military presence abroad. Yet rather than defining the norm, Americans should view this prospect as a sharp departure, entailing public debate and prior congressional authorization. Dismantling the Pentagon's sprawling network of existing bases promises to be a lengthy process. Priority should be given to those regions where the American presence costs the most while accomplishing the least. According to those criteria, U.S. troops should withdraw from the Persian Gulf and Central Asia forthwith.

Third, consistent with the Just War tradition, the United States should employ force only as a last resort and only in self-defense. The Bush Doctrine of preventive war—the United States bestowing on itself the exclusive prerogative of employing force against ostensible threats even before they materialize—is a moral and strategic abomination, the very inverse of prudent and enlightened statecraft. Concocted by George W. Bush to justify his needless and misguided 2003 invasion of Iraq, this doctrine still awaits explicit abrogation by authorities in Washington. Never again should the United States undertake "a war of choice" informed by fantasies that violence provides a shortcut to resolving history's complexities.

Were this alternative triad to become the basis for policy, dramatic changes in the U.S. national security posture would ensue. Military spending would decrease appreciably. The Pentagon's global footprint would shrink. Weapons manufacturers would see their profits plummet. Beltway Bandits would close up shop. The ranks of defense-oriented think tanks would thin. These changes, in turn, would narrow the range of options available for employing force, obliging policy makers to exhibit greater restraint in intervening abroad. With resources currently devoted to rehabilitating Baghdad or Kabul freed up, the cause of rehabilitating Cleveland and Detroit might finally attract a following.

Popular susceptibility to fearmongering by those always conjuring up new national emergencies might also wane and with it the average American's willingness to allow some freshly discovered "axis of evil" to dictate the nation's priorities. The imperial presidency's ability to evoke awe and command deference would likewise diminish. With that, the possibility of responsible and genuinely democratic government might present itself.

Of fundamental importance, the identity of the American soldier would undergo substantial revision. The warrior-professional brought home from distant provinces of empire might once again become the citizen-protector of the nation. Rather than serving as an instrument of the state, the soldier might simply defend the country—a cause to which Americans, regardless of class or political orientation, might once again see as their own.

This very prospect—the prospect of any departure from

the Washington rules reducing the privileges that Washington has long enjoyed—helps explain the tenacity of those intent on preserving the status quo.

POPULAR COMPLICITY

"War is the health of the State." So wrote Randolph Bourne nearly a century ago, as he contemplated the U.S. entry into World War I. Bourne's famous aphorism contains an essential truth, yet is too narrowly framed for present-day purposes. Not only war itself, but the preparation for, preoccupation with, and casual acceptance of war all serve today to enhance state power. In addition to the state itself, a constellation of individuals and institutions drawing sustenance from the state also prosper.

That Washington is the principal beneficiary of the national security consensus prompts critics—whether on the antiwar left or the anti-interventionist right—to conclude that Washington itself defines the problem. Change the way Washington works, as virtually every presidential candidate since Jimmy Carter has vowed to do, and the problem will fix itself.

This diagnosis accords with a hallowed practice of blaming dark and distant forces for whatever problems afflict American society, from air pollution and fatty foods to poverty and the erosion of moral standards. Wall Street, the Trusts, Big Oil, Big Pharma, Madison Avenue, Hollywood, and the Mainstream Media: The list of villains is an imposing one. Yet even when the charges levied are not without merit, they fall well short of being satisfactory. In blaming Leviathan, Americans conveniently give themselves a pass.

The Washington consensus persists in considerable

measure because it conforms to and reinforces widely accepted, if highly problematic, aspects of American civic culture. Put simply, if "they" routinely promulgate ill-advised national security policies, it's because "we" let them. Semiwarriors—whether Allen Dulles or Robert McNamara from an earlier era or their latter-day successors like defense secretaries Donald Rumsfeld and Robert Gates—get away with perpetuating the Washington rules because those rules draw upon, sustain, and help conceal the implications, moral as well as practical, of contemporary America's impoverished and attenuated conception of citizenship.

That conception privileges individual choice above collective responsibility and immediate gratification over long-term well-being. For Americans today, duties and obligations are few. Although the United States is not without "good citizens"—they exist in every community—active participation in civic life is entirely a matter of personal preference. The prevailing definition of citizenship requires simply that you pay your taxes and avoid flagrant violations of the law.

The Washington rules offer an approach to national security policy that hews closely to this minimalist definition of what it means to be a citizen. Americans once believed—or at least purported to believe—that citizenship carried with it a responsibility to contribute to the country's defense. In his "Sentiments on a Peace Establishment," written in the immediate aftermath of the American Revolution, George Washington offered the classic formulation of this proposition. "It may be laid down, as a primary position, and the basis of our system," the general wrote, "that every citizen who enjoys the protection of a free government, owes not only a proportion of his property, but even of his personal services to the defence of it."[13] Out of this proposal came the tradition of the citizen-soldier, the warrior who filled the ranks of citizen armies raised for every major war fought by the United States until that system foundered in Vietnam.

Since Vietnam, military and civilian authorities presiding over the capital that bears the old general's name have abandoned his position, radically revising—indeed severing—the relationship between citizenship and soldiering. As with owning a gun or getting an abortion, military service falls within the realm of activities governed by individual choice. To defend the country and its interests, the United States now relies on volunteers who fill the ranks of a professional military establishment only loosely connected to American society.

In General Washington's day this was known as a "standing army." To the extent that the pool of willing volunteers proves insufficiently deep, the Pentagon makes up the difference by outsourcing many functions that uniformed regulars once performed. In an earlier day, such hired auxiliaries were known as war profiteers or mercenaries, terms freighted with unsavory connotations. Today to conceal such unseemliness, the preference is to use anodyne terms like *private security firms* and *private contractors*.

The United States does not rely on this mix of military professionals and profit-oriented contractors because doing so delivers desired policy outcomes at an affordable price. Based on those criteria, the arrangement flunks, as the post-9/11 record amply demonstrates. Only when it comes to satisfying the ambitions of those wielding power and influence in Washington, while giving the American people a pass, can this system be said to work.

The Founders, the commander of the Continental Army

not least among them, disparaged standing armies as incon-
sistent with republican virtue while posing a potential
threat to republican institutions. Today, Americans evince
little interest in cultivating virtue, preferring instead the
frantic pursuit of happiness, defined more often than not in
terms of wealth, celebrity, and personal license. Washington
meanwhile concerns itself less with the well-being of republican institutions than with feathering its own nest, relying
on adventurism abroad to divert attention from chronic
dysfunction at home.

The so-called all-volunteer force satisfies the interests of
both, conferring on citizens a semblance of autonomy and
providing semiwarriors with an instrument well suited to
the pursuit of imperial ambitions. Individual Americans are
relieved of an unwanted duty, which many mistake as freedom. The semiwarriors also acquire a sort of freedom—to
employ American military might however they see fit. Both
parties in this arrangement profess to hold in high regard
the 0.5 percent of the population actually bearing the burden of military service. Neither party concerns itself with
the question of whether this arrangement accords with commonplace notions of fairness or efficacy. For the American
people and for Washington, the arrangement is simply convenient, and that suffices.

There is a second way in which the Washington consensus meshes with the prevailing civic culture. Privileging
the here and now at the expense of the future, those who
govern and those who are governed are one in refusing
to pay their bills. The matter can be simply stated: Washington wants guns; the American people want butter; massive and habitual deficit spending satisfies both appetites,
with responsibility for repaying that debt off-loaded onto
future generations.

Here the record of the post-9/11 period is especially instructive. When George W. Bush became president in 2001, the Pentagon budget amounted to $305 billion and the total national debt stood at $5.7 trillion. Over the next eight years, the red ink flowed. Military spending doubled while annual federal deficits averaged over $600 billion. By the time Bush left office, the national debt had reached $10.6 trillion.

During the first year of the Obama presidency, with defense spending and overall federal spending increasing even as tax receipts fell, the annual budget deficit hit an all-time high of $1.4 trillion or 10 percent of the total gross domestic product (GDP). The annual cost of servicing that debt reached a staggering $383 billion, equivalent to the GDP of Belgium, and continued to climb. So, too, did the resources funneled to the Pentagon: The Obama administration announced plans to increase military spending by 5 percent above what it had averaged during the Bush years.

For year two of the Obama presidency, the White House projected a federal budget deficit of approximately $1.3 trillion, an estimate to be taken with a grain of salt given the consistent tendency of previous administrations to lowball such matters. Stung by criticism from Republicans posing as fiscal conservatives, Obama promised to curb the federal government's spending habits. Yet this promise specifically exempted the Pentagon, the Department of Homeland Security, and other agencies falling under the rubric of national security, and therefore all but guaranteed deficits without end. A study by the nonpartisan Congressional Budget Office forecast trillion-dollar deficits for the next decade. Based on that analysis, by 2019 the total size of the national debt is likely to surpass $21 trillion, an amount substantially greater than the nation's GDP. By that time, expenditures required to service the national debt will exceed even the massive amounts spent annually by the Pentagon—the equivalent of the interest on your monthly credit card statement exceeding the size of your mortgage payment.[14]

This sorry spectacle of fiscal indiscipline has generated much finger-pointing by both Democrats and Republicans. In fact, the nation's headlong lunge toward insolvency has been a thoroughly bipartisan project, with both parties deeply implicated and few Americans raising serious objections. When public protest has occurred, as with the "tea party" movement, it has derived from barely concealed partisan considerations. Overall, members of the present generation have plundered the inheritance of their children and grandchildren as remorselessly as the disgraced financier Bernard Madoff bilked those who entrusted him with their money.

By satisfying the immediate demands of their constituents, regardless of cost, politicians buy popular deference, win reelection, and insulate the Washington rules from serious examination. A half century ago, with the United States a creditor nation, President Eisenhower understood that military expenditures exact social costs. Today, with the United States in hock up to its neck, politicians pretend that Americans can have guns and butter, thereby perpetrating fraud on a scale far greater than Mr. Madoff's. They have gotten away with this modern version of bread and circuses for the same reason that Madoff did: When you're selling something that seems too good to be true, nothing works like having a greedy and gullible clientele.

The bottom line is this: A minimalist conception of citizenship that relieves individual Americans of any obligation to contribute to the nation's defense allows Washington wide latitude in employing U.S. military power. Unnecessary and misguided wars are but one deleterious result. An insistence that, unlike other nations, the United States need not live within its means obviates any requirement to balance the books, with the country hurtling toward insolvency as a result.

To put it another way, if Washington pursues ruinous military and fiscal policies, Americans have no one but themselves to blame. Were they to define national defense as a collective responsibility (as George Washington urged) and were they to demand that the state operate on a pay-as-you-go basis (as common sense requires), the Washington rules would almost immediately become untenable.

CHOOSING

At a White House press conference on July 28, 1965, President Lyndon Johnson explained why it had become necessary to send thousands of U.S. combat troops to fight in South Vietnam. "We did not choose to be the guardians at the gate," he emphasized, "but there is no one else."[15]

Johnson's statement, expressing a sentiment widely shared in Washington then and now, was deeply misleading. LBJ's immediate predecessors in the White House *had* chosen. In the wake of World War II, with American wealth and power at their zenith, they had established "national security" as paramount among the purposes that government exists to serve. They imparted to "U.S. national security policy"—a phrase laden with weighty connotations—its abiding characteristics: a reliance on ideologically charged statements of intent and justification; an emphasis on coercive power held at the ready; and a penchant for global interventionism, both overt and covert.

Johnson had not invented this approach; he had merely

inherited it. Yet by escalating the U.S. military involvement in Indochina, he, too, signaled his fealty to the Washington rules. He, too, was choosing. His choice was to conform.

The consequences of that choice would prove to be fateful, not least of all for Johnson himself. The ensuing conflict—"that bitch of a war," as he called it—consumed the lives of fifty-eight thousand Americans to no avail and destroyed his presidency. Johnson had hoped that an ambitious domestic reform program known as the Great Society might define his legacy. Instead, he bequeathed to his successor a nation that was bitterly divided, deeply troubled, and increasingly cynical.

To follow a different course would have required Johnson to depart from the Washington rules. This he—although not he alone—lacked the courage to do.

Here lies the real significance—and perhaps the tragedy—of Barack Obama's decision, during the first year of his presidency, to escalate the U.S. military effort in Afghanistan. By retaining Robert Gates as defense secretary and by appointing retired four-star officers as his national security adviser and intelligence director, Obama had already offered Washington assurances that he was not contemplating a radical departure from the existing pattern of national security policy. Whether wittingly or not, the president now proffered his full-fledged allegiance to the Washington consensus, removing any lingering doubts about its durability.

In his speech of December 1, 2009, while explaining to the cadets at West Point why he felt it necessary to widen a war already in its ninth year, Obama justified his decision by appending it to a much larger narrative. "More than any other nation," he declared, "the United States of America has underwritten global security for over six decades—a time that, for all its problems, has seen walls come down, and markets open, and billions lifted from poverty, unparalleled scientific progress and advancing frontiers of human liberty."[16] Obama wanted it known that by sending tens of thousands of additional U.S. troops to fight in Afghanistan his own administration was carrying on the work his predecessors had begun. Their policies were his policies.

The six decades to which the president referred in his artfully sanitized rendering of contemporary history were the years during which the American credo and the sacred trinity had ascended to a position of uncontested supremacy. Thus did the president who came into office vowing to change the way Washington works make known his intention to leave this crucially important element of his inheritance all but untouched. Like Johnson, the president whose bold agenda for domestic reform presaged his own, Obama too was choosing to conform.

Still, we should be grateful to him for making at least one thing unmistakably clear: To imagine that Washington will ever tolerate second thoughts about the Washington rules is to engage in willful self-deception. Washington itself has too much to lose.

If change is to come, it must come from the people. Yet unless Americans finally awaken to the fact that they've been had, Washington will continue to have its way.

So the need for education—summoning Americans to take on the responsibilities of an active and engaged citizenship—has become especially acute. For me personally, education became possible twenty years ago at the Brandenburg Gate when I contemplated the disparity between what I had been conditioned to believe and what I was actually witnessing. The dissonance was too great to ignore. The ensuing process of confronting illusions (including my own) and of dissecting the contradictions besetting U.S. policy was sometimes painful and never easy. Yet it included moments of considerable exhilaration and its overall effect has been liberating. Self-awareness is a great gift. The ability to see things as they are, without blinders, is an even greater one.

Americans today must reckon with a contradiction of gaping proportions. Promising prosperity and peace, the Washington rules are propelling the United States toward insolvency and perpetual war. Over the horizon a shipwreck of epic proportions awaits. To acknowledge the danger we face is to make learning—and perhaps even a course change—possible. To willfully ignore the danger is to become complicit in the destruction of what most Americans profess to hold dear. We, too, must choose.

NOTES

INTRODUCTION: SLOW LEARNER

1. Henry Adams, *Democracy, Esther, Mont Saint Michel and Chartres, The Education of Henry Adams* (New York, 1983), p. 1066. This is the Library of America edition.
2. "Table of U.S. Nuclear Weapons, 1945–2002," Natural Resources Defense Council, http://www.nrdc.org/nuclear/nudb/datab9.asp.
3. Henry R. Luce, "The American Century," *Life*, February 7, 1941.

1. THE ADVENT OF SEMIWAR

1. "President-Elect Obama's Grant Park Speech," November 5, 2008, http://blogs.suntimes.com/sweet/2008/11/obamas_grant_park_speech.html.
2. "Foreign Policy Address at the Council on Foreign Relations," July 15, 2009, http://www.state.gov/secretary/rm/2009a/july/126071.htm.
3. "Transcript of Theodore Roosevelt's Corollary to the Monroe Doctrine," December 6, 1904, http://www.ourdocuments.gov/doc.php?flash=old&doc=56&page=transcript.
4. Tony Capaccio, "Congress Approves $636.3 Billion Defense Measure," December 19, 2009, http://www.bloomberg.com/apps/news?pid=20601209&sid=aCyW2U1Ze0uY. Among the expenditures not

included in this appropriation are those related to nuclear weapons programs, veterans' benefits, covert operations, and the costs of expanding the war in Afghanistan. Total military outlays surpass $700 billion—and that qualifies as a conservative estimate.

5. "Number of American Servicemen and Women Stationed Overseas," May 28, 2008, http://www.ppionline.org/ppi_ci.cfm?knlg AreaID=108&subsecID=900003&contentID=254647.

6. Department of Defense Base Structure Report, Fiscal Year 2008, http://www.acq.osd.mil/ie/download/bsr/BSR2008Baseline .pdf. This report does not count classified facilities of which there are many.

7. The phrase is Chalmers Johnson's from his book *The Sorrows of Empire* (New York, 2004).

8. U.S. Pacific Command vision statement, http://www.pacom .mil/web/site_pages/uspacom/regional%20map.shtml.

9. Gen. David Petraeus, "Posture Statement" (testimony before the Senate Armed Services Committee), April 1, 2009, http://www .centcom.mil/en/about-centcom/posture-statement/.

10. "Mission," http://www.eucom.mil/english/mission.asp.

11. "AFRICOM Mission," http://www.africom.mil/AboutAFRICOM .asp.

12. "Our Goals," http://www.southcom.mil/AppsSC/pages/ourMis sion.php.

13. "Overview," http://www.fas.org/spp/military/program/nssrm/ initiatives/usspace.htm.

14. "Exercises and Other Engagements," http://www.pacom.mil/ web/site_pages/uspacom/facts.shtml.

15. "U.S. Strategic Command," http://www.stratcom.mil/.

16. Michael J. Hogan, *A Cross of Iron: Harry S. Truman and the Origins of the National Security State, 1945–1954* (Cambridge, England, 1998), p. 74.

17. Roger Morris, "Take the Myth and Mystery Out of Foreign Policy," *New York Times*, January 29, 1980, p. A19.

18. "Eisenhower's Farewell Address to the Nation," January 17, 1961, http://mcadams.posc.mu.edu/ike.htm.

19. This sketch of Dulles and the CIA draws on the following works: James Srodes, *Allen Dulles: Master of Spies* (New York, 1999); Evan Thomas, *The Very Best Men: Four Who Dared* (New York, 1995);

and Tim Weiner, *Legacy of Ashes: The History of the CIA* (New York, 2007).

20. Srodes, *Allen Dulles*, p. 457.
21. Cabell Phillips, "Allen Dulles of the 'Silent Service,'" *New York Times Magazine*, March 29, 1953, p. SM12.
22. "The Man with the Innocent Air," *Time*, August 3, 1953, pp. 12–15.
23. Srodes, *Allen Dulles*, p. 439.
24. Srodes, *Allen Dulles*, p. 384.
25. William Colby, *Honorable Men* (New York, 1978), p. 73.
26. Allen Dulles, *The Craft of Intelligence* (New York, 1963), p. 54.
27. Dulles, *The Craft of Intelligence*, pp. 44, 50.
28. Thomas, *The Very Best Men*, p. 37.
29. Dulles, *The Craft of Intelligence*, p. 264.
30. Weiner, *Legacy of Ashes*, p. 76.
31. This sketch of LeMay and SAC draws on the following works: William S. Borgiasz, *The Strategic Air Command: Evolution and Consolidation of Nuclear Forces, 1945–1955* (Westport, Connecticut, 1996); Thomas M. Coffey, *Iron Eagle: The Turbulent Life of General Curtis LeMay* (New York, 1986); and Curtis LeMay, *Mission with LeMay: My Story* (Garden City, New York, 1965).
32. LeMay, *Mission with LeMay*, pp. 494–495.
33. Tami Davis Biddle, "Shield and Sword: U.S. Strategic Forces and Doctrine Since 1945," in *The Long War: A New History of U.S. National Security Policies Since World War II*, ed. Andrew J. Bacevich (New York, 2007), p. 142; Borgiasz, *Strategic Air Command*, p. 12.
34. Coffey, *Iron Eagle*, p. 255.
35. Steven L. Rearden, "U.S. Strategic Bombardment Doctrine Since 1945," in *Case Studies in Strategic Bombardment*, ed. R. Cargill Hall (Washington, D.C., 1998), p. 403.
36. LeMay, *Mission with LeMay*, p. 454.
37. LeMay, *Mission with LeMay*, p. 436. Italics in the original.
38. Francis V. Drake, "On Guard!," *Reader's Digest*, August 1953, pp. 11–12.
39. George Barrett, "On Patrol with 'The Weapon,'" *New York Times Magazine*, April 6, 1958, p. SM16.
40. Richard S. Meryman, Jr., "The Guardians," *Harper's*, October 1955, pp. 38–39.

41. "The Man the Kremlin Fears the Most?," *U.S. News & World Report*, May 2, 1958, p. 62.

42. "Here Comes LeMay," *Time*, April 15, 1957, p. 33.

43. Ernest Havemann, "Toughest Cop in the Western World," *Life*, June 14, 1954, pp. 145, 147.

44. "Second Best in Air Is Not Good Enough," *Life*, May 14, 1956, pp. 53–56.

45. LeMay, *Mission with LeMay*, p. 381.

46. David Alan Rosenberg, "The Origins of Overkill: Nuclear Weapons and American Strategy, 1945–1960," *International Security* 7 (Spring 1983): 50, 55, 58.

47. Henry Adams, *The Education of Henry Adams* (New York, 1983), p. 1027.

48. LeMay, *Mission with LeMay*, p. 380.

49. "U.S. Cold War Overflights," http://www.rb-29.net/HTML/77ColdWarStory/09.01apndxD.htm.

50. Richard H. Kohn and Joseph P. Harahan, eds., *Strategic Air Warfare* (Washington, D.C., 1988), p. 109.

51. LeMay, *Mission with LeMay*, p. 481.

52. Theodore Shackley, *The Third Option: An American View of Counterinsurgency Operations* (New York, 1981), p. 13.

2. ILLUSIONS OF FLEXIBILITY AND CONTROL

1. Maxwell D. Taylor, *Swords and Plowshares* (New York, 1972), p. 170.

2. Maxwell D. Taylor, *The Uncertain Trumpet* (New York, 1960), pp. xi, 4, 5, 6, 146.

3. "Excerpts of a Speech by Senator John F. Kennedy," American Legion Convention, Miami, Florida, October 18, 1960, http://www.jfklink.com/speeches/jfk/oct60/jfk181060_miami03.html.

4. "Speech by Senator John F. Kennedy," VFW Convention, Detroit, Michigan, August 26, 1960, http://www.jfklink.com/speeches/jfk/aug60/jfk260860_vfwadvance.html.

5. Lawrence S. Kaplan, Ronald D. Landa, and Edward J. Drea, *The McNamara Ascendancy, 1961–1965* (Washington, D.C., 2006), p. 69.

6. Russell F. Weigley, *History of the United States Army* (New York, 1967), pp. 538, 543–544, 561, 569.

7. "Who Fights Brush-Fire Wars?," *Life*, January 13, 1961, p. 43.

8. Taylor, *Uncertain Trumpet*, p. 108.

9. Robert S. McNamara, *In Retrospect: The Tragedy and Lessons of Vietnam* (New York, 1995), p. 25.

10. Robert J. Watson, *Into the Missile Age, 1956–1960* (Washington, D.C., 1997), pp. 473–495.

11. McNamara, *In Retrospect*, pp. 6, 22.

12. Quoted in *The Fog of War: Eleven Lessons from the Life of Robert S. McNamara*, a 2003 film by Errol Morris, http://www.imdb.com/title/tt0317910/.

13. LeMay, *Mission with LeMay*, p. 8. Emphasis in the original.

14. Deborah Shapley, *Promise and Power: The Life and Times of Robert McNamara* (Boston, 1993), pp. 106–107.

15. Ernest R. May and Philip D. Zelikow, eds., *The Kennedy Tapes: Inside the White House During the Cuban Missile Crisis* (Cambridge, Massachusetts, 1997), p. 32.

16. "Herman Kahn's Escalation Ladder," http://www.texas chapbookpress.com/magellanslog41/escalation.htm.

17. Kaplan et al., *The McNamara Ascendancy*, p. 322.

18. Shapley, *Promise and Power*, pp. 194–195.

19. David MacIsaac, "Strategy: Nuclear Warfare Strategy and War Plans," in *The Oxford Companion to American Military History* (New York, 1999), p. 694.

20. For a recent account of the entire episode, see Howard Jones, *The Bay of Pigs* (New York, 2008).

21. Letter From the Chairman of the Cuba Study Group (Taylor) to President Kennedy, June 13, 1961, *Foreign Relations of the United States, 1961–1963*, volume X, Cuba, 1961–1962 (Washington, D.C., 1997), p. 575; hereafter cited as *FRUS, Cuba*.

22. "Memorandum No. 2 From the Cuba Study Group to President Kennedy," June 13, 1961, *FRUS, Cuba*, pp. 600–602.

23. "Memorandum No. 4 From the Cuba Study Group to President Kennedy," June 13, 1961, *FRUS, Cuba*, p. 606.

24. Editorial Note, *FRUS, Cuba*, p. 666. This reprints extracts from a handwritten note prepared by Robert Kennedy on November 11, 1961.

25. Memorandum from the Chief of Operation in the Deputy Directorate for Plans (Helms) to Director of Central Intelligence (McCone), Subject: Meeting with the Attorney General of the

United States Concerning Cuba, January 19, 1962, *FRUS, Cuba*, p. 720. The memo contains verbatim quotes from Robert Kennedy.

26. Memorandum from the Chief of Operations, Operation Mongoose (Lansdale), to Members of the Caribbean Survey Group, January 20, 1962, *FRUS, Cuba*, p. 721.

27. Program Review by the Chief of Operations, Operation Mongoose (Lansdale), January 18, 1962, *FRUS, Cuba*, pp. 710–718.

28. Paper prepared in the Department of State, August 10, 1962, *FRUS, Cuba*, p. 922.

29. Memorandum from the Deputy Secretary of Defense (Gilpatric) to President Kennedy, January 31, 1962, *FRUS, Cuba*, p. 735.

30. Memorandum, August 21, 1962, *FRUS, Cuba*, p. 956. The document's author is identified as John A. McCone, successor to Allen Dulles as director of central intelligence.

31. Memorandum from the Chief of Operations, Operation Mongoose (Lansdale), to the Deputy Assistant Secretary of State for Inter-American Affairs (Goodwin), March 6, 1962, *FRUS, Cuba*, p. 767.

32. Sam Dolgoff, *The Cuban Revolution: A Critical Perspective* (Montreal, 1977), pp. 63, 67.

33. Theodore C. Sorensen, *Kennedy* (New York, 1965), p. 308.

34. Ted Sorensen, *Counselor: A Life at the Edge of History* (New York, 2008), p. 321.

35. Arthur M. Schlesinger, Jr., *A Thousand Days: John F. Kennedy in the White House* (Boston, 1965), p. 297.

36. Tim Weiner, *Legacy of Ashes: The History of the CIA* (New York, 2007), p. 180.

37. Memorandum from the Central Intelligence Agency Operations Officer for Operation Mongoose (Harvey) and the Acting Chairman of the Board of National Estimates (Smith) to the Chief of Operations, Operation Mongoose (Lansdale), August 17, 1962, *FRUS, Cuba*, p. 942.

38. May and Zelikow, eds., *The Kennedy Tapes*, pp. 666–675.

39. Dean Rusk, *As I Saw It* (New York, 1990), p. 242.

40. Plan for Cuba, undated [1961], *FRUS, Cuba*, p. 681.

41. James G. Blight and Janet M. Lang, *The Fog of War* (Lanham, Maryland, 2005), p. 40.

42. James G. Hershberg, "Before 'The Missiles of October': Did

Kennedy Plan a Military Strike Against Cuba?," *Diplomatic History* 14 (Spring 1990): 163–198.

43. Sorensen, *Kennedy*, pp. 3, 696.

44. May and Zelikow, eds., *The Kennedy Tapes*, pp. 177–178.

45. John F. Kennedy, "American University Commencement Address," June 10, 1963, http://www.americanrhetoric.com/speeches/jfk americanuniversityaddress.html.

46. May and Zelikow, eds., *The Kennedy Tapes*, p. 198.

47. McNamara, *In Retrospect*, p. 96.

48. The centerpiece of the U.S. counterinsurgency effort during this period was the Strategic Hamlet Program, which yielded disappointing results. George C. Herring, *America's Longest War: The United States and Vietnam, 1950–1975* (New York, 1979, 4th ed., 2002), pp. 103–109.

49. By the time of Kennedy's assassination, American helicopters were ferrying South Vietnamese troops into battle, while American pilots in aircraft with South Vietnamese markings were flying close air support missions.

50. Herring, *America's Longest War*, p. 104.

51. In November 1961, at the conclusion of the so-called Taylor-Rostow Mission, General Taylor was already advocating for the commitment of U.S. combat troops to South Vietnam. The report endorsed the reigning precepts of the domino theory, declaring that "if Vietnam goes, it will be exceedingly difficult if not impossible to hold Southeast Asia"; such a defeat would lead others to question whether "the United States has the will and the capacity to deal with the Communist offensive in that area." Quoted in Stanley Karnow, *Vietnam: A History* (New York, 1983), p. 252.

52. "Kennedy Considered Supporting Coup in South Vietnam," August 1963, National Security Archive, http://www.gwu.edu/~nsarchiv/NSAEBB/NSAEBB302/index.htm.

53. McNamara, *In Retrospect*, p. 164.

54. Telegram from the Embassy in Vietnam to the Department of State, January 6, 1965, *Foreign Relations of the United States, 1964–1968*, volume II, Vietnam, January–June 1965 (Washington, D.C., 1996), pp. 12–19; hereafter cited as *FRUS, Vietnam*.

55. Telegram from the Embassy in Vietnam to the Department of State, January 6, 1965, *FRUS, Vietnam*, p. 24. Although published

as a separate document, this is a continuation of the cable cited above.

56. Memorandum from the President's Special Assistant for National Security Affairs (Bundy) to President Johnson, January 27, 1965, *FRUS, Vietnam*, pp. 95–97. Emphasis in the original.

57. Telegram from the Department of State to the Embassy in Vietnam, January 30, 1965, *FRUS, Vietnam*, p. 114. The text identifies Bundy as the author of the cable.

58. Brian VanDeMark, *Into the Quagmire: Lyndon Johnson and the Escalation of the Vietnam War* (New York, 1995), p. 63.

59. Memorandum from the President's Special Assistant for National Security Affairs (Bundy) to President Johnson, February 7, 1965, *FRUS, Vietnam*, pp. 174–181.

60. Paper by the Members of the Bundy Mission (A Policy of Sustained Reprisal), undated [February 8, 1965], *FRUS, Vietnam*, pp. 184–185. Emphasis added.

61. Memorandum for the Record, February 8, 1965, *FRUS, Vietnam*, pp. 192–197. The author of the memorandum was CIA director John McCone. Bundy was presiding in the president's absence.

62. Memorandum from the President's Special Assistant for National Security Affairs (Bundy) to President Johnson, February 7, 1965, *FRUS, Vietnam*, p. 175.

63. Memorandum from Senator Mike Mansfield to President Johnson, February 8, 1965, *FRUS, Vietnam*, p. 204.

64. Memorandum from Senator Mike Mansfield to President Johnson, February 8, 1965, *FRUS, Vietnam*, p. 204.

65. Letter from the President's Special Assistant for National Security Affairs (Bundy) to Senator Mike Mansfield, February 9, 1965, *FRUS, Vietnam*, pp. 208–211.

66. Memorandum from Senator Mike Mansfield to President Johnson, February 10, 1965, *FRUS, Vietnam*, pp. 226–227. Emphasis in the original.

67. Letter from the President's Special Assistant for National Security Affairs (Bundy) to Senator Mike Mansfield, February 11, 1965, *FRUS, Vietnam*, pp. 237–238.

68. David Halberstam, *The Best and the Brightest* (New York, 1972), p. 462.

69. Telegram from the Embassy in Vietnam to the Department of

State, February 7, 1965, *FRUS, Vietnam*, p. 165. The author of this cable was John McNaughton.

70. Telegram from the Commander, Military Assistance Command, Vietnam (Westmoreland) to the Commander in Chief, Pacific (Sharp), February 23, 1965, *FRUS, Vietnam*, p. 351.

71. Telegram from the Chairman of the Joint Chiefs of Staff (Wheeler) to the Commander in Chief, Pacific (Sharp), February 27, 1965, *FRUS, Vietnam*, p. 380.

72. Telegram from the Office of the Secretary of Defense to the Embassy in Vietnam, March 2, 1965, *FRUS, Vietnam*, p. 395.

73. Paper by the Assistant Secretary of Defense for International Security Affairs (McNaughton), March 10, 1965, *FRUS, Vietnam*, p. 430. Emphasis in the original.

74. Johnson Report Outline, March 14, 1965, *FRUS, Vietnam*, p. 439.

75. Memorandum by the President's Special Assistant for National Security Affairs, March 16, 1965, *FRUS, Vietnam*, p. 447.

76. Telegram from the Embassy in Vietnam to the Department of State, March 18, 1965, *FRUS, Vietnam*, pp. 454–457.

77. Memorandum from the Joint Chiefs of Staff to Secretary of Defense McNamara, March 20, 1965, *FRUS, Vietnam*, p. 466.

78. National Security Action Memorandum No. 328, April 6, 1965, *FRUS, Vietnam*, p. 538.

79. Kaplan et al., *The McNamara Ascendancy*, p. 531.

3. THE CREDO RESTORED

1. J. William Fulbright, *The Arrogance of Power* (New York, 1966), pp. 3–4.

2. Fulbright, *Arrogance*, pp. 3, 15.

3. Fulbright, *Arrogance*, pp. 32, 121, 248, 252.

4. Fulbright, *Arrogance*, pp. 138, 248.

5. Fulbright, *Arrogance*, pp. 14, 21.

6. Fulbright, *Arrogance*, pp. 20, 134–135, 217.

7. Fulbright, *Arrogance*, pp. 5, 127, 185, 199.

8. Fulbright, *Arrogance*, pp. 202, 250.

9. Fulbright, *Arrogance*, pp. 253, 256.

10. For an admiring profile, see Howard Jablon, "General David M. Shoup, USMC: Warrior and War Protester," *Journal of Military History* 60 (July 1996): 513–538.

11. The quotes come from a speech Shoup made at the Tenth Annual Junior College World Affairs Day, Pierce College, Los Angeles, California, May 14, 1966, reprinted in Senate Foreign Relations Committee, *Present Situation in Vietnam*, March 20, 1968, pp. 44–51.

12. "General Shoup Derides U.S. Stand on Vietnam," *Washington Post*, December 19, 1967.

13. For a complete transcript of this exchange, see Senate Foreign Relations Committee, *Present Situation in Vietnam*, March 20, 1968, pp. 1–44.

14. David M. Shoup, "The New American Militarism," *The Atlantic*, April 1969.

15. Seymour M. Hersh, "Huge C.I.A. Operation Reported in U.S. Against Anti-War Forces, Other Dissidents in Nixon Years," *New York Times*, December 22, 1974, p. A1. This is the story that revealed CIA domestic spying activities.

16. Gerald K. Haines, "The Pike Committee Investigations and the CIA," https://www.cia.gov/library/center-for-the-study-of-intelligence/kent-csi/pdf/v42i5a07p.pdf.

17. Russell F. Weigley, *History of the United States Army* (New York, 1967), p. 569.

18. "Military Basic Pay and Allowances," http://www.dfas.mil/militarypay/militarypaytables/militarypaypriorrates/1965.pdf.

19. "Withdrawal of Troops Asked," *Evening Prescott* [Arizona] *Courier*, May 16, 1966, http://news.google.com/newspapers?nid=918&dat=19660516&id=ZP4KAAAAIBAJ&sjid=aFADAAAAIBAJ&pg=4110,354870.

20. Don Oberdorfer, *Senator Mansfield* (New York, 2003), pp. 311–313.

21. The War Powers Act of 1973 (Public Law 93-148), http://www.thecre.com/fedlaw/legal22/warpow.htm.

22. For a discussion of the U.S. military reform project after Vietnam, see Andrew J. Bacevich, *The New American Militarism: How Americans Are Seduced by War* (New York, 2005), pp. 34–68.

23. Anthony Lake, ed., *The Vietnam Legacy: The War, American Society, and the Future of American Foreign Policy* (New York, 1976), p. xxiii.

24. Lake, ed., *The Vietnam Legacy*, p. 120.

25. Lake, ed., *The Vietnam Legacy*, p. xii.

26. Lake, ed., *The Vietnam Legacy*, p. 64.

27. Lake, ed., *The Vietnam Legacy*, p. 91.

28. Lake, ed., *The Vietnam Legacy*, p. 354.

29. Lake, ed., *The Vietnam Legacy*, p. 410.

30. Lake, ed., *The Vietnam Legacy*, pp. xiii, xvii, xxi.

31. Martin Luther King, "Declaration of Independence from the War in Vietnam," April 1967, www.h-net.org/~hst203/documents/King.html.

32. Lest the reader think that Lake's *Vietnam Legacy* is unique, see also W. Scott Thompson and Donaldson D. Frizzell, eds., *The Lessons of Vietnam* (New York, 1977). The cast of characters differs, but the approach and the conclusions are the same.

33. Republican Party Platform of 1980, http://www.presidency.ucsb.edu/showplatforms.php?platindex=R1980. The document contains brief references to the nation of Vietnam, condemning its human rights record.

34. Ronald Reagan, "Address to the Veterans of Foreign Wars Convention in Chicago," August 18, 1980, http://www.presidency.ucsb.edu/ws/index.php?pid=85202.

35. "The Munich Analogy," http://www.americanforeignrelations.com/E-N/The-Munich-Analogy-Reagan-bush-and-the-gulf-war.html.

36. For the record, Clinton fought and lost a war in Somalia, intervened in Haiti, Bosnia, and Kosovo, and bombed the Sudan, Afghanistan, and Iraq, the latter on innumerable occasions. Clinton's version of maintaining a global military presence included stationing U.S. troops in Saudi Arabia, which set the stage for the Khobar Towers bombing of June 25, 1996, and ordering the USS *Cole* to visit Yemen, providing the target for a devastating terrorist attack on October 12, 2000.

37. In a speech justifying the bombing of Serbia, Clinton asked, "What if someone had listened to Winston Churchill and stood up to Adolf Hitler earlier? How many people's lives might have been saved? And how many American lives might have been saved?" Quoted in Timothy Garton Ash, "The New Adolf Hitler?" *Time*, April 5, 1999.

38. Henry A. Kissinger, "Lessons of Vietnam," ca. May 12, 1975, http://www.ford.utexas.edu/library/exhibits/vietnam/750512b.htm. This draft memorandum to the president was apparently never sent.

39. Elaine Sciolino, "Madeleine Albright's Audition," *New York Times Magazine*, September 22, 1996, p. SM67.

40. "Interview on NBC-TV 'The Today Show' with Matt Lauer," February 19, 1998, http://secretary.state.gov/www/statements/1998/980219a.html.
41. Colin Powell, *My American Journey* (New York, 2005), p. 576.
42. Interview on *60 Minutes*, May 11, 1996.
43. Sciolino, "Madeleine Albright's Audition."
44. "Farewell Remarks by Secretary of State Madeleine K. Albright," January 19, 2001, http://usinfo.org/wf-archive/2001/010119/epf503.htm.

4. RECONSTITUTING THE TRINITY

1. David Vine, *Island of Shame: The Secret History of the U.S. Military Base on Diego Garcia* (Princeton, New Jersey, 2009).
2. Secretary Cohen's Remarks at the Foreign Policy Association Medal for Leaders, April 2, 1998, http://www.defenselink.mil/transcripts/transcript.aspx?transcriptid=791.
3. James R. Blaker, *Transforming Military Force: The Legacy of Arthur Cebrowski and Network Centric Warfare* (Washington, D.C., 2007), pp. 82, 74, 84.
4. Operation Northern Watch, http://www.globalsecurity.org/military/ops/northern_watch.htm, accessed September 12, 2009; Operation Southern Watch, http://www.globalsecurity.org/military/ops/southern_watch.htm.
5. Department of Defense, *Conduct of the Persian Gulf War: Final Report to Congress*, April 1992, p. 19, http://www.ndu.edu/library/epubs/cpgw.pdf.
6. Dan Balz and Rick Atkinson, "Powell Vows to Isolate Iraqi Army and Then 'Kill It,'" *Washington Post*, January 24, 1991, p. A1.
7. Department of Defense, *Conduct of the Persian Gulf War*, pp. 22, 24, 25.
8. Department of Defense, *Conduct of the Persian Gulf War*, p. 38.
9. There is a vast literature on the Revolution in Military Affairs, much of it predating 9/11 and most of it now largely discredited. To sample that literature, see the compendium assembled by the Project on Defense Alternatives, available at http://www.comw.org/rma/. For an exceptionally instructive primer, see *Joint Vision 2010*, a document published by the Joint Chiefs of Staff in 1996 and available at http://www.dtic.mil/jv2010/jv2010.pdf.

10. Norman Podhoretz, *World War IV: The Long Struggle Against Islamofascism* (Garden City, New York, 2007).

11. "Building a Military for the 21st Century," http://avalon.law .yale.edu/sept11/testimony_002.asp. This document provides the text of written testimony that Wolfowitz presented to the House and Senate Armed Services Committee on October 3 and 4, 2001.

12. Remarks at the Citadel in Charleston, South Carolina, December 11, 2001, http://externalaffairs.citadel.edu/presbush01.

13. "Text of Bush Speech," May 1, 2003, http://www.cbsnews.com/ stories/2003/05/01/iraq/main551946.shtml.

14. "Cheney Declares Iraqi Freedom 'Most Extraordinary Military Campaign,'" May 1, 2003, http://www.defenselink.mil/news/ newsarticle.aspx?id=29033.

15. "Prepared Statement for the Defense Transformation Act of the 21st Century," May 6, 2003, http://www.defenselink.mil/speeches/ speech.aspx?speechid=388.

16. "Operation Enduring Freedom/Iraqi Freedom Intelligence Lessons Learned," April 13, 2004, www.oss.net/ . . . /Mazzafro %20on%20OSINT%20and%20All%20Source.PPT.

17. Williamson Murray and Robert H. Scales, *The Iraq War: A Military History* (Cambridge, Massachusetts, 2003), p. 145.

18. "Secretary Rumsfeld Interview with *Meet the Press*," April 13, 2003, http://www.defense.gov/Transcripts/Transcript.aspx ?TranscriptID=2383.

19. Donald Rumsfeld, "Pentagon Town Hall Meeting," April 17, 2003, http://www.defense.gov/Speeches/Speech.aspx?SpeechID=370.

20. Thomas Donnelly, "Toward a Global Cavalry," *AEI Outlook Series*, July 2003, http://www.aei.org/outlook/17783.

21. Statement of Lieutenant General Robert Wagner, Senate Subcommittee on Terrorism, Unconventional Threats, and Capabilities, February 26, 2004, http://www.iwar.org.uk/rma/resources/ transformation/02-26-2004-wagner.htm.

22. "U.S. Casualties in Iraq," http://www.globalsecurity.org/military/ ops/iraq_casualties.htm.

23. "The President's News Conference," April 13, 2004, http://www .guardian.co.uk/world/2004/apr/14/iraq.usa2.

24. "Rumsfeld Interview with Chris Matthews," April 29, 2004,

http://www.defense.gov/transcripts/transcript.aspx?transcrip
tid=2555.

25. "Feith Speech at the American Enterprise Institute," May 4, 2004,
http://www.america.gov/st/washfile-english/2004/May/
20040507124856sjhtrop0.1972315.html.

26. "Bush's Statement at Pentagon," May 10, 2004, http://www
.nytimes.com/2004/05/10/politics/10CND-TEXT.html?page
wanted=1.

27. "Fletcher Conference Remarks as Delivered by Deputy Secretary
of Defense Paul Wolfowitz," November 14, 2001, http://avalon
.law.yale.edu/sept11/dod_brief89.asp.

5. COUNTERFEIT COIN

1. "General Foresees 'Generational War' Against Terrorism," *Washington Times*, December 13, 2006, http://www.washingtontimes
.com/news/2006/dec/13/20061213-010657-5560r/.

2. "Rumsfeld's War-on-Terror Memo," October 16, 2003, http://
www.usatoday.com/news/washington/executive/rumsfeld
-memo.htm.

3. Max Boot, "It's Not Over Yet," *Time*, September 3, 2006.

4. Bob Egelko, "Pelosi's First Priority Is to Halt Iraq War," *San Francisco Chronicle*, December 10, 2006, http://www.sfgate.com/cgi
-bin/article.cgi?f=/c/a/2006/12/10/BAGJGMSTAQ1.DTL#ixz
z0U0BWyLWi.

5. "President's Address to the Nation," January 10, 2007, http://
georgewbush-whitehouse.archives.gov/news/releases/2007/01/
20070110-7.html.

6. Paul Krugman, "Things to Come," *New York Times*, March 18, 2003,
http://www.nytimes.com/2003/03/18/opinion/things-to-come
.html?pagewanted=1.

7. Gen. Sir Rupert Smith, *The Utility of Force: The Art of War in the Modern World* (New York, 2007), pp. xiii, 291.

8. Rick Atkinson, "The Long, Blinding Road to War," *Washington Post*, March 7, 2004, http://www.washingtonpost.com/ac2/wp
-dyn/A36843-2004Mar6?language=printer.

9. David Howell Petraeus, "The American Military and the Lessons of Vietnam: A Study of Military Influence and the Use of

Force in the Post-Vietnam Era" (unpublished Ph.D. dissertation, Princeton University, 1987), p. 305.

10. Petraeus, "The American Military and the Lessons of Vietnam," p. 241.

11. Petraeus, "The American Military and the Lessons of Vietnam," p. 13.

12. "FM 3-24 Available in Hard Copy," *Small Wars Journal* (May 8, 2007), http://smallwarsjournal.com/blog/2007/05/-fm-324-the -new/.

13. http://www.press.uchicago.edu/Misc/Chicago/841519.html.

14. FM 3-24/MCWP 3-33.5, *Counterinsurgency* (December 2006): ix, 1-4; hereinafter cited as FM 3-24.

15. FM 3-24, pp. 1-27, 1-28. In all likelihood, Petraeus himself is the author of the paradoxes. They bear a close similarity to the lessons enumerated in "Learning Counterinsurgency," an article that Petraeus contributed to the journal *Military Review* in January–February 2006.

16. Col. David Petraeus et al., "Why We Need FISTs—Never Send a Man When You Can Send a Bullet," *Field Artillery Journal* (May–June 1997): 3–5.

17. FM 3-24, pp. 1-29, 2-2.

18. FM 3-24, p. 1-21.

19. Indeed, ample precedent exists for putting civilians in charge: In 1900, with the recently annexed Philippine Islands racked by an insurgency, President William McKinley appointed William Howard Taft, a federal judge without military experience, to direct U.S. efforts to pacify the archipelago. American generals in the Philippines took their orders, however unenthusiastically, from Taft.

20. William B. Caldwell, "FM 3-07, Stability Operations: Upshifting the Engine of Change," *Military Review* (July–August 2008), http://findarticles.com/p/articles/mi_m0PBZ/is_4_88/ai_ n28048846/.

21. Steven Lee Myers, "Deadly Blasts Rock Shiite Mosque in Baghdad," *New York Times*, September 12, 2009, http://www.nytimes .com/2009/09/13/world/middleeast/13iraq.html.

22. Elisabeth Bumiller, "General Sees a Longer Stay in Iraq Cities for

U.S. Troops," *New York Times*, May 8, 2009, http://www.nytimes
.com/2009/05/09/world/middleeast/09military.html?_r=1.

23. FM 3-24, p. 1-14.

24. Frederick W. Kagan and Kimberly Kagan, "The Patton of Coun-
    terinsurgency," *Weekly Standard* 13 (March 10, 2008), http://www
    .weeklystandard.com/Content/Public/Articles/000/000/014/
    822vfpsz.asp.

25. Jeffrey Bell, "The Petraeus Promotion," *Weekly Standard*, May 5,
    2008, http://www.weeklystandard.com/Content/Public/Articles/
    000/000/015/038lzirr.asp.

26. FM 3-24, p. x.

27. "Petraeus Cites Areas of Improvement in Baghdad," *PBS News-
    Hour*, April 4, 2007, http://www.pbs.org/newshour/bb/middle_
    east/jan-june07/petraeus_04-04.html.

28. Quoted in Barbara Tuchman, *The March to Folly: From Troy to Viet-
    nam* (New York, 1985), p. 326.

29. Walter LaFeber, *America, Russia, and the Cold War* (New York,
    1976), p. 100.

30. Address at the Veterans of Foreign Wars Convention, Phoenix,
    Arizona, August 17, 2009, http://www.whitehouse.gov/the_press
    _office/remarks-by-the-president-at-the-veterans-of-foreign
    -wars-convention/.

31. The quotations come from Nagl's foreword to the University of
    Chicago Press edition of FM 3-24, p. ix.

32. John Kerry, "A New Approach to Fighting Terrorism," July 31,
    2008, speech delivered at the Center for American Progress,
    http://www.americanprogressaction.org/issues/2008/kerry_
    event.html.

33. Bruce Hoffman, "Terrorism's Twelve Step Program," *The National
    Interest Online*, January 13, 2009, http://www.nationalinterest
    .org/Article.aspx?id=20592.

34. Bennet Sacolick, "Character and the Special Forces Soldier," *Spe-
    cial Warfare* (January–February 2009): 8–9.

35. Daniel S. Roper, "Global Counterinsurgency: Strategic Clarity
    for the Long War," *Parameters* (Autumn 2008): 106.

36. Figures are taken from *The CIA World Factbook*, https://www.cia
    .gov/library/publications/the-world-factbook/geos/ym.html.

37. "Obama Approves Afghanistan Troop Increase," February 18, 2009, http://www.cnn.com/2009/POLITICS/02/17/obama.troops/index.html.

38. Ann Scott Tyson, "Top U.S. Commander in Afghanistan Is Fired," *Washington Post*, May 12, 2009, http://www.washington post.com/wp-dyn/content/article/2009/05/11/AR2009051101864.html.

39. Dexter Filkins, "Stanley McChrystal's Long War," *New York Times Magazine*, October 14, 2009, http://www.nytimes.com/2009/10/18/magazine/18Afghanistan-t.html?ref=magazine.

40. Evan Thomas, "McChrystal's War," *Newsweek*, October 5, 2009, http://www.newsweek.com/id/216237.

41. Mark Thompson, "A New General, and a New War, in Afghanistan," *Time*, July 10, 2009, http://www.time.com/time/world/article/0,8599,1909261-1,00.html.

42. These included Stephen Biddle and Max Boot of the Council on Foreign Relations, Anthony Cordesman of the Center for Strategic and International Studies, Frederick Kagan of the American Enterprise Institute, and John Nagl of the Center for a New American Security.

43. *Lou Dobbs Tonight*, November 2, 2009, http://transcripts.cnn.com/TRANSCRIPTS/0911/02/ldt.01.html.

44. Frederick W. Kagan and Kimberly Kagan, "The Cost of Dithering," *Weekly Standard*, November 11, 2009, http://weeklystandard.com/Content/Public/Articles/000/000/017/197pvvru.asp?pg=1.

45. The complete text of "COMISAF's Initial Assessment," August 30, 2009, is at http://media.washingtonpost.com/wp-srv/politics/documents/Assessment_Redacted_092109.pdf?sid=ST2009092003140.

46. Gen. Barry McCaffrey speaking on *Meet the Press*, October 11, 2009, http://www.realclearpolitics.com/articles/2009/10/11/senators_levin__graham_generals_myers__mccaffrey_on_meet_the_press_98669.html.

47. John F. Burns and Alan Cowell, "McChrystal Rejects Lower Afghan War Aims," *New York Times*, October 1, 2009, http://www.iiss.org/whats-new/iiss-in-the-press/october-2009/mcchrystal-rejects-lower-afghan-aims/.

48. Alessandra Stanley, "Situation Report: The Dilemma of Afghanistan," *New York Times*, October 12, 2009, http://www.nytimes.com/ 2009/10/13/arts/television/13stanley.html.

6. Cultivating Our Own Garden

1. Dwight D. Eisenhower, "The Chance for Peace," April 16, 1953, http://www.edchange.org/multicultural/speeches/ike_chance_ for_peace.html.

2. John Winthrop, "A Model of Christian Charity" (1630), http:// religiousfreedom.lib.virginia.edu/sacred/charity.html.

3. "Washington's Farewell Address" (1797), http://avalon.law.yale .edu/18th_century/washing.asp.

4. "John Quincy Adams on U.S. Foreign Policy" (1821), http://www .fff.org/comment/AdamsPolicy.asp.

5. William James, "Address on the Philippine Question" (1903).

6. Randolph Bourne, *War and the Intellectuals* (New York, 1964), p. 45.

7. George F. Kennan, *Memoirs, 1950–1963* (Boston, 1972), p. 84.

8. George F. Kennan, *Realities of American Foreign Policy* (Princeton, New Jersey, 1954), p. 115. This book reprints a series of lectures that Kennan gave at Princeton University in 1954.

9. J. William Fulbright, *The Arrogance of Power* (New York, 1966), pp. 4, 81, 217–218, 247.

10. Quoted in Eric Miller, *Hope in a Scattering Time: A Life of Christopher Lasch* (Grand Rapids, Michigan, 2010), p. 300. The quotation comes from a 1983 essay published in *Harper's*.

11. Martin Luther King, "A Time to Break Silence," April 4, 1967, http://www.americanrhetoric.com/speeches/mlkatimetobreak silence.htm.

12. Martin Luther King, "It's a Dark Day in Our Nation," April 30, 1967, http://www.informationclearinghouse.info/article16183.htm.

13. George Washington, "Sentiments on a Peace Establishment," May 2, 1783, http://www.history.army.mil/books/RevWar/ss/ peacedoc.htm.

14. Treasury Direct, http://www.treasurydirect.gov/NP/NPGate way; Lawrence Kadish, "Taking the National Debt Seriously," *Wall Street Journal*, October 12, 2009; Project on Defense Alternatives, "An Undisciplined Defense," January 18, 2010, http://www .comw.org/pda/fulltext/1001PDABR20exsum.pdf; *CIA World*

Factbook,   https://www.cia.gov/library/publications/the-world
-factbook/rankorder/2001rank.html; Council on Foreign Relations, "U.S. Interest vs. Defense Spending," October 26, 2009,
http://blogs.cfr.org/geographics/2009/10/26/interest-expense/.

15. *The Pentagon Papers*, Gravel ed., vol. 4 (Boston, 1971), pp. 632–633.
16. "Remarks by the President on a New Way Forward in Afghanistan and Pakistan," December 1, 2009, http://www.whitehouse
.gov/the-press-office/remarks-president-address-nation-way
-forward-afghanistan-and-pakistan.

Acknowledgments

I wish to express my gratitude to all those who enabled me to pursue my project of belated self-education. At the very top of the list of those to whom I am indebted are John Wright, Tom Engelhardt, and Sara Bershtel. Literary agents, editors, and publishers don't come any better. To each, I say simply this: Thank you for encouragement, counsel, and friendship.

Rita Quintas and Jason Ng shepherded the manuscript through the production process with cool efficiency. Lucky for me and the book Melanie DeNardo continues to contribute the skills of a first-class publicist.

My young research assistants Paul Roche, Sibyl Kirkpatrick-McKee, and Larissa Forster did a superlative job in tracking down stray facts. Larissa, you are in a league of your own.

For timely advice, I am grateful to Casey Brower, Gian Gentile, Bob Griffith, and especially Dick Kohn, one of the wisest and most generous people I've ever been privileged to know.

My debt to the Lannan Foundation grows apace. Toward the end of this project, a Lannan Writing Residency Fellowship allowed me to spend a very productive month in Marfa, Texas. Special thanks to Douglas Humble and Ray Freese for doing so much to make the time spent in Marfa pleasant and rewarding. Since my wife, Nancy, was able to come along, that made Marfa even better. When she is near, things are good. It's that simple.

Fortunate indeed is the academic who lands a post at Boston University, where students and colleagues create a stimulating environment in which to teach and think. I am especially grateful to Dean Gina Sapiro and to my departmental chairs Charles Dellheim, Erik Goldstein, and Bruce Schulman for their superlative leadership and for granting me leave so that I could finish this project and get started on the next one.

The dedication of this book is to three remarkable young women who bring joy to the life of a very proud and loving father.

Index

About the Author

ANDREW J. BACEVICH, a professor of history and international relations at Boston University, retired from the U.S. Army with the rank of colonel. He is the author of *The Limits of Power* and *The New American Militarism*. His writing has appeared in *Foreign Affairs*, *Atlantic Monthly*, *The Nation*, *New York Times*, *Washington Post*, and *Wall Street Journal*. He is the recipient of a Lannan Award and a member of the Council on Foreign Relations.

THE AMERICAN EMPIRE PROJECT

In an era of unprecedented military strength, leaders of the United States, the global hyperpower, have increasingly embraced imperial ambitions. How did this significant shift in purpose and policy come about? And what lies down the road?

The American Empire Project is a response to the changes that have occurred in America's strategic thinking as well as in its military and economic posture. Empire, long considered an offense against America's democratic heritage, now threatens to define the relationship between our country and the rest of the world. The American Empire Project publishes books that question this development, examine the origins of U.S. imperial aspirations, analyze their ramifications at home and abroad, and discuss alternatives to this dangerous trend.

The project was conceived by Tom Engelhardt and Steve Fraser, editors who are themselves historians and writers. Published by Metropolitan Books, an imprint of Henry Holt and Company, its titles include *Hegemony or Survival* and *Failed States* by Noam Chomsky, *The Blowback Trilogy* by Chalmers Johnson, *The Limits of Power* by Andrew Bacevich, *Crusade* by James Carroll, *Blood and Oil* by Michael Klare, *Dilemmas of Domination* by Walden Bello, *Devil's Game* by Robert Dreyfuss, *A Question of Torture* by Alfred McCoy, *A*

People's History of American Empire by Howard Zinn, *The Complex* by Nick Turse, and *Empire's Workshop* by Greg Grandin.

For more information about the American Empire Project and for a list of forthcoming titles, please visit www.american empireproject.com.